BRILLIANT
JEWELS FROM EUROPEAN COURTS
EUROPE

BRILLIANT
JEWELS FROM EUROPEAN COURTS
EUROPE

EDITED BY

Diana Scarisbrick, Christophe Vachaudez and Jan Walgrave

ING   MERCATORFONDS

This book is published in conjunction with the exhibition *Brilliant Europe: jewels from European courts.* Organized as part of the europalia.europa festival.

ING Cultural Centre, Place Royale 6, Brussels, 24 October 2007 – 17 February 2008

© 2008 ING Belgium and Mercatorfonds, Brussels.
www.mercatorfonds.be

Distributed outside the USA, Canada, Belgium, The Netherlands and
Luxembourg by:

Thames & Hudson Ltd.
44 Clockhouse Road
Farnborough
Hants GU14 7QZ
United Kingdom

Tel.: +44 (0) 1252 541602
Fax: +44 (0) 1252 377380
www.thameshudson.co.uk

ISBN 978 90 6153 774 8
D/2007/703/66

Contents

Cleopatra's pearl: 14
jewellery and the European courts
LUC DUERLOO

The Middle Ages 28
JOHN CHERRY

The Renaissance: 62
between uniformity and internationalism
ELISABETH SCHMUTTERMEIER

The seventeenth century: the reign of the diamond 120
JAN WALGRAVE

The jewellery of absolutism 154
DIANA SCARISBRICK

Empire and romanticism: Napoleon and George IV 200
DIANA SCARISBRICK

The European monarchies in splendour 256
CHRISTOPHE VACHAUDEZ

Bibliography 290

6

Pforzheim, Schmuckmuseum
Pforzheim, Sparkassenstiftung
Edmond Rochtus
Rueil-Malmaison, Musée National des Châteaux
    de Malmaison et de Bois-Préau
Soleure, Musée de l'Ancien Arsenal
Stockholm, Nordiska Museet
Stockholm, Statens Historiska Museet
Stuttgart, Landesmuseum Württemberg
Tokyo, Albion Art Collection
Van Cleef & Arpels
Versailles, Châteaux de Versailles et de Trianon
Vienna, Kunsthistorisches Museum, Bibliothèque
Vienna, Kunsthistorisches Museum, Kunstkammer
Vienna, Museen des Mobiliendepots
Wrocław, Muzeum Narodowe we Wrocławiu
    (National Museum)

ING would like to thank all the museums and
private collectors in Belgium and elsewhere who
loaned items for this exhibition.

Insurance
    Aon Artscope International
    Aon France Conseil et Courtage
    Axa Art Insurance
    Axa Servicio Assurazzione
    Consulting Europeo de Riesgos
    FidesSecur München
    Kuhn & Bülow
    Léon Eeckman
    Lübke Gmbh
    Nationale Suisse
    Realty Insurance
    Uniqa

Transport
    Arteria
    Constantine
    Haller
    Hasenkamp
    HSart
    Hungart
    Kortmann
    LP ART
    SID
    Mobeltransport
    Mobull
    MTAB
    Renesans Trans
    RN Trans
    Via Mat
    Welti Furrer
    Yamato Transport

CATALOGUE

Editors
    ING Belgium
    Fonds Mercator, Brussels

Authors
    Vincent Bastien (VB)
    Marie-Claire Berkemeier (MCB)
    Pierre Cambier (PC)
    Florence Carlier (FC)
    John Cherry
    Luc Duerloo
    Christina Egli (CE)
    Annica Ewing (AE)
    Ulrich Feldhahn (UF)
    Liene Geeraerts (LG)
    Fernando Martín García (FMG)
    Karine Huguenaud (KH)
    Franz Kirchweger (FK)
    Erika Kiss (ERK)
    Ettele Kiss (EK)
    Béatrix Kriller (BKE)
    Jacques Jeanmart (JJ)
    Claudette Joannis (CJ)
    Frédéric Lacaille (FL)
    Markus Leutenegger (ML)
    Wim Luyckx (WL)
    Leonor Orey (LO)
    Muriel Prieur (MP)
    Georges Sanders (GS)
    Diana Scarisbrick (DSC)
    Elisabeth Schmuttermeier
    Dirk Syndram (DS)
    Juliette Trey (JT)
    Christophe Vachaudez (CV)
    Luc Vanackere (LV)
    Jan Walgrave (JW)
    Jacek Wittecki (JWi)

Production
    Tijdsbeeld & Pièce Montée, Ghent
    Supervised by Ronny Gobyn

Coordination
    Patricia De Peuter, ING
    Hannelore Duflou, Tijdsbeeld, Ghent
    Roseline Lessens, ING
    Ann Mestdag, Fonds Mercator, Brussels
    Anne Petre, ING

Layout
    Griet Van Haute, Ghent

Typesetting
    Karakters, Ghent

Photogravure, printing and binding
    Lannoo, Tielt

Translation
    Mark Carlson
    Elisabeth Lyman
    Trista Selous

Editing
    Kate Bell

Aalst Fabrique de l'Église Saint-Martin, © KIKIRPA, Brussels : 73 (bottom), 131

Aix-la-Chapelle Trésor de la Cathédrale, Photo BPK © Jochen Remmer : 30

Amsterdam Rijksmuseum : 124

Antwerp Diamond Museum Province of Antwerp : 135, 192 (top)

Apeldoorn Paleis Het Loo Nationaal Museum, Apeldoorn, © Photo E. Boeijinga : 153 ; © Photo Tom Haartsen : 148

Arenenberg © Musée Napoléon, Arenenberg : 39 (bottom)

Basle © Historisches Museum Basel, Photo : HMB P. Portner : 56, 57

Bazel Fabrique d'Église, on loan from the Diamond Museum Province of Antwerp : 213

Beloeil Château de Beloeil, le Prince de Ligne : 240

Berlin SAR Georg Friedrich Prince de Prusse, © Stiftung Preussische Schlösser und Gärten, Berlin Brandenburg. Photo : Jörg P. Anders : 172 ; © SPSG, Roland Handrick : 19

Bruges © H. Maertens Fotograaf, Bruges. All rights reserved. Private collection : 53, 208 (bottom) ; Noble Confrérie du Saint-Sang : 59

Brussels © Musées royaux d'Art et d'Histoire : 52 (top), 128, 190 (top), 190 (bottom) ; © Musées royaux des Beaux-Arts de Belgique, Photo : Speltdoorn : 78, 89, 127 ; Musées royaux d'Art et d'Histoire, Musée du Cœur Boyadjian : 139 (left) ; Musée de la Ville de Bruxelles – Hôtel de Ville : 141 ; Musée royal de l'Armée : 207

Budapest Musée national de Hongrie : 75 (right), 85 (top), 85 (bottom), 129, 134, 138 (left), 140 (left), 145 (centre) ; © Musée des Arts appliqués, Budapest : 101, 103, 118, 139 (right)

Cambridge Fitzwilliam Museum, © The Fitzwilliam Museum, University of Cambridge : 114

Cumbria UK Levens Hall : 208 (top)

Dijon © Musée des Beaux-Arts de Dijon : 50

Dresden Staatliche Kunstsammlungen Dresden, Grünes Gewölbe, © Photo Karpinski : 177, 178, 179, 182, 184 ; Staatliche Kunstsammlungen Dresden, Gemäldegalerie Alte Meister : 159 ; © Photo Estel : 175 ; © Photo H-P. Klut : 176 ; © Photo Jürgen Karpinski : 154 ; Staatliche Kunstsammlungen Dresden, Rüstkammer : 185

Edinburgh National Museums of Scotland, Photo : Ken Smith, Edinburgh : 113

Eichenzell Hessische Hausstiftung, Kronberg i.T., © Hessische Hausstiftung, Museum Schloss Fasanerie, Eichenzell, Germany : 218, 238

Florence Galleria Palatina, Photo © Scala Florence, courtesy Ministero Beni e Attività Culturali : 64 ; Museo degli Argenti, Palazzo Pitti : 96 (top), 97 (top), 97 (bottom), 102, 117

Gaasbeek © Gaasbeek Castle : 48

Geneva © Cartier S.A., Photo : L. Tirilly : 282

Innsbruck Château Ambras, Photo © AKG-images/Erich Lessing : 157

Karlsruhe Badisches Landesmuseum : 279

La Haye Collectie Gemeentemuseum Den Haag, © Stichting Beeldrecht : 142 (left) ; Stichting Historische Verzamelingen van het Huis Oranje-Nassau, Photo BPK © Hermann Buresch : 68

Lille Palais des Beaux-Arts, © Photo RMN – © Jacques Quecq d'Henripret : 70

Lisbon © Museu Nacional de Arte Antiga, Divisão de Documentação Fotográfica – Instituto Português de Museus, Photo : Giorgio Bordino : 136 ; Photo : José Pessoa : 145 (left), 168, 170, 193 (bottom) ; Palácio Nacional da Ajuda, courtesy of Palácio Nacional da Ajuda, Lisbon/IGESPAR/Photo : Henrique Ruas : 165 ; Photo : Manuel Silveira Ramos : 24, 181, 187, 215

London © A.C. Cooper, London : 94, 137 (bottom), 137 (top), 143, 150, 241 ; V&A Images/Victoria and Albert Museum : 108, 123 (right) ; London, The Trustees of Sir John Soane's Museum, Photo : A.C. Cooper, courtesy of the Trustees of Sir John Soane's Museum : 116 ; S.J. Phillips : 169, 171, 235 (bottom) ; D.S. Lavender (Antiques) Ltd. : 212 ; Sandra Cronan Ltd. : 246 ; Photo © National Maritime Museum : 109

Luxembourg Collection Grand-ducale : 249, 286

Madrid Monasterio de las Descalzas Reales, Patrimonio nacional, © Patrimonio Nacional : 76, 77 ; Museo del Prado : 26 ; Photo © Scala Florence : 67 ; Photo © AKG-images/Joseph Martin : 122 ; Museo Nacional de Artes Decorativas : 126, 163, 165, 167

Memmingen Strigel-Museum : 60

Munich Bayerische Verwaltung der staatlichen Schlösser, Gärten und Seen, Residenz München, Schatzkammer : 162, 265 ; © Copyright 2007 – Wittelsbacher Ausgleichsfonds, 266 ; Photo : George Meister : 264 ; Alte Pinakothek, Photo BPK © Jochen Remmer : 120

Namur Musée diocésain. Trésor de la cathédrale Saint-Aubin, © Photo : Vincent Everarts, Brussels : 42

8

Foreword

In 2007 Europe celebrates its fiftieth anniversary – fifty years of political equilibrium and democratic agreement, fifty years of solidarity and growing prosperity. To mark the event, ING is staging an exhibition in which our glittering European cultural heritage bears witness to the stability of Europe today. 'Jewels from European courts' is a subject that appeals to almost everyone because of the symbolic meaning that these pieces carry with them.

Europe's roots are inextricably bound up in the endless struggle for balance between the political powers. If an ambitious monarch overstepped his territorial bounds he could be sure that a coalition of the other member states would soon be waging war against him. The politics of marriage among the young princes and princesses of the European courts – along with extravagant displays of gifts and wedding jewels – provided a guarantee of peace and the consolidation of power. Alliances were ratified by making friendly monarchs members of royal orders and by showering them with insignia and decorations.

In this context, expensive gifts and jewels were constantly exchanged between rulers and members of the royal courts or inherited by other European branches of the royal houses. Monarchs' private jewels became currency in their political undertakings; later on, the family or dynastic jewels became part of a country's treasury and as a result they were sometimes consigned to a perilous existence.

There were countless numbers of jewels in Europe – many with a fascinating story to tell – but those that have survived the turbulence of the years are rare. Jewels were frequently altered to satisfy the whims of fashion and stones were reused in new 'trinkets' or sold to make money. The 230 magnificent pieces that we see here provide a wealth of information about the symbolism used among European courtiers. The fragility of these ultimate symbols of power is self-evident.

The expertise and the trust of the lenders are essential in mounting an exhibition such as this. ING Cultural Centre called on the experience of three outstanding specialists in the history of European jewels. Jan Walgrave, former Chief Curator of the Museums of the Province of Antwerp, knows the curators in the most important European museums better than anyone. Thanks to his involvement, the Grünes Gewolbe, the Museo degli Argenti, the Pforzheim, the Louvre, the Palacio de Ajuda and many others, have entrusted some of their most precious objects to this exhibition. Diana Scarisbrick has an unrivalled knowledge of the English aristocracy and museums, which enabled us to gain access to the most amazing collections. We may say with pride that a great many royal jewels glittering here in the European capital have never before left the British Isles. Finally, sincere thanks are due to Christophe Vachaudez, the leading specialist in the jewels of the royal houses of the nineteenth and twentieth centuries, who has coordinated a dazzling gallery of tiaras that will captivate everyone.

This exhibition would have been impossible without the close co-operation of several departments in ING: the security, buildings, press, communication, marketing and public relations departments play a crucial role in supporting initiatives like this. It has meanwhile become second nature for ING employees to meet this challenge with technical perfection and to keep the initiative on the right track. As the new Chairman of this organization I am extremely proud of this and I wish to express my sincere thanks to everyone concerned.

Eric Dralans
Chairman ING Belgium

Foreword

Welcome to the *europalia.europa* festival, the twenty-first in a highly successful series stretching back to 1969 which has marked europalia out as one of Europe's premier cultural events. Unlike all previous festivals, which focused on the culture of individual states, this year we are pleased to present for the first time an ambitious programme that incorporates all twenty-seven member states of the European Union and encompasses all artistic disciplines. The choice, of course, is not accidental; 2007 marks the fiftieth anniversary of the signing of the Treaty of Rome and continues into early 2008, the anniversary of the year of its implementation. The Treaty and its successors have brought today's European Union to the fullest realization, east and west, of Robert Schumann's vision of creative reconciliation between the states and peoples of Europe. Yet our sense of Europe is both older and deeper than its contemporary political and institutional expression; it is the exploration of this sense of Europe that is our festival's point of departure.

For the occasion, ING Cultural Centre has taken the excellent initiative in organizing an exhibition about jewellery from the European courts. *Brilliant Europe* explores 800 years of jewellery history in Europe and enlightens us about their symbolic role.

I would like to convey my warmest thanks to Diana Scarisbrick, Jan Walgrave, Christophe Vachaudez, Patricia De Peuter and Anne Petre, curators of this exhibition, as well as the team at ING Cultural Centre for this splendid contribution to the *europalia.europa* festival.

It has been a privilege and a pleasure for me, as President of the International European Movement and past President of the European Parliament, to be associated with this wonderful festival as Commissioner General. *Europalia.europa* encompasses a whole range of exciting exhibitions and performances, incorporating all the arts from music and dance to film and literature. The festival reflects cultural Europe in all its rich diversity and is the result of many months of painstaking preparation, hard work and dedication. Enjoy it!

Pat Cox
Commissioner General
europalia.europa

14

Cleopatra's pearl: jewellery and the european courts

LUC DUERLOO

In his *Natural History* Pliny the Elder tells the story of a bet that Cleopatra, Queen of Egypt, made with Mark Antony. He had defied her to serve a dinner costing more than ten million sesterces. The following night Cleopatra appeared, dressed in the finest clothes and jewellery. She was of course wearing her famous earrings, adorned with the two largest pearls known to the ancient world, which were in themselves quite priceless. In marked contrast to her dazzling appearance, she served her guest a modest meal. Just as Mark Antony was starting to swagger, thinking he had won his bet, the servants brought the queen a cup filled with vinegar. Cleopatra casually dropped one of her enormous pearls into the cup, knowing perfectly well that it would dissolve in the acid, and then drank it down. Dumbfounded and defeated, Mark Antony was more impressed than ever by the wealth and power of the Egyptian sovereign.

The truth of this story is far from certain. Pliny relates it a century after the event, and in the intervening time many legends grew up around the last queen of Egypt. True or not, what is certain is that this story inspired the artists of the Renaissance and Baroque periods as it did their royal patrons. For them the story of the pearl was a story of royal power, wealth and ostentation, and also of a sovereign's greatness. Crucially it illustrates the function of jewels in the royal lifestyle. Cleopatra uses her priceless pearls as a tool. They are the necessary attributes of royalty. Only a republican parvenu like Mark Antony worries about the intrinsic value of a jewel. A true sovereign can surround herself with the most select, valuable objects without becoming attached to them in that way. For her, they are tools of power, nothing more. Gold and silver, precious stones and pearls are part of her image. The sovereign exerts power by divine right. Brilliant jewels are there to impress others, not to dazzle the kings themselves.

From this point of view royal jewels are inextricably linked to European history. For centuries, sovereigns and royal houses dominated the process by which European states were created. Until the early twentieth century monarchy was the most widespread political regime. The preponderance of monarchical states exerted a profound influence on political culture. In reality there is a paradox here. The Europe of sovereigns was divided at the political level, but at the same time it showed a remarkable cultural unity. It is precisely this tension between division and unity that lent crown jewels, chivalric orders and other royal decorations their meaning and function.

For a thousand years the sovereigns and royal houses were the main agents in the formation of states. Most of the dynasties laid the foundations of their power during the decline of the Carolingian period. They did this by attributing to themselves capacities that they had initially exercised in the name of their sovereign. Power and the exercise of power then became private property, something that could be inherited according to the rules of private law, like a piece of land. Moreover, it was not enough for a monarch to pass his inheritance intact to his successor; he had to expand and increase the dynastic patrimony. He could do this by making an advantageous marriage or he could buy another king's possessions; however, the most usual method was war. The constant quest to expand and maintain the family estate played a large part in determining the positions of borders. However, this notion requires qualification. A European sovereign could not take up arms at the drop of a hat, with no other form of process. The Middle Ages created a distinction between licit and illicit violence. The fundamental idea was that peace was the norm and war the exception, to be avoided. This idea is less obvious than it first seems. In many non-European cultures it was war that was the normal state; the Ottoman Empire is almost certainly the best-known example of this. In Europe, however, a serious reason was needed to break the peace. Only defence of the faith or the protection of hereditary rights were admissible. During the Renaissance, reasons of state emerged as a pretext for licit war, and gradually supplanted the others, so that religious wars lost their legitimacy after the mid-seventeenth century.

In the following century, the legitimacy of dynastic claims was in turn eroded as international politics underwent a

< Giovanni Battista Tiepolo, *The banquet of Cleopatra*, 1757 (detail).

process of secularization and revision. Secularization occurred because religion was no longer a factor of division in international politics and revision because the constraining power of historical rights was weakening. At the same time the European royal houses were gradually losing the monopoly they had once had over international politics. Reasons of state were no longer linked to the person of the sovereign or to his dynasty, but dictated by the country over which he reigned.

The formation of the European states depended in the first instance on the establishment of a monopoly of violence. Internally the state projected itself as the only authority capable of effectively controlling the violence inherent in society. Order must reign in the public space. Subjects do not have the right to take their rights into their own hands. The pacification of European societies went hand in hand with a civilizing offensive. A network of conventions obliged Europeans to control themselves more effectively or, as it was put at the time, to act in a civilized manner. The emerging state and royal courts in particular played a major role in this. In reality, for centuries it was the courts that defined what was distinguished and desirable. From the late fifteenth to the late eighteenth century, the cultural element common to all of Europe was primarily that of the court. However, it would be wrong to see this cultural offensive and the pacification of the society as processes led exclusively from on high. The urban middle classes also played an active part. The rejection of violence and respect for certain forms of social relations were values of primordial importance for the protection of their commercial interests, ethics and bourgeois culture. So the bourgeoisie was an objective ally in the process of forming states.

Clearly, however, the establishment of a monopoly of violence also had a dark side. The state gradually eliminated competition from the aristocratic and urban militia. Soon, it alone had an effective military force at its disposal, which grew in size and regularly increased its strike power. In this way a spectacular shift can be seen. Violence within states decreased, but at the same time it seems to have drained outwards, becoming greatly increased at the international level. Wars became ever more intense, absorbing many more men and much more money, placing an ever-growing burden on civilian populations. Some authors regard this point as the start of the arms race between states. Moreover, at this stage monarchies had a comparative advantage over republics – at least until the French Revolution and perhaps long after that. Because sovereigns had traditionally been military leaders, their relationship

to war was much more direct. This is also why their decision-making processes tended to favour military solutions.

The European royal houses were in fact engaged in bitter rivalry with each other. In itself there is nothing surprising in this. On other continents, too, dynasties competed for power. However, what distinguishes the formation of the European states is that, after the Carolingian empire had fragmented, no other empire ever managed to rule the entire continent. During the sixteenth century the spectacular advance of the Habsburg dynasty raised the fear that it might aspire to universal monarchy. In the second half of the seventeenth century similar ambitions were attributed to Louis XIV. After the French Revolution Napoleon Bonaparte in his turn tried to create a European empire. Each time, the other European sovereigns did their utmost to block such dreams. So it is possible to speak of a kind of underlying solidarity, which acted as a corrective whenever one sovereign state appeared too threatening to another. During the negotiations that led to the Peace of Utrecht (1713), this solidarity mechanism was given a name: the European balance of power. It came down to a single principle: one could seek to consolidate one's own power position, but not totally to destroy the enemy. Whoever failed to respect that understanding could expect to face war with a coalition.

This mechanism still functions indirectly today. It is thanks to the balance of power that Europe still has a multitude of states of all sizes. The process of state formation described above occurred in a series of relatively restricted settings, leading to a great diversity, which in turn gives the Old Continent its richness. This diversity has also had a fundamental impact on the process of European union. On the one hand – if only due to the small size of the states – it has advanced the cause of European unification and determined its architecture. On the other it also acts as a brake on that cause.

This is far from the only paradox in this regard. It is equally paradoxical that the royal houses, in their quest for expansion, should have acted in a manner that guaranteed a multiplicity of states. It is paradoxical that they should each have built a state with its own identity, and yet been the vehicles of a court culture common to the whole of Europe. Lastly, it is equally paradoxical that they should have been at once rivals and partners. For the solidarity of sovereigns is also exerted at another level. In practice the legitimacy of kings depends largely on their mutual recognition within a very closed club. The constant diplomatic exchanges that developed in fifteenth-century Italy and then extended to the rest of Europe were fundamentally based on a principle of reciprocity: the parties could only negotiate if they recognized each other's sovereignty. In the modern period all kinds of tools were developed to express this recognition. Sovereigns went so far as to bare their heads in the presence of

< Peter Paul Rubens, *The marriage by proxy of Marie de' Medici and Henry IV, in Florence on 5 October 1600*, 1624–1625.

an ambassador and repeated this action at each mention of the name of the sovereign whose emissary he was. Diplomatic reports specify the number of steps that a sovereign took in coming forward to greet the ambassador. There was disproportionate excitement over access to the *Salia regia* or the *Sala ducale* of the pontifical palaces, the protocol of the seating order in the chapel of the imperial court, the titles used in correspondence and the rules of precedence for carriages of the diplomatic corps. All these things reflect the importance given to degrees of mutual respect. At the same time royal solidarity could be expressed in forms of exclusion. Other political regimes were regarded with a degree of disdain. At the Congress of Vienna, Tsar Alexander I dismissed the proposal to restore the former Italian city republics with the quip, 'Republics have gone out of fashion'. This was solidarity in support of established dynasties. Newcomers – the Bonapartes, the Karadordevics in Serbia and Petrovic Njegos in Montenegro – found it hard to become accepted. Significantly, Tsar Nicholas I addressed the new Emperor Napoleon III with the slightly condescending 'my dear friend' instead of 'my brother', as protocol required.

The marks of honour in diplomatic exchanges were part of a wider idiom. European royals set themselves apart by their use of language, by the rituals that structured their lives, the images and myths that they appropriated, and the architectural language they employed. This list is far from exhaustive. They also set themselves apart, for example, through the minutely calculated exchange of gifts between royal houses and the symbolic subjection of nature in hunting or the training of horses. The idiom of European royalty was marvellously adapted to creating distinctions. It elevated the sovereign above his subjects. It underlined the obviousness of his divine right to exert power. It made the sovereign and his entourage sacred by making their everyday life sacred. It created a parallel existence that legitimized monarchy. This royal idiom created a distinction not only between the king and his subjects, but also between European kings and the rest. The latter acted according to the standards specific to their culture and were not generally aware of European customs, or insufficiently so. They communicated in a completely different way and expected quite different proofs of esteem. In this sense the idiom of the European courts provides an indisputable example of a culture common to the entire continent. In reality it could only function effectively if it extended beyond state borders. At the same time it indicated where the frontiers of European culture lay at any given time.

Up until the French Revolution the monarchy seemed a fact of life. Most European states were governed by a king. It is not so easy to translate this into figures, since the situation on the ground was often highly complex. In practice many regions were condominiums, or states governed by several sovereigns.

One example was the city of Maastricht, which was ruled partly by the Dutch States General and partly by the principality of Liège. In addition there were many personal unions, in which a sovereign had power over a series of regions. In the late eighteenth century the head of the House of Habsburg was thus at once emperor of the Germanic Holy Roman Empire, king in Hungary and Bohemia, archduke of Austria, duke of Milan and governor of the Southern Netherlands. Another problem is that of the member states of the Holy Roman Empire. In theory these were fiefs granted by the emperor, so that the holder of the monarch's title was not sovereign in the strict sense. But if these states are not included, the king of Prussia must be left out. Including all the principalities and independent cities of the Holy Roman Empire, in 1789 there were at least 265 entities, of which almost 22 per cent were republics or cities of empire. All the others were governed by a sovereign, of which there was a huge variety: emperors, kings, electors, grand dukes, dukes, landgraves, margraves, princes and a whole series of counts of empire. There were also no fewer than eighty ecclesiastical sovereigns, from the pope to the ecclesiastical electors, bishop-princes, grand masters of chivalric orders, prince-abbots and princess-abbesses.

The Revolution produced a further paradox. It caused monarchy to seem less obvious. It countered the idea of reign by the grace of God with the concept of the sovereignty of the people. Napoleon brought these two extremes together in his own title, proclaiming himself 'by the grace of God and the Constitutions of the Republic, Emperor of the French'. But the Revolution also gave the republican system a highly negative reputation. Throughout the nineteenth century the term 'republic' was synonymous with radicalism, arbitrary violence and instability. It is no coincidence that, on the eve of the First World War, Europe had only four republics out of twenty-five independent states. Switzerland and tiny San Marino had been republics for centuries. France had been a republic since 1870 and Portugal since 1910. We should also mention the condominium of Andorra and the three independent Hanseatic cities of the German empire. The other countries of the Old Continent were governed by – including the German sovereigns – four emperors, seventeen kings, six grand dukes, five dukes and nine princes. There was also a long list of dynasties that had lost their thrones in the course of the political upheavals of the nineteenth century. Some of these were removed from the political map during the French Revolution, as were almost all the ecclesiastical sovereigns. Others had fallen victim to Italian and German unification. These families were described as 'mediatized', because they were now strictly speaking subjects of another regime. In practice these unfortunate cousins retained their places in the great family of European monarchs. They enjoyed diplomatic status and their names appeared in the bible of European titles, the *Almanach de Gotha*.

To an outside observer they appeared as one big family. Queen Victoria of England and King Christian IX of Denmark were known as the grandmother and grandfather of Europe. In the course of two generations their numerous descendants came to occupy many European thrones. However, some relationships were more direct than others. All or almost all these people were related, but a genealogist would sometimes have to go a very long way back in the family tree to identify the relationship. Overall there were two fairly separate sets of families. Catholic princes rarely married outside their own faith, but the line between Protestant and Orthodox was less strict. This is why, for example, the Tsar of Russia was related to the royal family of the Netherlands, but not to that of Belgium. Of course the Sultan occupied an altogether different sphere. However, religious differences were not the crucial factor. The most important element was royal solidarity: the proverbial world of 'well-known people'.

Monarchical Europe ultimately gave way under the blows of the First World War. The twilight of the kings, in November 1918, was as abrupt as it was unexpected. In the preceding months the Central Powers were still placing kings on the thrones of Lithuania and Finland. A week before the Armistice, they created a Baltic duchy in the territory of Estonia and Lithuania. A few weeks later the German sovereigns were packing their bags and leaving their ancestral homes. Once the ground had been cleared it was possible to carry out a fundamental reorganization of frontiers and political regimes. By 1919 Europe had thirty-two states, of which sixteen were republics. Furthermore Hungary was a kingdom on paper only. No reigning emperors remained; there was only one grand duchy and two principalities. The twelve surviving kingdoms were concentrated in north-western and southern Europe, with the position of the latter most unenviable. Greece and Spain were republics for a while, Albania passed from one regime to another, while in Yugoslavia, Romania and Bulgaria the monarchy was sliding towards dictatorship. In north-western Europe the trend was in the opposite direction. The royal houses were coming to terms with the advance of democracy and, by remaining above and outside the political mêlée, they ensured their own survival beyond the Second World War.

Throughout the millennium separating the dissolution of the Carolingian empire from the twentieth-century twilight of the kings, the European sovereigns and royal houses were at once the creators and vectors of a common culture. This culture made very considered use of material supports. Objects were tools that enabled them to legitimate, display, exert and perpetuate their power. As a general rule such objects were

Samuel Theodor Gericke, *The alliance of the three kings*, 1709.

The coffin holding the body of Emperor Francis Joseph I of Austria as it lay in state in the Hofburg Chapel in Vienna in 1916 is flanked on the left by the replica of Saint Stephen's crown of Hungary and on the right, partially concealed by the candles, by the replica of Emperor Rudolph II's crown.

< Anton von Maron (workshop), *Maria Theresa of Habsburg, Empress of Austria, Queen of Hungary and Bohemia, in widow's dress, presenting the crowns of Bohemia and Hungary and the Imperial crown*, c. 1772.

extraordinarily valuable, due either to the rarity of their materials or the virtuosity with which they were made. Items of sacred, magical, historical or allegorical significance, masterpieces and otherwise unique items were all metaphors for the exceptional state of grace that was royal power. But more than any other material aspect of royal culture, it was the art of jewellery that encapsulated all the facets of European royalty.

Of all the decorations that were part of the royal panoply in Europe, it was the regalia, or crown jewels, that most fired the imagination. More than all the rest, they carry monarchy's pretensions to sacredness. The names of the medieval crowns were already highly revealing in this respect. Both the German emperors and the French kings asserted that they wore the crown of Charlemagne. The Hungarian crown was attributed to Saint Stephen, that of Bohemia to Saint Wenceslaus and that of England to Saint Edward. In each case liberties were taken with history: the origins of each of these famous crowns were more recent than the period claimed. The association with a

holy predecessor gave them the status of relics. This is particularly apparent in the case of the crown of Wenceslaus, which dates only from the fourteenth century, but which is preserved, as instructed by the papal bull of foundation, on top of the skull of Saint Wenceslaus. In this way it too became a relic by contact. In the early seventeenth century the bonnet of the Austrian archdukes was similarly preserved with the relics of Saint Leopold. The link between relics and crown jewels is even more explicit in the case of the iron crown of Lombardy. It was said that the thin ribbon of iron holding its different elements together was forged from a nail from the Holy Cross. In Catholic monarchies this close link between crown jewels and relics was maintained until the end of the *ancien régime*. In Protestant kingdoms on the other hand, the association was quite logically abandoned during the sixteenth century. Even so, in these kingdoms the regalia retained a special power of attraction, if only because they were very rarely seen in public. In Hungary, which was deeply split along religious lines, Saint Stephen's crown came to be regarded as an emanation of royalty; it was known as the Holy Crown of Hungary and was even given the status of a legal person.

In the sixteenth century the emergence of new monarchies was also reflected in the form adopted by royal crowns. In the Middle Ages, in principle it was only the emperor who had the right to a closed crown, in other words a crown surmounted by a diadem. This element expressed the imperial claim on the highest level of temporal power. Gradually the new monarchies began to attribute to themselves the supranational authority of the pope or emperor. The kings of France and England – forerunners in this respect – started from the principle that they exerted the power of emperors in their own kingdoms, and expressed the fullness of their power by adding diadems to their crowns. So the form taken by royal jewellery closely follows political evolution.

It was therefore no coincidence that during the French Revolution the crown jewels were subjected to symbolic violence. In October 1793 Reims became the setting for the ceremonial destruction of the Holy Phial, which contained the chrism (consecrated oil) with which the kings of France were anointed. Other jewels from the crown of France suffered the same fate. However, the royal symbols of the Holy Roman Empire were moved – with some difficulty – from Nuremberg to Vienna in time to save them. Somewhat ironically it can be observed that this revolutionary period and the following decades, in which the insignia of the power of the *ancien régime* were banned, saw the manufacture of more crowns, sceptres and royal orbs than ever before. For the map of Europe was continually being redrawn. Once the fires of revolution had died down, France granted its allies a whole network of new titles. The Bonapartes established themselves – albeit temporarily – in parts of Italy and Germany. A similar process occurred with the Congress of Vienna, which entirely updated the political system along with the map. The powers at the disposal of the state apparatus were now greatly extended. But when it came to giving external form to the image of royalty, there was a systematic return to the *ancien régime*. Indeed this form was now turning into a stereotype. Though one crown may have had a more imposing design than another, or been more outrageously studded with gems, in shape they were all alike. There had been a great deal more variety before the Revolution. Republican iconoclasm thus ultimately led to the standardization of the idiom of monarchy.

After this the only changes to occur pertained to the materials from which crowns were made. For example, in 1881, having previously seen its sovereignty attacked, the Romanian monarchy had a crown made from the steel of a canon captured from the Ottomans. Twenty-five years later Serbia followed suit : this time it was the bronze from a canon that was incorporated into the new royal crown. The weapon in question had been in use about a century earlier during the first Serb rebellion. In many respects these two crowns can be compared to military decorations such as the German Iron Cross (1813) or the British Victoria Cross (1865), whose more rugged material precisely highlights an act of exceptional bravery.

Like crown jewels, chivalric orders were imbued with an important symbolic capital. However, there is a major difference. While the former mainly served to raise the sovereign above his subjects, chivalric orders had their origins in the notion of brotherhood. This was quite expressly true of the first dynastic orders – such as the Order of the Garter in England (1348) or the Burgundian Order of the Golden Fleece (1430) – whose members were seated in order of seniority rather than birth. Moreover, initially it was not the grand master but the assembly of the chapter of the order who had the right to appoint new members. Membership was tightly restricted to twenty or thirty people at most. The subject who was made a knight of the order was admitted to the closest circle of the royal entourage. The conferring of the order on a foreign sovereign was in itself a proclamation of a political alliance. But when, in 1614, Duke Charles-Emmanuel of Savoy threw his chain of the Golden Fleece into the face of the Spanish ambassador, everyone understood that war had been declared.

By the sixteenth century however, brotherhood had to give way to the growing needs of the states that were then in the process of formation. It was now the sovereigns themselves who selected those they would admit to their chivalric orders. The conquest of new territories and the growth of the state apparatus required that these orders be opened up to a large number of new members, or that additional orders be created. Over time we see the establishment of distinctions for specific actions – mainly military honours – or designed for a particular group, including orders reserved for women. Smaller states that did not have their own orders of chivalry established some, or claimed they were reviving a long forgotten corporation. The numbers speak for themselves. At the start of the eighteenth century the Austrian monarchy had only two orders : the Golden Fleece and the Ladies' Order of the Starred Cross. By 1815 there were already six. In addition to the first two there were now the Military Order of Maria Theresa (1757), the Order of Saint Stephen of Hungary (1764), the Order of Leopold (1808) and the Order of the Iron Crown (1815). The same trend can also be seen in other states. In addition, most of these orders were now divided into several different classes, so that the number of decoration holders increased far more than that of the orders themselves.

Once again the French Revolution led to a degree of standardization. The Legion of Honour, created in 1802, provided the model. During the nineteenth century most states created an order of merit of this kind, comprising five classes. Even the design of the insignia shows a growing uniformity. The typical

> Orazio Gentileschi, *Public Felicity surmounting perils*, 1625. 22

23

decoration appears as a Maltese cross decorated with a central medallion. Palms and laurel leaves appear obligatory and even the small crowns seem interchangeable. It is extraordinary that, at a time when the theory of state sovereignty was being put into practice in the most radical manner, the image those states chose to adopt was usually borrowed from an idiom that all could recognize and share.

However, hasty extrapolations should be avoided. There is no reason to suppose that the changes apparent in crown jewels and orders of chivalry also applied to the much broader phenomenon of royal jewellery. Crown jewels and the insignia of orders represent a highly specific symbolic capital. They are very direct material expressions of power, bearing an obvious historical charge. Jewels, meanwhile, shine with all their brilliance. It is perhaps because of this that the adjective 'brilliant' is so often associated with courts or the life of palaces. Jewellery impresses because of the very rare materials from which it is made, the extraordinary size of the stones, or a combination of both. Although a piece of jewellery is not timeless in itself – it bears the recognizable marks of a style – the stones with which it is usually set have an air of eternity. All in all, the language of jewellery is of a different order. It does not carry the same degree of history, unless, of course, mysterious powers are attributed to particular precious stones.

However it is striking to note the extent to which sovereigns adorned themselves with a multitude of precious stones until late into the eighteenth century, whereas their successors in the nineteenth wore almost none. In the first third of the eighteenth century Augustus the Strong, King of Poland and Elector of Saxony, could choose between parures of rubies, sapphires, emeralds and diamonds. Each set comprised a sword, a cane, an aigrette for his hat, shoe and garter buckles, one or several chivalric insignia and an unbelievable quantity of buttons. Each piece was abundantly decorated with stones of the required type. In later generations sovereigns increasingly dressed in military uniform. This new custom admirably expressed the fact that in many respects the acquisition of the monopoly of violence had become the driving force behind the formation of European states, but it did not leave much room for the wearing of jewellery. In practice there was room only for the insignia of orders set with diamonds. So indirectly the display of jewellery thus became the business of the dynasty's women. In response to their wishes the jewellers created the most spectacular parures throughout the nineteenth century. However, it must be noted that in its essence the concept of parure implies a form of standardization. These may offer little more than hints, but they nevertheless suggest that in this area as well, there was a break between the periods that preceded and followed the French Revolution.

Eduard von Engerth, *Francis Joseph, Emperor of Austria*, 1863.

< Domingos Antonio de Sequeira, *Portrait of John VI, last king of Portugal with his insignia.*

26

Jewellery was not simply for impressing others ; royal jewels had other purposes too. The symbolic and monetary capital went hand in hand. For centuries they were highly prized as gifts. They were given as rewards to devoted subjects or placed on altars as votive offerings. Moreover, in addition to their symbolic value, royal jewels represented a very concrete capital that was easy to transport. They were useful for settling inheritances and debts. In cases of urgent need they could serve as collateral. When necessary they could simply be pawned or sold. It was no coincidence that the many victims of the 'twilight of the kings' of 1918 took their jewels into exile. They were the tools of European royalty and as such were used with great pragmatism.

When the Infanta Isabella Clara Eugenia learned of the death of her husband, Archduke Albert, in 1621, she immediately took off her earrings and gave them as a gift to her nearest lady-in-waiting. She had no more need of them. Her decision to take the habit of the Third Order of Saint Francis was already made. Although she continued to govern the Habsburg Netherlands as Regent for the next twelve years, she never again wore any kind of jewellery. In practice she was no longer a sovereign ; she was now a member of the lay branch of a mendicant order. Although affairs of state forbade her from withdrawing completely from the world, she wanted at the least to show that her heart lay elsewhere. The sobriety of her dress was ostentatious, since her entourage continued as before to wear the most splendid jewellery. In a sense Isabella's decision never to wear jewellery again was a final act of royal extravagance. Her display of sobriety raised her above the level of common mortals. For her contemporaries the message was instantly understandable. The French ambassador to Brussels found the gift – or abandonment – of the earrings sufficiently eloquent to mention it the following day in a dispatch. Like the Infanta, the other European sovereigns and their courtiers, he understood why she had done it. He knew that royal jewels were tools, and that their value had thus to be expressed in symbolic rather than monetary terms.

< Alonso Sanchez Coello, *Portrait of the Infanta Isabella Clara Eugenia with Magdalena Ruiz, holding the cameo of Phillip II*, 1580

The Middle Ages

JOHN CHERRY

INTRODUCTION

'The sapphire is the finest of gems, and the most precious and suitable for the fingers of Kings', wrote Bartholomew the Englishman in the mid-thirteenth century. Those words exemplify the appeal of jewellery and regalia, from medieval times to the present day. Gems were admired for their rarity, translucence and for their regal qualities, but they were also worn to ward off evil and protect from disease. Above all, however, they were prized as tokens of loyalty or status.

'Gems', wrote Alexander Neckham in the twelfth century, 'are commended by the wondrous power of their virtues, their sparkling light and the elegance of their beauty. I call them the miracles of nature, grateful gifts, a delight, a study and a treasure.'

CHARLEMAGNE

On Christmas Day in the year 800, the coronation of Charlemagne by Pope Leo III took place in the Basilica of Saint Peter in Rome. It was one of the key events of the Middle Ages. Wearing the crown emphasized the status of the ruler and indicated a respect for his historical legacy, while looking forward to a new period in history. In a bronze equestrian statue, formerly in Metz Cathedral, Charlemagne (or possibly his grandson, Charles the Bald) is shown crowned and holding an orb. This portrayal may be derived from Roman equestrian statues such as that of Marcus Aurelius in Rome, which was then thought to be a statue of the first Christian emperor Constantine crushing paganism. The little bronze may, therefore, be intended to show Charlemagne as a 'new Constantine'.

Few gems associated with Charlemagne have survived. A large, square sapphire, mounted on the twelfth-century Shrine of the Three Kings at Cologne Cathedral, is the only known existing Carolingian gemstone cameo. Showing a half-length beardless Christ, it indicates Carolingian interest in the sapphire as a symbol of the heavenly Jerusalem. For many early authors of treatises on stones, the sapphire was the colour of the sky and therefore associated with heaven and its inhabitants. The Talisman of Charlemagne also bears a large sapphire (possibly originally one of two), set amidst other stones. This hollow, golden vessel, which contains a relic, probably a hair of the Virgin Mary, was made in imitation of a Palestinian ampulla. Both shape and relic provide links with the earthly Jerusalem, while the sapphire draws a closer connection with the eternal city of God.

ORB AND SCEPTRE

The orb held by the figure of Charlemagne was an ancient imperial emblem, signifying Roman rule and sovereignty over the whole empire, and was much used in Byzantine portraiture of rulers. Charlemagne may not have carried an orb, but later emperors, such as Charles the Bald, are depicted in manuscripts holding one. Ottonian emperors are shown holding an orb on their seals, and orbs were often used as part of the ceremonies at imperial coronations. At the coronation of the Emperor Henry II in 1014, Pope Benedict VIII presented him with a golden orb decorated with a band of precious stones and surmounted by a cross. The finest surviving medieval golden orb, now in the Treasury of Vienna, is made of gold with two broad vertical bands decorated with filigree, precious stones and pearls. On top there is a cross set with a sapphire intaglio, indicating the heavenly world that can be attained through the cross. Probably made in the Rhine-Meuse area, it dates from the end of the twelfth or early thirteenth century. In 1227, Pope Gregory IX wrote a letter to the Emperor Frederick II stating that 'the spherical shape, which has neither beginning nor end, signifies Divinity and the Lord's mercy which lasts from Eternity to Eternity and to which had been promised the Empire everlasting'.

The sceptre signified the royal power of command, as opposed to the rod or staff, which indicated the royal duty of pastoral care. The Sceptre of Hungary is one of the finest early surviving sceptres in Europe. Dating from the tenth century, it is a short golden rod topped by a Fatimid rock crystal ball, carved with three lions couchant. From its upper and lower mounts hung little golden balls suspended by chains, which tinkled as

< Frans Pourbus the Younger, *The virgin of the family of Vic*, detail depicting Charlemagne, shortly after 1617.

29

the ruler moved. A later, impressive, bejewelled sceptre is that of the kings of France, now in the Louvre. It was first mentioned in 1379/80 during the reign of Charles v of France, who both revised the French coronation and fostered the cult of Charlemagne. Above the staff of the sceptre, there is a knop (ornamental knob) with scenes from the history of Charlemagne, taken from the Chronicle of Bishop Turpin, surrounded by precious stones in high collets and circles of stones that once had diamonds in the middle. A fleur-de-lis, originally covered with opaque white enamel, leads the eye from the knop up to the seated statue of Charlemagne as emperor, wearing a cloak and holding a sceptre and an orb surmounted by a cross.

A ring sometimes played a part in coronation rituals. In England, the ruby became the traditional stone for coronation rings, the earliest belonging to Henry iii. In medieval eyes the ruby was the grandest and most beautiful of all precious stones, inspiring reverence and love towards a lord and embodying the virtue of all other precious stones.

CROWN

Byzantine crowns were often closed and were based on the civil cap of Constantine. The arched crown first appears in the West in the ninth century. Edward the Confessor is shown on his coins wearing an arched crown with pendants and the crown later known as Saint Edward's crown, used at English coronations, is probably a later version of this type. The arched crown of William i of England, ordered for his coronation in 1066, was described as a stemma : 'a noble crown of a fitting sort made for him by the artifice of gold and gems.' The band was set with twelve collets each containing a different precious stone, probably chosen to represent the twelve stones that God named to Moses for the decoration of the breast ornament of Aaron ; they may have represented an invocation of divine assent and protection for William's rule.

Henry ii of England (1154–1189) was the first English king to be depicted wearing an open lily crown with fleurons. Philip Augustus of France (1180–1223) had a similar crown consisting of four large gold plates, each surmounted with a fleur-de-lis. From 1271 this was thought to have been the crown of Charlemagne. Louis ix (Saint Louis) also had a crown of this type, which he presented to the Abbey of Saint Denis. The stylized fleur-de-lis motif illustrates the medieval fascination with religious symbolism : Moses was directed by God to adorn the candlestick in the Tabernacle with lilies of gold (Exodus 25 : 31ff.).

Bust of Charlemagne.
The crown was created by a Prague-based goldsmith and presented at the coronation of Emperor Charles iv in Aix-la-Chapelle in 1349.

Although empresses in the East wore crowns in the fifth century, queens in the West did not follow suit until the eighth century. Up until the fifteenth century, queen's crowns were invariably open circlets, although from the end of the thirteenth century these simple crowns became more elaborate and were surmounted by fleurs-de-lis. Two of the finest examples are those of Anne of Bohemia, Richard II of England's queen (d. 1396) and of Margaret of York (d. 1503) now in Aix-la-Chapelle (Aachen). The former was certainly worn by a queen; the latter may have been made for Margaret in 1468, when she married Charles the Bold, Duke of Burgundy, or for Margaret to give as a votive offering to the late fourteenth-century cult image of the Virgin at Aix-la-Chapelle. The enamelled white roses could equally well serve as an emblem for the House of York or for the Virgin.

SAINT LOUIS

Louis IX, King of France (1226–70), was an outstanding patron of the arts. He created a tradition of artistic patronage for succeeding French kings, which was much imitated by other European kings. He had an international reputation for justice and piety, for which he was canonized in 1297, and his patronage made Paris the centre of Gothic art, architecture and metalwork. Some twenty years before his birth, the sack of Constantinople in 1204 had brought the possession of many relics into the hands of the Latin Emperor Baldwin. In 1238 Louis purchased these relics, which included Christ's Crown of Thorns, via the Venetians, and constructed the Sainte Chapelle in Paris in which to house them. This chapel, one of the great triumphs of Gothic architecture, is like a giant reliquary, imitating goldsmiths' work in its elegant perpendicular structure with light streaming through the windows. The importance of light in Christian belief is demonstrated by the stained-glass windows telling the story of the salvation of mankind through Christ's Passion. By reflecting and refracting light, precious stones, like stained glass, were considered to be both manifestations and condensations of the essence of the stars.

The veneration devoted to the Christ's Crown of Thorns revived the idea of the reliquary crown. After the crown had been placed in the Sainte Chapelle, Louis gave four reliquary crowns to four religious houses. Other crown-shaped reliquaries survive. One contains two thorns from the crown of Christ sent by Henry of Flanders, brother of Emperor Baldwin, to his other brother, Philip II, Count of Namur, and given by him to Namur

Sceptre of the King of France, Charles V, said to have belonged to Charlemagne, from the Abbey of Saint Denis, 1364–1380.

Crown of the Germanic Holy Roman Empire, 10th–12th century.

Cathedral. Another, sent by Louis to the Dominicans of Liège, contains a thorn from the Sainte Chapelle. Other relics of the Passion were mounted in the votive reliquary crown of 1320–30 from the Abbey of the Paraclet. Medallions containing relics are interspersed between hexagonal mounts with translucent enamels depicting secular scenes of monsters, ladies and rabbits. These have their closest parallels in the work of secular goldsmiths, in which sacred and secular themes were combined, a characteristic of fourteenth-century imagery.

THE GREAT CITIES

Under Louis IX, Paris had grown into the greatest and most important city of the Middle Ages. A tax list from 1292 records the presence of 116 goldsmiths and jewellers. Jean de Garlande in his *Dictionary* described the goldsmiths of Paris at the time of the birth of Saint Louis: 'The goldsmiths sit before their fur-

naces and tables on the Grand-pont and make hanaps [goblets] of gold and silver and brooches and pins and buttons, and choose garnets and jasper, sapphires and emeralds for rings.'

A similar expansion of the goldsmiths' and jewellers' craft in other French towns led to the introduction of makers' marks to show the place of origin. Unlike silver, jewellery was only marked very occasionally. Goldsmiths and jewellers flourished in other great towns of Europe such as Bruges, Utrecht, Lübeck, London, Florence and Strasbourg. Cologne, in particular, had a large number of goldsmiths; in 1395, 122 masters were recorded.

The precious stones that gave medieval jewellery its glow, and later its sparkle, were set in gold and gilded silver. The principal sources of rubies were India and Ceylon, while sapphires came from Ceylon, Arabia and Persia. Emeralds came from Egypt, turquoises from Persia or Tibet and amethysts from Germany or Russia. Diamonds were rare in the early Middle Ages but became more common in the late fourteenth and fifteenth centuries. The natural octahedron of the diamond had long

32

been divided to give a pointed shape and in the late fourteenth century more elaborate cutting was attempted. From this point the emphasis moved to the glitter of cut stones rather than the more subtle use of reflection of light through translucent enamel.

Much of the trade in precious stones was in the hands of Jews with Italian merchants often acting as intermediaries. The rich inventories of Jean Duke of Berry, (d. 1416) brother of Charles v of France, record that he obtained rubies, emeralds, pearls and diamonds from Nicolas Pigace, a Genoese merchant, and that in 1412, Louis Gradenigo of Venice sold him two famous diamonds and presented him with a third as a gift.

The difficulty of assigning a fine piece of jewellery to a particular centre of goldsmiths' work is well illustrated by the crown from Sroda Slaska, Poland (German Neumarkt). Found with other treasures in Silesia, it may have been made in Prague by a French or Italian goldsmith, or was possibly brought to Bohemia from Paris. The golden queen's crown, decorated with eagles holding rings in their beaks and fleurons, was originally adorned with 193 gemstones including garnets, spinels, sapphires, aquamarines and pearls, together with cloisonné enamel and *émail de plique*. The hoard also contained a gem-set ring brooch with an eagle cameo, pendants, rings, 3,924 silver coins and 39 gold coins. This amazing discovery shows the importance of jewellery as security; it is likely that these treasures belonged to the Bohemian kings and were pawned to the Sroda Jews in exchange for a loan to the Emperor Charles iv (1346–78). Like hoards from Erfurt and Colmar, it was probably hidden at the time of the Black Death for which the Jews were blamed.

COURTLY JEWELLERY

There was an extraordinary vogue for richly ornamented goldsmiths' work at the end of the Middle Ages. The taste for luxury goods and their conspicuous display were demonstrated by the use of silver and gold dining implements for feasts and a fondness for lavish dress adornments. Dress became more fashionable in the 1340s with the introduction of cutting on the bias, which emphasized the shape of the body. Marriages such as that of Valentina Visconti to Louis, Duke of Orleans, the brother of Charles vi in 1389, were great occasions for the wearing of fine dress and jewellery. As part of the dowry, Valentina brought with her from Italy a great gold brooch set with a large ruby in the centre, five other rubies, twenty-three sapphires, six diamonds and fifty-four large pearls. The earlier clasp found at Motala gives an idea of the impression such a large and bejewelled brooch would have made.

Many brooches of this period, including some of the smaller examples from Valentina's dowry, were enamelled with figures of animals, birds or people. The rich, white enamel technique

Thirteenth-century crown with three fleurons, featuring cabochons and pearls. 'Crown of Charlemagne modelled after the crown in the Abbey of Saint Denis in France'.

33

known as '*émail en ronde bosse*' was much used around 1400. In 1392 Philip the Bold gave his nephew Charles VI a gold brooch as a New Year's gift. Decorated with a white lady and several broomcods (a heraldic device), the jewel was enamelled in the royal colours of white and green and set with a magnificent diamond, a large ruby and several big pearls. The remarkable series of secular brooches preserved in the Treasury of Essen, which includes white ladies, may also have served as New Year's gifts.

BURGUNDY

The marriage of Philip the Bold, Duke of Burgundy (d. 1404), in 1369 to Margaret, only daughter of Louis of Male, Count of Flanders, led to the expansion of the house of Burgundy into Flanders. By shrewd acquisitions, Philip the Good (d. 1467), son of John the Fearless (d. 1419) built up a major power, finally linking the original dukedom with Flanders. The ambition of Charles the Bold (d. 1477) to join them, however, later caused the collapse of Burgundy. All the dukes were great patrons of the arts and none more so than Philip the Good.

ORDERS OF CHIVALRY

The courts of the fourteenth and fifteenth century were marked by elaborate ritual, in which the creation of new orders of chivalry to bind major nobles in loyalty to the king was an important element. The ornaments and jewellery that were produced for them were often impressive. The order of the Garter founded by Edward III, King of England, in 1348 was marked by its symbol and badge of the Garter. These were sometimes bejewelled and one of the most remarkable was found among the Burgundian Treasure at Grandson, where Charles the Bold was defeated in 1476.

The most famous of these orders is that of the Golden Fleece. Founded by Philip the Good in 1430, on the occasion of his marriage to Isabella of Portugal, it became a symbol of the wealth of Burgundian society. The collar of the order was composed of links showing the fire steels of Burgundy and the flints on which the flames were struck, with a golden fleece hanging from the collar. Possibly it represented the Golden Fleece won by Jason in the legend of the Argonauts, but it may have been a reminder of the fleece that Gideon spread on the ground recounted in the Bible (Judges 6 : 36–40).

Pierced, four-lobed clasp from the Colmar treasury, second quarter of the 14th century.

Talisman of Charlemagne (see p. 39).

34

Crown of Wenceslaus, worn by the king of Bohemia in 1346.

THE END OF THE MIDDLE AGES

Our understanding of medieval jewellery has been extended by the discovery of jewellery buried in tombs such as the silver-gilt and copper crown of Marie of Anjou, embellished with stones and found at Nagyvarad in Hungary. Other crowns, like those buried with the emperors at Speyer, were fairly simple – Frederick II at Palermo was buried with a silver gilt crown. According to legend, when Otto III opened the tomb of Charlemagne in 1000 the body was discovered enthroned, clad in golden garments and with a golden crown on its head. This legend was not accepted in Aix-la-Chapelle but was believed at Saint Denis, which already claimed to have relics of the emperor. The continuing interest in Charlemagne is shown by the reliquary bust at Aix-la-Chapelle, which was probably commissioned by the Emperor Charles IV, making it a Bohemian work of the mid-fourteenth century.

Many great jewels were given names : a ruby owned by Jean Duke of Berry was known as the 'Heart of France' ; Ludovico Sforza owned a jewel known as 'il Lupo' (the 'Wolf'). One of the most famous jewels was the 'Three Brothers' made before 1420 for Philip the Good or his father. It consisted of three large table-cut rubies (the brothers) set around a large pointed and faceted diamond. Inherited by Charles the Bold in 1467, it was lost in the battle of Grandson in 1476. A drawing made after its rediscovery shows it as rather an inelegant jewel. Sold to Edward VI of England in 1551, it was worn by James I of England as a hat badge. In this way the sparkling quality of some medieval jewels continued to ornament dress into the Renaissance, although belief in their magical and heavenly qualities started to decline.

BIBLIOGRAPHY : Steingraber 1957 ; Twining 1967 ; Evans 1970 ;
Ottawa 1972 ; Paris 1981 ; Cherry 1992 ; Lightbown 1992 ;
Scarisbrick 1993 ; Scarisbrick 1994 ; Munich 1995 ; Gajewska-Prorok 1996 ;
Paris 2001 ; London 2003 ; Paris 2004 ; Leuven 2005 ; Paris 2007.

*First chapter of The Order of the Golden Fleece held by Philip III the Good,
Duke of Burgundy, in St Peter's church in Lille, 22nd November 1431.*

> *John the Fearless, Duke of Burgundy,* early 15th century.

Statuette of Emperor Charlemagne on horseback

Recent copy

Plaster, 25 cm

Paris, Musée du Louvre (inv. SN 911)

This statuette may be the model for a larger work. It depicts the emperor wearing a crown, and holding a globe and sceptre. The horse's foreleg is raised, much like the horse in the statue of Marcus Aurelius (AD 121–180), at the Capitoline Museums in Rome – a work that served as a model for most effigies of kings on horseback until the seventeenth century.

Charlemagne is considered the first truly European sovereign, in the sense that he inherited and conquered the greater part of the continent, but perhaps most importantly because he wanted to give it an efficient legal and administrative structure. He was born in 742 and became supreme sovereign of the kingdom that he had inherited from his father, Pepin the Short, which extended to the Atlantic Ocean and the North Sea. By waging war against neighbouring powers, Charlemagne extended his empire considerably, as far as Hamburg and Budapest in the east, all the way to the centre of Italy in the south. In 795, he seized part of Catalonia from the Moors. He was crowned emperor by Pope Leo III in 800, and was recognized as such by Byzantium in 812. He died in Aix-la-Chapelle (Aachen) on 28 January 814, and was buried the same day in the Palatine Chapel. At his death the kingdom was divided and Charlemagne's dream of a Greater Europe disappeared. JW

BIBLIOGRAPHY : Aken 1965, pp. 9–10.

Drawing of the talisman of Emperor Charlemagne

Louis Napoleon Bonaparte, signed 'Pour copie conforme' [Certified true copy], NAPOLÉON LOUIS B' after 1831

Watercolour on paper, 24 x 15 cm

Arenenberg, Musée Napoléon

Talisman de Charlemagne.

Today, the talisman of Charlemagne is in the collections of the Palace of Tau in Reims. It was thus to the cathedral that had witnessed so many coronations of the kings of France – and not to Aix-la-Chapelle – that the Empress Eugenie, widow of Napoleon III, chose to 'return' this relic in 1919. In September 1804, when Napoleon I and his wife Josephine were visiting Aix-la-Chapelle (Aachen), Bishop Marc Antoine Berdolet, a Frenchman, offered the talisman of Charlemagne to the empress. Upon her death in 1814,

< Crown-Reliquary of the Holy Thorns.

it passed to her daughter Hortense, who placed it amongst her many other souvenirs of the emperor at her residence in Switzerland.

In 1842, Louis Napoleon Bonaparte, Hortense's youngest son and the future Emperor Napoleon III, made an unsuccessful attempt – while imprisoned for life in the fortress of Ham – to sell the talisman to Tsar Nicholas I. It was perhaps at this time that he used this illustration and description of the reliquary. The handwriting of Bishop Berdolet was copied to attest to the piece's authenticity; in addition, the prince had signed it 'Pour copie conforme [Certified true copy], NAPOLÉON LOUIS B', quite possibly in order to facilitate the sale of the object.

The collections of the Napoleon Museum at Arenenberg contain a portrait of Queen Hortense done by Felix Cottrau (1799–1852). Seated at an organ or harmonium in the chapel at Arenenberg, she proudly embodies the role she has been given: that of assuming the legacy of Napoleon I. Napoleon did not hesitate to place himself in the tradition of Charlemagne, the only other emperor to have reigned over the French. Since he did not believe that his son – the King of Rome (1811–32) – would ever ascend to the throne of France, he designated the sons of his adopted daughter as his successors; it was they who were given the heavy responsibility of bearing the torch that their mother had passed to them. Hortense's intention here is quite plain: she wears the talisman of Charlemagne as the fastening to her cloak, its prominent position chosen specifically to attract attention. Since it was never mounted on a chain, what we see is a painterly adaptation by Felix Cottrau. Hortense died on 5 October 1837, before Napoleon III came to power, and thus did not live to see her dream fulfilled. CE

BIBLIOGRAPHY : Arenenberg 2003.

Engraving of the crown of the Germanic Holy Roman Empire

Inscription in the lower left-hand corner :
IOH. ADAM DELSENBACH, DEL. ET SCULP.
Coloured copper engraving, 47 x 64 cm
Vienna, Kunsthistorisches Museum, Bibliothèque (inv. 35.326/I)

Engraving of sceptre, holy-water sprinkler, four globes and spurs of the Germanic Holy Roman Empire

Inscription in the lower left-hand corner : DELSENBACH FEC.
Coloured copper engraving, 47.5 x 64.5 cm
Vienna, Kunsthistorisches Museum, Bibliothèque (inv. 35.326/IV)

From Johann Adam Delsenbach : *Exact Delineation of the Imperial Ornaments of the Holy Roman Empire of the German Nation. Kept in the free imperial city of Nuremberg. Drawn and engraved by Johann Adam Delsenbach at the expense of Senator Hieronymus Wilhelm Ebner von Eschenbach. With the Holy Relics engraved after drawings by Frederick Iuvenell*, Nuremberg, Gottlieb Schneider, 1790.

These two engravings are from a series of twelve coloured engravings on copper, depicting the imperial jewels (insignia, ornaments, relics), as well as three portraits of kings in their coronation robes. They are the work of the painter and engraver Johann Adam Delsenbach (1687–1765), one of Nuremberg's most important illustrators. The idea for the engravings came from Jerome Ebner of Eschenbach (1673–1752), who was a member of the delegation from Nuremberg that was sent to the coronation celebration. The mounts date from 1790, after Christoph Weigel and Adam Gottlieb Schneider, art and book dealers in Nuremberg, acquired the engravings.

With the exception of the engravings of garments, Delsenbach's representations of the objects are life-sized and extremely precise, both in terms of the materials and the details of their execution. These engravings are best understood in a context of scientific interpretation of the imperial treasures. This intellectual framework continued throughout the eighteenth century, and stood in opposition to a more legend-based (and Catholic) explanation of the their origins. The copper engravings – for which several preparatory studies by Delsenbach have come down to us – present the state of the imperial jewels as they were at the outset of the Early Modern era, shortly before the 1796 evacuation of the Nuremberg treasury and the loss of several pieces.

The first engraving shown here illustrates the most important item from the imperial ornaments, the imperial crown, which dates from the Middle Ages. The second engraving depicts two sceptres (one of them a holy-water sprinkler), four globes and golden spurs. The two simple globes, one of which may be seen in Albrecht Dürer's portrait of Charlemagne, and the spurs, which were not used for imperial coronations in the Early Modern period, are now lost. FK / BKE

BIBLIOGRAPHY : Nuremberg 1986, pp. 42ff., no. 37 ; Gall, FFM, 1994, p. 170 ; Bauer 2003, p. 92 ; Palermo 2006, pp. 84ff. ; Berlin/Magdebourg 2006, pp. 266ff.

Reliquary of the right arm of Saint Louis

France (?), c. 1275

Gilt and silver-plated copper, cabochons and coloured glass,

400 x 100 mm

Midi-Pyrénées, Mairie de Prudhomat

The upright arm of Saint Louis is clad in the sleeve of a ceremonial garment decorated with engraved medallions ; the upper and lower edges are decorated with a gilt border set with semi-precious stones. The sleeve, decorated with a fold pattern, has a grilled opening cut into it, which proves that it was a later addition. The thumb and index finger are almost touching, while the other fingers are straight. This is sometimes – incorrectly – seen as a hand of justice, which in France symbolized royal judicial power. The gesture has many other meanings, however : the desire for a lovers' rendezvous, an amulet to ward off danger, or a symbol of protection – a natural gesture for a king.

We know of other similar reliquaries, particularly one in the parish church of Saint-Gildas-de-Rhuys in Morbihan, France, in which the hand forms a gesture of benediction: thumb, index and middle fingers are extended, while the other two are folded to the palm. This arrangement of the fingers is also evocative of the hand of justice. Two other arm-reliquaries are in the collection of the Saint Kunibert church in Cologne. Both have all five fingers extended, in prayer or submission. The meaning may thus vary slightly from one place to another. The arm shown here contains a relic of Louis IX, known as Saint Louis (1214/15–1270), who earned his surname fighting against France's heretics and unbelievers. He also launched two Crusades: one in 1249 in Palestine, to liberate the Holy Land – during which he was taken prisoner and was forced to pay his own ransom – and the second in 1270 in Tunisia, in an attempt to convert the Sultan, during which Louis died at the foot of the ramparts of Tunis.

The Crusades, which took place from the eleventh to the thirteenth centuries, were military undertakings in which the pope brought together several European sovereigns. The principal objective of the Crusades was the liberation of the Holy Land, so that Christians could resume their pilgrimages. From a religious point of view, the Crusades had the added advantage of fostering a feeling of unity within Europe. JW

BIBLIOGRAPHY : Morel 1988, pp. 42–4 ; Daoulas 1991, no. 165, 166, 167, 169 ; Brussels 1992, p. 345 ; Antwerp 1995, no. 80.

> ## Crown-Reliquary of the Holy Thorns
> After 1206
>
> Gold, precious stones and natural pearls, 33 x 207 mm
>
> Namur, Musée Diocésain, Trésor de la Cathédrale Saint-Aubain
> (inv. 4)

The crown-reliquary of the Holy Thorns is incontestably the most precious and prestigious piece in the treasury of Saint-Aubain Cathedral, Namur. The relics for which it was made came from the Bucoleon, the imperial palace in Constantinople built by Constantine in the fourth century AD. At the initiative of Pope Innocent III (1160–1216), the Fourth Crusade set sail from Venice for Constantinople. Prince Alexios dreamed of retaking the throne of his father Isaac II, who had been deposed. In exchange for their help, he promised the crusaders money and an army, and that he would bring the Greek Orthodox Church under the authority of the Church of Rome. But he did not keep his promises and, exasperated, the crusaders sacked the city in 1204, massacring its population, pillaging its treasuries and removing its most precious relics. Baldwin I then founded the Latin Empire of Constantinople. His reign came

to an abrupt end in 1205, and his brother Henry, Count of Flanders and Hainaut, succeeded him, initially as regent. Henry charged Daniel d'Ecaussines with carrying a gift of inestimable value to his brother, Philip the Noble, Count of Namur. Among other items, the package contained a large fragment from the True Cross and two thorns from Christ's crown, which were given to the Chapter of Saint-Aubain.

The crown-reliquary of the Holy Thorns was created to give the thorns a splendour befitting their importance. It is not known whether the crown was meant to be worn, although in practical terms this is impossible. The crown consists of eight hinged gold plates, each topped by a fleur-de-lis, like other crowns from this period. Two rectangular capsules, mounted one on each side, serve to contain the thorns. The decoration is sumptuous: fleurons and filigree-work surround the stones, all of them precious, which is rare for the period. A line of pearls emphasizes the contours and hinges. On the front plate, an Indian emerald and a large sapphire complement each other harmoniously. Several other sapphires, some of them pierced, have been re-employed in this piece. Amethysts, turquoise and a tourmaline complete a sophisticated palette of colours. The crown, which weighs 550 grams, has come down to us in a remarkable state of preservation. It is missing only a few cabochons, three rows of pearls and nine fleurons. The results of a 1973 restoration are barely noticeable.

The crown has been wrongly attributed to the Mosan goldsmith Gerard, who worked in Constantinople as part of the entourage of Emperor Henry. Its style is more reminiscent of an artist from the Upper Moselle who had been influenced by French art. However, comparison with the cross-reliquary from the Abbey of Saint Vincent de Laon, now in the Louvre, suggests that its origins are even more likely to be Parisian. The fact that Philip the Noble married the daughter of Philip II of France adds weight to this argument. In an inventory of the treasury of Saint-Aubain from 1218, mention is made of a 'corona Domini spinea'. This may be a reference to the current crown-reliquary, or it could simply be the mention of the Crown of Thorns, in which case the date of creation could be moved forward to 1225–30.

The case in which the crown has been kept since the thirteenth century is also remarkable. Octagonal in shape and fitted with a handle, it is made of oak or covered in leather. It is decorated with twenty-five *champlevé* Limousin enamel discs, all of which, with the exception of the one in the centre of the cover, are decorated with a motif from a Romanesque bestiary. JJ

BIBLIOGRAPHY : Lanotte 1969, pp. 20–6 ; Didier 2003 ; Wilhelmy 2004 ; Wilhelmy 2004b.

< Eagle crown of Blanche of Valois

Paris (?), early 14th century

Gold, precious stones, pearls and enamel, 62 x 160 mm

Wroclaw, Muzeum Narodowe we Wroclawiu (inv. v-2333)

This queen's crown consists of ten articulated sections, linked by pins topped with elaborate fleurons. Each of these trapezoidal sections consists of a double gold leaf. An openwork technique has been used to create the trefoil and quatrefoil pattern on the inward-facing leaves. The outer leaves have been enhanced with precious stones and pearls in gold settings, as well as with trefoil ornaments in relief that were at one time enamelled. An eagle with spread wings, sometimes holding a ring in its beak, sits atop each of the ten sections. In all, 193 precious stones, including garnets, sapphires, spinels, pearls, tektites and aquamarines enhance this crown, which has been attributed to expert goldsmiths and jewellers in either Paris or Prague.

The eagle motif suggests that the crown was intended for a marriage ceremony. This is the only known example of an 'eagle crown', a style made popular by the Staufen dynasty in the thirteenth century. The last recorded example was the 'Corona Rica', which was made for Isabella the Catholic in Valencia in the fifteenth century. A description of Isabella's crown – now lost – suggests that it was very similar to that of Sroda, which was missing at that time. Both crowns appear to have drawn on similar sources of inspiration to convey the message of royal and imperial power.

The present example was discovered on 24 May 1988 during excavation work in the centre of Sroda Slaska in Silesia, southwest Poland. It was found in the medieval foundations of a house in the town's ancient Jewish quarter. The excavation also turned up a large brooch featuring a central cameo with an eagle, a pair of decorated pendants, a bracelet, three rings, 3,924 silver coins, 39 gold coins and a piece of stamped gold leaf. The crown was broken when it was found, but it was restored and the missing fragments (two section bases, four eagles and two fleurons) were reconstructed. Historical research has shown that the jewellery was probably hidden in the mid-fourteenth century. The Jewish community of this town – located near Wroclaw, capital of the duchy – were persecuted in 1349 and disappeared entirely from Sroda after the pogrom of 1362. The duchy of Wroclaw had belonged to the Bohemian crown since 1335, following a succession agreement between Henry IV the Good and John I of Bohemia. The wealthy Jewish merchants of Wroclaw and Sroda had close ties with the court in Prague, and they were able to obtain privileges and letters of credit in exchange for loans to John I and his son Charles IV. Charles's secretary and chancellor, Johann von Neumarkt – the original name of the town of Sroda – was an efficient and discreet intermediary. Some of the jewels are unquestionably of royal or imperial origin. They were probably part of the treasury of Prague under Charles IV, and were given as collateral against a loan.

The last owner of this crown may have been Blanche of Valois, the first wife of Charles IV, King of Bohemia, and half-sister of Philip VI of France. She died in 1348, shortly after this treasure was buried, then lost. This is the first time that the crown has been shown outside Poland. JWI / CV

BIBLIOGRAPHY : Sachs 1991 ; Wroclaw 1996 ; Pietrusinski 1996 ; Wachowski/Witkowski 1996 ; Gajewska-Prorok 2001 ; Warsaw 2001 ; Dresden 2002 ; Valladolid 2004 ; Arbeteta Mira 2004, pp. 169–86, 273–5, no. 52 ; Golinski 2006, pp. 67–70 ; Sroda Slaska.

'Aquila Vitrix' brooch

Italy (?), first half of the 13th century

Gold, precious stones, pearls and chalcedony cameo, 129 mm

Wroclaw, Muzeum Narodowe we Wroclawiu (inv. v-2334)

The central motif of this round brooch (or fibula) – a cameo with a figure of an eagle in the 'Aquila Vitrix' imperial style – is characteristic of Sicilian workshops around 1240. This kind of eagle representation has its roots in Byzantine imperial art. The round construction is typical but is designed here with outstanding artistic quality, emphasizing the contrast between the simple, flat polished surface of the outer ring and the complex settings of the gemstones and pearls. Such brooches were used as a fastening for ceremonial robes and were usually worn on the wearer's chest. This one was probably made in a workshop connected with the Staufen Italian court. A similar design has been found in a later example from Split made towards the end of the thirteenth century.

The brooch was found in 1988 during excavation works in the centre of Sroda Slaska in Silesia along with other jewels and coins including a queen's crown. It probably came from the Prague Treasury of Charles IV and was hidden during the persecution of Jews in the middle of the fourteenth century. JWI

BIBLIOGRAPHY : Sachs 1991, pp. 71–5 ; Pietrusinski 1996, pp. 9–63 ; Wachowski/Witkowski 1996, pp. 99–125 ; Wroclaw 1996 ; Gajewska-Prorok 2001, pp. 25–56 ; Warsaw 2001 ; Dresden 2002 ; Valladolid 2004 ; Arbeteta Mira 2004, no. 53, pp. 275–6 ; Golinski 2006, pp. 67–70.

> Motala clasp

Paris (?), early 14th century

Gold, sapphires, rubies and amethysts, 192 mm

Stockholm, Statens Historiska Museum (inv. Shm 423)

This gold clasp was found in 1818 by a fisherman casting for eels in Motala River in the parish of Kimstad, Östergötland, Sweden. The clasp consists of an arched gold disc set with cabochon-cut sapphires, rubies, amethysts and small cast-gold figures. The many empty settings suggest that the clasp was also originally decorated with sixty pearls, which have presumably dissolved from the years submerged in water.

The design resembles the rose window of a Gothic cathedral. The decoration at the centre of the disc is constructed like a six-petalled flower with a large sapphire in the middle. Each petal holds both a sapphire and a gold figure in the form of a centaur. The spaces between the petals are decorated with octagonal rubies. The central flower motif in three concentric circles is surrounded by gold figures in the shape of lions, eagles,

griffins and chimerae, and semi-precious stones (rubies, sapphires and amethysts). The origins of the clasp are unknown. Due to its extraordinary quality, it is possible that it was made in Paris, the leading artistic centre for goldwork at this time. No information about the original ownership of the clasp has been discovered, however, the considerable value and the secular nature of the decoration suggest that it belonged to a person from the highest levels of the aristocracy or a member of the royal family. AE

BIBLIOGRAPHY : Montelius 1912 ; Rosenberg 1918 ; Andersson 1984.

< ## Bust of Isabella the Catholic

Spain, Saragossa (?), 16th and 19th centuries
Silver, silver gilt and semi-precious stones, 45.5 x 42 x 27 cm
Gaasbeek Castle (inv. 648)

Isabella of Castile (1451–1504), daughter of King John II of Castile and Isabella of Portugal, was the half-sister of the future King Henry IV of Castile. In 1469 at Valladolid, she married Ferdinand, heir to the throne of Aragon. When Henry died in 1476, Isabella became Queen of Castile. The ascension of her husband Ferdinand to the throne of Aragon in 1479 created a double monarchy. The royal couple, to whom Pope Alexander VI in 1494 gave the title 'The Catholic Monarchs', succeeded in stimulating economic development while reining in the power of the nobility. Ferdinand's foreign policy and Columbus's discovery of the New World formed the basis of the vast empire of the future Charles V.

Isabella and Ferdinand instituted the Inquisition – originally intended for the Jewish section of the population – and in 1492 successfully completed the *Reconquista* (the recapture of the Iberian peninsula from the Arabs) with the fall of Granada, hitherto the epicentre of Moorish culture. In that same year, the Jews of Spain were expelled. The vigorous campaign of religious re-conquest that followed marked the end of a long period of integration and ended with an unprecedented intellectual decline. On the other hand, it heralded the triumphant birth of a culturally unified empire.

This full-face bust was probably created in Saragossa as a relic, after Isabella's death. The plaited hair, gilt crown and necklace, garments laden with ornaments, and the intarsias (mosaic woodwork) are all characteristic of Spanish silverwork in the late Gothic period. Nevertheless, several doubts remain about the authenticity of the bust, which was purchased in 1893 by the last Marquise of Gaasbeek at the famous Spitzer auction in Paris. In the catalogue *La collection Spitzer* (Paris, 1890), it was described as a 'Reliquary in the shape of a head, 15th century', with a matching piece explicitly identified as a bust of

Ferdinand of Aragon. On the basis of this information, in 1899, the piece was listed in the inventory of Gaasbeek Castle as a bust of Isabella. The dating, identification and description of the piece remain imprecise. The absence of inscriptions or hallmarks, and the comparison with portraits of the queen from the same period, serve only to reinforce feelings of ambivalence. From both an iconographic and metalworking point of view, arguments tend to lean in favour of a partial 'transformation' of the object in the nineteenth century. More in-depth research will be required to determine if this piece dates from the late Middle Ages, if it was overzealously restored, or whether it is a high-quality copy. LV

BIBLIOGRAPHY : Silio Cortes 1960 ; De Azcona 1964 ; Ballesteros-Gaibrois 1964 ; Renson/Casteels 1979, pp. 170–1 ; Innsbruck 1992, pp. 404ff. ; Thomas/Stolz 1995 ; Gent 1999, p. 168, no. 7 ; Bonn/Vienna 2000, pp. 121–2, no. 19.

Crown of the dukes of Burgundy

France, between 1404 and 1419

Gilt and silvered copper, cabochon stones and coloured glass,

150 x 220 mm

Dijon, Musée des Beaux-Arts, (inv. CA 1467)

This copper crown comprises a closed band with a decoration of silver suns with fiery rays alternating with vertically-set pairs of coloured stones. The band is surmounted by fleurs-de-lis alternating with three trefoil motifs on pierced triangular bases, interspersed with roses and three-pronged elements. Both the fleurs-de-lis edged in turned metal and the three-pronged elements are surmounted by stars and enhanced with three coloured stones held in place by claw-shaped settings.

Formerly in the collection of the scholar Louis-Bénigne Baudot, who worked to save certain endangered pieces from the crown jewels during the French Revolution, this crown was given to the museum by his widow in 1856. In 1857 its provenance was officially recorded as the tomb of Margaret of Bavaria (1363–1423), wife of the duke of Burgundy known as John the Fearless (1371–1419). However, it had previously been described in an inventory of the sacristy of the Champmol Charterhouse dated 1791, apparently proving that it had not been in the princess's burial vault : 'a crown of gilt copper with a few silver fleurons and more or less precious stones.' As some experts have rightly noted, the materials used are out of step with the magnificence of the Burgundian court and it therefore seems likely that the crown was not made to be worn, a practice which, in any case, was preserved for rare, exceptional occasions. Furthermore, there is no mention of the crown in the inventories of Philip the Bold (1404) or John the Fearless (1420). This has given rise to the hypothesis that the crown may have surmounted the duke's catafalque or stood for his status during a funeral ceremony, although the practice of replacing the duke's body with his crown was not traditional at the Burgundian court. Despite the many uncertainties, this crown can be dated to between 1404 and 1419. A crown symbolizes royal, ducal or princely power more than any other ornament and for this reason it can, in some cases, stand in for the absent potentate who wears it, hence its importance in the history of the monarchies of the Old Continent. cv

BIBLIOGRAPHY : Magnin 1883, note 1467 ; Monget 1898, vol. III, p. 65 ; Beaulieu/Baylé 1956 ; Twining 1960, p. 225, ill. 78d ; Dijon 2004, no. 84.

Ring of John the Fearless, Duke of Burgundy

Paris, c. 1410

Gold, enamel, agate, jet, emerald and rubies, 15 x 23 mm

Paris, Musée du Louvre, Département des Objets d'Art

(inv. OA 9524)

The raised bezel of this gold ring is set with a portrait of John the Fearless, Duke of Burgundy (1371–1419). His profile in white agate is topped with a large hat carved out of jet and his emerald garment is embellished with two rubies, one of which is now missing. The duke's emblem – a carpenter's plane in orange enamel – may be seen inside the ring, along with an obliterated inscription : VERE [FILIUS DEI ERAT] ISTE ('Truly, this was the Son of God' : Matthew 27 : 54). All that remains of the inscription on the outside of the ring is the letter c. This luxurious ring proves that the fashion for wearing cameos disguised as attributes of power – which was adopted by Renaissance kings and queens – had already begun in Paris, led by the dukes of Burgundy, who were great art lovers. The portrait is comparable to a miniature of John the Fearless receiving the author of *Le Livre des Merveilles du Monde*, in the collections of the Bibliothèque Nationale de France (Ms.fr. 2810 fol. 226).

The ring was found in the tomb of John the Fearless, which was opened in 1792 during reorganization work after the Champmol Charterhouse was closed in the wake of the French Revolution. DSC

BIBLIOGRAPHY : Paris 2004, no. 66.

Insignia of the Golden Fleece

Southern Netherlands (?), 16th century

Gold, 54 x 23 mm

Brussels, Musées Royaux d'Art et d'Histoire (inv. 3858)

The ram's fleece hangs from a simple ring beneath a Burgundian standard. The early insignia were fairly plain. It was not until the seventeenth century that the Knights of the Golden Fleece, like those of the other great chivalric orders, began to commission two versions, one simple, to be suspended from a ribbon worn around the neck, and the other richly decorated and accompanied by an imposing chain for grand occasions. The Order of the Golden Fleece was founded in 1430 by Philip the Good, Duke of Burgundy, and for centuries maintained a strong solidarity among the high aristocracy of all the countries under Habsburg domination. JW

BIBLIOGRAPHY : Antwerp 1995, no. 24.

> Collar of the Golden Fleece

Hans Boxhammer, Wroclaw, 1623–55

Silver and silver gilt, 680 mm

Private collection

The piece bears two stamps : the letter w in an oval, for Wroclaw and the monogram B in an oval for the master jeweller Hans Boxhammer

Founded in Bruges by Philip the Good in 1430, the prestigious Order of the Golden Fleece was designed to bring the Burgundian nobility closer to the duke. It could only be passed through the male line or, where there was no male heir, to the husband of the female heir. The order accordingly passed to the Habsburg monarchy when Charles v was made a knight in 1517. But, on the emperor's subsequent abdication, the Order of the Golden Fleece passed to the Spanish branch of the family. It was not until 1712 that it also returned to the Austrian Habsburgs. Since then, as international law has never settled in favour of either, there have been two coexisting orders of the Golden Fleece : the Austrian order, which has retained an aristocratic and religious character, and the Spanish order, which has been open to non-Catholics and to commoners since the nineteenth century. Albert II, King of the Belgians is one of the few European catholic heads of state to be a knight of both the Spanish and Austrian orders of the Golden Fleece.

The order's insignia consists of a ram's fleece, recalling the Greek legend of the Golden Fleece. This tells the story of an immortal ram with a golden fleece, which was given by Zeus to the inhabitants of Iolcos.

Knights of the order may also wear the insignia on a red ribbon around the neck, or on the small or large ceremonial collar.

The owner's initials, engraved when the piece was made along with its weight, and the indication of the place (Wroclaw) and period (1623–1655) of its making have enabled the holder of this collar and insignia of the Golden Fleece to be identified. The initials RGS are those of Heinrich Wilhelm von Starhemberg (RGS), Count of the Holy Roman Empire, who was born in Riedegg, Austria, on 28 February 1593, and died in Vienna on 2 April 1675. He became a count of the Holy Roman Empire in 1643 and the 423rd dignitary to be received into the Order of the Golden Fleece in 1647. Grand Marshal of the court of Ferdinand III, he was also a member of the Privy Council. FC/PC

BIBLIOGRAPHY : Maurice 1665 ; Bruges 1962, p. 45, no. 423 ; Brussels 2004, p. 246, no. 236 ; Valencia 2007, pp. 36–7, no. 7.

< ### Chain of Michelle of Valois
First quarter of the 15th century
Silver gilt, garnets and enamel pearls, chain : 909 mm ;
rosettes : 31 mm ; height of crowned letters : 30 mm
Soleure, Musée de l'Ancien Arsenal Voor de Vertaling :
Solothurn, Museum Altes Zeughaus (inv. MAZ 1143)

This silver-gilt chain dates from the first quarter of the fifteenth century. Research carried out in 1980 revealed that the stones are garnets rather than rubies. In its current state, the chain consists of fourteen rosettes and thirteen links in the form of the letter M topped by a crown. At one extremity an M is missing, and both ends of the chain thus end in a rosette. The chain once had a clasp, but this is also now missing. The rosettes that have survived intact consist of rings encircling diagonally placed crosses. The arms of each cross are decorated with a five-petalled flower bud. At the centre, the crosses feature an eleven- or sometimes ten-pointed star. The stars are topped with foliage consisting of six elements, at the centre of which is a cut garnet, the setting for which is generally composed of nine segments. Originally, the fields between the arms of the crosses featured pearls of enamel. The middle of the chain is marked by an M link that has been enhanced with three garnets. The backs of the links are numbered and there are two brazed hooks.

The origin of this chain is unknown. Since the nineteenth century it has been thought to be part of the 'Burgundian booty' seized by the confederate armies from the riches of Charles the Bold, Duke of Burgundy, after the three great battles of Grandson, Morat and Nancy (1476–7). The attribution of this chain to Michelle of France (1395–1422), the first wife of Philip the Good, Duke of Burgundy, is explained by the presence of the M topped

with a crown, as well as by the agreement of dates. The style of the silverwork nevertheless allows for other interpretations : for example, the chain may have been used to decorate a statue of the Virgin Mary. ML

BIBLIOGRAPHY : Deuchler 1963, pp. 131ff. ; Munich 1995, pp. 265ff.

>> ### Four paintings of the jewellery of Charles the Bold, Duke of Burgundy
c. 1500
Watercolour on parchment, 21.6 x 45.1 cm ; 17 x 13 cm ;
34.5 x 26 cm ; 22 x 19 cm
Basle, Historiches Museum (inv. 1916.475–478)

These four watercolours, painted on parchment around 1500, are exceptional documents since they are life-sized representations of four of the most beautiful pieces of jewellery of Charles the Bold, Duke of Burgundy (1433–1477). On 3 March 1476, the confederate army defeated Charles at the Battle of Grandson and seized a number of splendid elements from a chancellery, a chapel and a treasury worthy of a king. However, the troops from Basle did not hand over the four pieces of jewellery at Lucerne with the rest of the booty, which they were permitted to divide equally between all the victors. It was only a quarter of a century later that they had the pieces assessed and drawn in order to sell them. The jewels were bought in 1504 by Jacob Fugger, a wealthy and renowned banker from Augsburg, for the sum of 40,200 florins. The four pieces are listed below.

The 'Three Brothers' clasp
The jewel takes its name from the three 70-carat balas rubies that surround a central diamond. It is listed in the 1419 testamentary inventory of John the Fearless. Eva Kovács's discovery of the invoice proves, however, that the king's goldsmith, Jehan Ruissel, made this piece in Paris in 1398 for Charles the Bold's great grandfather, Philip the Bold, Duke of Burgundy. Fugger resold the 'Three Brothers' in 1543 to the king of England, Henry VIII. Portraits depicting Elizabeth I and James I wearing the 'Three Brothers' document the existence of this piece in the British royal collections. The piece disappeared around 1630.

The 'Federlin'
This precious clasp once adorned a lavish duke's hat owned by Charles the Bold. It is decorated with seventy pearls mounted in openwork, five rubies, four diamonds and three large pearls. In 1471 the goldsmith Gerard Loyet made a jewel of this type for Charles the Bold. Real feathers can be attached to the clasp. One of these hats, also adorned with pearls and rubies, was also

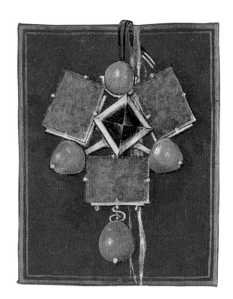 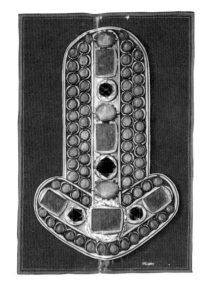 

part of the Basle booty from Grandson sold to Jacob Fugger. Fugger resold that piece as well, along with the clasp (probably as separate pieces) to Emperor Maximilian I of Austria, whose first wife had been Mary, Charles the Bold's daughter.

The 'White Rose'

The symbol of the House of York, this jewel may have come into Charles the Bold's possession after his third marriage to Margaret of York, Edward IV's sister, in 1468. The style of this piece is characteristic of the work of a British silversmith, and not of a Parisian jeweller of the first half of the fifteenth century. The ruby centre (a spinel) is surrounded by petals in white enamelled gold. However, clasps in the shape of white roses are also mentioned in inventories of the court of Burgundy from the fourteenth century.

'The Order of the Garter'

Charles the Bold became a member of the Order of the Garter thanks to his brother-in-law, Edward IV of England, at Gand on 4 February 1469. Set amongst eleven diamonds and precious stones, the letters of the motto HONNY SOYT QUY MAL Y PANSE are also formed by cut stones. The watercolour is all the more valuable as it is the only documented appearance of the Order of the Garter in the fifteenth century : no original example has come down to us. Around 1515, Jacob Fugger sold the order to the Emperor Maximilian I for 8,000 florins. **MCB**

BIBLIOGRAPHY : Wackernagel 1894, pp. 57–68 ; Burckhardt 1931, pp. 247–59 ; Deuchler 1963 ; Bern 1969 ; Van der Velden 2000 ; Kovács 2004, pp. 388–9.

> Johan de Critz, *Portrait of James I, King of England*, c. 1605.

> Jacob Fugger, coloured engraving of the 'Federlin' hat clasp, c. 1500.

> Jacob Fugger, coloured engraving of the 'Three Brothers' clasp, c. 1500.

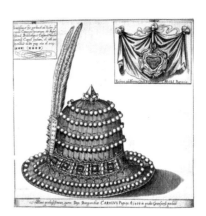

Ring with the initial M

Burgundy (?), late 14th century (?)

Gold and diamonds, 23 mm

Vienna, Kunsthistorisches Museum, Kunstkammer (inv. KK 131)

This gold ring is distinctive for the prominent letter M formed by eleven diamonds. It is mounted in a separate setting, on both sides of which are engraved a crown and the letters CHI (or CLI). According to recent tradition, this ring belonged to Mary of Burgundy (1457–1482), and was the engagement ring offered to her in 1477 by the future Emperor Maximilian I, however, there is no evidence to support this proposal. The ring is not an ancestral possession of the Habsburgs, since it entered the collections only in 1845. In 1866, it was suggested that the ring had belonged to Queen Mary of Hungary (1371–1395), the first wife of Sigismund of Luxembourg. According to Tillander, such an early date is supported by the simple cut of the diamonds. It has not been clearly established whether the M was an original part of the setting of the ring, as we know it today, but the style of the engraving decorating the sides of the setting does not exclude a late-fourteenth-century dating. Nevertheless, there is no solid basis for any further connection with Mary of Hungary. In addition, at present we have no convincing interpretation of the engraved word CHI (Christ ?) or CLI. FK

BIBLIOGRAPHY : Tillander 1995, p. 84 ; Malines 2005, no. 61, p. 187.

> Crown of Mary of Burgundy

Southern Netherlands (?), third quarter of the 15th century

Silver gilt, enamel, pearls and coral, 180 x 100 mm

Bruges, Edele Confrerie van het Heilig Bloed

(Noble Brotherhood of the Holy Blood)

This small crown is composed of a bandeau embellished with medallions – notably one of Saint Catherine and the monogram IHS – imitation stones in enamel and five upright blue enamel fleurs-de-lis decorated with coral and pearls. The piece was reduced in the nineteenth century to be mounted on a reliquary. It is believed that the crown was placed on the coffin of Mary of Burgundy when her body was transferred to Notre-Dame for the funeral service. It was common practice not to bury royals with their crown jewellery but to replace these with funerary objects of lesser value. This silver-gilt crown set with imitation gemstones was created in haste and was probably never even placed on Mary's head. In contrast, the crown presented by her mother Margaret of York at Aix-la-Chapelle cathedral was crafted with much more care and is opulently decorated with precious stones. JW

BIBLIOGRAPHY : Beaune 2000, p. 41 ; Mechelen 2005, no. 11.

Portrait of Emperor Maximilian I and his family

Period copy by Bernhard Strigel (1460–1528), 1515–16

Oil on canvas, 56 x 47 cm

Memmingen, Strigel-Museum

Emperor Maximilian I is positioned to the left of the painting, turning to the right to meet the gaze of his first wife, Mary of Burgundy, at whose side stands Philip the Handsome, their son. The emperor's arm is wrapped around his grandson Ferdinand, who stands next to Maximilian's other grandson, Charles. Near Mary is Maximilian's adopted son, Louis of Hungary. Maximilian, his son, and his grandsons are all wearing the chain of the Order of the Golden Fleece – except for Louis, who was only made a knight during the Chapter of Brussels in 1516. Philip and Charles are both wearing ornaments on their hats, while Mary is wearing a long bodice chain and a necklace with a large red stone. Louis wears a chain with a rosette set with a square-cut diamond.

Maximilian skilfully arranged political marriages for his descendants, and took advantage of these unions to increase his own territory. He himself married Mary of Burgundy in 1477, after a long series of diplomatic discussions. The empress died after a fall from a horse in 1482, and the following year he married Bianca Maria Sforza, daughter of the late Duke of Milan. He thus obtained the help of Milan in the war against the Turks, which the emperor financed almost entirely with the immense artistic treasure given to him by his wife's uncle, Ludovico Sforza, so that Ludovico could retain the throne of Milan.

His son Philip's flattering title – 'the Handsome' – in fact, signified that he was a beloved sovereign, going so far as to defend the interests of his Dutch subjects against the wishes of his father. Philip inherited Burgundy and the Netherlands through his mother, and he married Joanna of Castile, whose parents had united Castile and Aragon. He was thus also King of Spain, but he died in 1506 at the age of twenty-eight. Subsequently, Maximilian's grandson Charles – the future Emperor Charles v – became sole heir to his parents' vast kingdom : the Holy Roman Empire, Spain and its overseas territories, and the Netherlands (Burgundy having meanwhile been recaptured by the French). In 1521, his brother Ferdinand married Anne of Bohemia, thus linking the fate of this country with that of the Habsburgs for nearly four centuries (until 1918). Ferdinand was made Holy Roman Emperor in 1556. Louis, successor to the Hungarian throne, was betrothed to Mary of Habsburg, Maximilian's adopted granddaughter, before he was even born. The marriage was only consummated in 1522. Louis ii died in 1526 during the Battle of Mohács, which was won by the Turks. He was barely twenty years old.

Bernhard Strigel also painted the original work, now in the collection of the Vienna Kunsthistorisches Museum (Gemäldegalerie, inv. 832), which had a depiction of the Holy Family on the back of the panel. The two sides have now been separated so that they may be admired side by side. Clearly, Maximilian did not have an ounce of modesty, since he did not baulk at putting his family on the same level as that of Christ. JW

BIBLIOGRAPHY : Hamann 1988, pp. 66–8, 102–5, 200–3, 382–5 ; Utrecht 1993, pp. 30–1, Vienna 2000, pp. 112–13.

The Renaissance:
between uniformity and internationalism

ELISABETH SCHMUTTERMEIER

Of all periods, it was during the Renaissance that members of the upper classes were most given to the wearing of jewellery, yet we know surprisingly little about the designers or the places where these objects were made. The stylistic features of many jewels are documented in funerary objects and portraits of royalty, aristocrats and wealthy bourgeois, while inventories provide their descriptions,[1] yet it remains impossible to establish the origins of most pieces, since there was at that time no law requiring them to be marked and the similarities are so great. Renaissance jewellery followed an international style. There are many reasons for this, of which a few here are provided.[2]

The output of the Italian, English, German and Dutch jewellery workshops was distributed across the whole of Europe: jewels were appreciated as gifts by men of state and were frequently included in dowries. Through embassies and European dealers, these pieces soon gained an international reputation. Furthermore, artists and craftsmen were often asked to work for foreign courts, or were obliged to leave their own countries to escape the religious wars that recurred throughout the sixteenth century, seeking asylum elsewhere. They continued to work in their own styles, but were also open to influences from their new surroundings. The account books preserved in some court archives reveal the names of many gold and silversmiths and jewellers, however, only a very few of the pieces preserved today can be attributed to a particular person or workshop. While some jewellery descriptions include indications of nationality such as 'of a Spanish, German or French kind', it is impossible to be any more precise regarding their provenance.

During the sixteenth century, publishers realised there was good business to be made from sourcebooks of ornamental engravings and distributed them widely, helping to define a uniform style across the whole of Europe. This style established itself quickly in some places, while in others the particular interests and importance of patrons rendered its advance more hesitant. Wood and copper engravings and etchings documented ornaments and personal items in every field of art, enabling craftsmen based outside the main artistic centres to become familiar with the latest fashions[3] and to respond quickly to new trends.

The many similarities characterizing jewellery of this period can also be explained by the fact that fashions in clothing were similar across the different countries and within each social class, so fashions in jewellery logically followed suit. In the fifteenth and early sixteenth centuries it was fashionable for women to wear bright colours, low-cut necklines and generous drapery complemented by appropriate jewellery.[4] This included long or short chains decorated with pendants and long belts or chatelaines enhanced with various ornaments. Men liked to wear rings, chains and medallions on their hats (enseignes). Towards the end of the fifteenth century women abandoned their medieval head-coverings, and now that their ears were free they started to wear earrings, mainly pearls.[5] They also plaited strings of pearls and fine chains into their hair or wore them around their heads. In the second half of the sixteenth century the body would be tightly enclosed in very straight, all-covering garments with almost no folds. From 1560 to 1620 members of the European upper classes wore 'Spanish dress'[6] of obligatory and quintessentially neutral black, providing the perfect background on which to display pieces enamelled in bright colours or set with precious stones.

Garments were edged with expensive embroideries in contrasting colours and the whole would be completed with a parure of multicoloured stones in a comparatively uniform style. While men were more likely to wear jewellery in the first half of the sixteenth century, women wore more in the second half. At first pieces were used primarily to hold together the openings in a garment, such as split sleeves, but they gradually lost this function. At royal courts in the late sixteenth century, garments would be covered in rosettes of different sizes, sometimes sewn to the fabric in an ostentatious, exuberant fashion to emphasize the status of the wearer. Sometimes the sovereign

< Joos van Cleve, *Eleanora of Habsburg, Queen of France (1530–1547)*, c. 1530.

CATERINE DE MEDICIS
REYNE DE FRANCE

64

or city authorities would rein in this profusion of jewels with regulations requiring a particular form of dress. Some parures have come down to us as a result of their 'second life'. Jewellery was also often attached to religious objects, decorations and relics.

Despite the great similarities that characterize jewellery from the second half of the sixteenth century to the first half of the seventeenth, the regional and local origins of these miniature works of art – and the artists and craftsmen who made them – can to some extent be determined though analysis of their motifs or themes and the techniques used in their manufacture. Sovereigns were primarily responsible for attracting well-known artists to their courts and commissioning these valuable items.

The Renaissance art of jewellery has its origins in Italy during the second half of the fifteenth century. The rediscovery of the art of the Greeks and Romans introduced a new vision of nature and the place of humanity within it, and also a new interpretation of artistic expression. Human beings were once again the centre of attention : their bodies and clothes, and so too the jewellery that they wore, had to form a harmonious whole, as conceived by the humanists of antiquity. After emerging in Florence these ideas spread through the rich courts of the princes of Ferrara, Mantua, Urbino and Milan, along with other Italian cities ruled by major patrons of the arts. Ancient mythology became an ever-growing feature of the pictorial repertoire, replacing the traditionally biblical iconography. Renaissance jewellery was not based on the original ancient pieces, since at that time they had not yet been discovered or studied, but on ancient architecture and sculpture. Painting, sculpture and jewellery-making shared the same affinities : artists such as Lorenzo Ghiberti (c. 1378–1445), Filippo Brunelleschi (1377–1446), Sandro Botticelli (1445–1510) and Andrea del Sarto (1486–1530) began their artistic careers as apprentice gold and silversmiths. The techniques described by Benvenuto Cellini (1500–1571) in his treatises on goldwork and sculpture are still relevant today.[7]

At this time Venice and Genoa were centres for the importation of precious and semi-precious stones, including pearls, and major dealers, such as the Fugger family of Augsburg, were based there. The Fuggers also owned a workshop in Venice, where the stones they had bought were mounted in gold and silver by German smiths before being sold on.[8] Venice also had a flourishing trade in imitation pearls and paste jewellery. Milan was another important Italian centre for jewellery-making and stonecutting under both the Sforzas and the Habsburgs.[9] Erudite, humanist members of the upper classes collected ancient gems, which were sometimes worn as jewellery mounted in the Renaissance style. As demand was so high, the stonecutters' cameos and intaglios based on classical tradition were much copied and imitated.

After his victory over the Swiss confederation at Marignano in 1515, Francis I of France (1494–1547) briefly took possession of the Duchy of Milan and the Renaissance style made its way into France. The tastes and preferences of the French king were adopted by members of the nobility and exerted a major influence over the arts. Francis I brought Italian artists to his court, including Leonardo da Vinci (1452–1519) and Benvenuto Cellini, and also Italian master gold and silversmiths, who worked with the French jewellery-makers. In a decree of 15 June 1530, the king declared certain particularly important pieces – which were not the personal property of the ruling family – to be 'crown jewels', and so part of the inalienable heritage of the crown.[10] This idea had supporters among his contemporaries. However, the concept of 'crown jewels' applied only to the precious stones, which were sometimes given names and regarded as having special powers, and did not concern their mounts. These stones were often re-cut as jewellery adapted to the fashions of each new period. Moreover, the establishment of the inalienability of the heritage did not prevent precious stones from being pawned in cases of financial need, and it sometimes happened that they could not be recovered from the lenders.[11]

Two types of Renaissance jewellery are particularly linked to the French court. The first is the hat medallion (enseigne), also known as an *agrafe*. Evolving out of a combination of medieval pilgrims' badges and military insignia, the hat medallion was one of the most characteristic pieces of the early Renaissance.[12] At first these circular or oval medallions showed images of the saints whose protection was being invoked, but over the years religious scenes began to appear, followed by motifs taken from ancient mythology. Portraits and original pieces from the period reflect the variety of these motifs. This French innovation spread rapidly across the whole of Europe, and particularly to Italy.

The other piece linked to the French court was the *commesso*, consisting of stones and enamelled gold. The combination of these materials made it possible to depict scenes and characters from ancient mythology and portraits. This type of art, which had been popular at the Burgundian court as early as the fourteenth and fifteenth centuries, gained a new lease of life at the court of Francis I, who was an avid collector.[13] The most remarkable examples of *commessi* in which the art of the stonecutter and jeweller are perfectly combined, were made by the Fontainebleau School in the reign of Francis I's successor Henry II (1519–1559). These miniature works of art were generally kept in cabinets but could also be sewn to hats or other garments, or worn as medallions.

< French school of the 16th century, *Catherine de' Medici*, 1547–1559.

Circle of Sofonisba Anguissola, *Portrait, probably Margherita of Savoy (1589–1655), wife of the Duke of Mantua.*

Like Italy, the Germanic Holy Roman Empire was composed of many states of varying size and political importance. Italian jewellery in the Renaissance style seems to have made its first appearance in the Habsburg empire as part of the dowry of Bianca Maria Sforza (1472–1510), who married Emperor Maximilian I (1459–1519) in Innsbruck in 1494, although pieces of similar importance had already entered the family through Maximilian's first wife, the rich heiress Mary of Burgundy (1457–1482). At this time the German gold and silversmiths were still working in the Gothic style and their creations mainly illustrated religious themes. The fashion for the Renaissance style coincided with the Counter-Reformation. Pieces in this style, notably 'large link chains', can clearly be seen in the paintings of Lucas Cranach the Younger (1515–1586), as can bracelets, usually worn in pairs. Centres of jewellery-making included Nuremberg and Augsburg, which were Protestant cities, and Catholic Munich. It should be noted that Nuremberg and Augsburg both had the advantage of a long tradition of high quality craftsmanship and were also free cities of the empire. They sent goods of all kinds to the assemblies of the Imperial Diet and, despite their own Protestant persuasions, to Catholic as well as Protestant courts.[14] Although over time Nuremberg lost its importance as a centre of gold and silverwork in comparison to Augsburg, ornamental engravings continued to be made and printed there.

Production in Munich was at its height during the reign of Albert V (1528–1579), younger brother and successor to Charles V and husband of Anna, daughter of Emperor Ferdinand I (1503–1564). His family ties to the emperor made Albert one of the most important Catholic regents in Europe. He followed the example of Francis I of France in amassing his own collection of jewellery and founding the Treasury of the Residence of Munich. This jewellery collection, of which nothing has been preserved, is mentioned by the court painter Hans Mielich (1516–1573) in an illustrated inventory produced between 1552 and 1555.[15] Most of the pieces were pendants which Anna had received as gifts around 1549, or that she received a little later on the occasion of her marriage.[16] The creators of these pieces are unknown, but they could have been works by the so-called 'minor masters'. Some inventories list the names of gold and silversmiths, but the little information we have does not make it possible to state with any certainty that it was these masters who made them, or whether they simply acted as intermediaries.

The largest collection of all belonged to Emperor Rudolf II (1552–1612) in Prague, who was particularly interested in the arts and sciences of his day. During his reign Prague became the most important city for jewellery-making in the German empire. Rudolf collected precious stones because he believed they had magical powers and brought members of a family of specialist stonecutters, the Miseronis, to his court. Jan Vermeyen (before 1559–1608) and his craftsmen, and Andreas Osenbruck[17] made mounts for cameos, which were worn as pendants or simply appreciated as miniature works of art.[18] Some parts of Rudolf's collection are now preserved in Vienna at the Treasury and at the Kunsthistorisches Museum.

King Henry VIII of England (1491–1547), an enlightened sovereign and keen promoter of art, maintained a fierce, personal rivalry with that other great collector, Francis I of France. Henry wanted to beat Francis in every area and, following his break with the pope in Rome, amassed the necessary astronomical sums by confiscating the wealth of the Catholic institutions. Henry had a jewellery collection of excellent quality at his disposal, since Hans Holbein the Younger (1479–1543) was among those creating the pieces.[19] Henry's daughters Mary Tudor (1516–1558) and Elizabeth I (1533–1603) inherited part of his collection after his death.

Following her marriage to Philip II of Spain (1527–1598), all the portraits of Mary Tudor show her adorned with the jewellery she had been given as wedding gifts by her father-in-law Charles V and her husband. Meanwhile, Elizabeth I had a marked fondness for pearls and precious stones. Portraits show her dressed in garments glittering with jewels. At New Year she liked to exchange gifts of precious stones with those close to her at court. She was particularly keen on emblematic jewellery, whose allegorical meaning was known only to a select few. One of the innovations seen at her court were the pendants and medallions showing miniature portraits and cameos – including the 'Drake Jewel' – whose creator was none other than the goldsmith and miniaturist Nicholas Hilliard (1547–1619). Elizabeth's successor, James IV of Scotland and I of England (1566–1625), had a marked preference for diamonds, which were so important that they were given names, such as the 'Three Brothers'.

In the sixteenth century Spain, Portugal and the Netherlands were all ruled by the Habsburgs and experienced a phenomenal economic boom. The trade links to the Habsburg possessions in the New World provided Europe with large quantities of gold and precious stones. The ports of Barcelona, Lisbon[20] and Antwerp became great commercial centres. Like his father Charles V, Philip II of Spain favoured the Italian masters – Naples, Sicily and Milan were then part of the Habsburg empire. Charles V had been brought up in the Netherlands and, despite the religious differences, close relations had been established with the north. In Spain, the influence of the Netherlands was felt primarily in painting and jewellery making. If the court inventories and correspondence are to be believed, messengers and other agents brought a phenomenal quantity of jewellery into every court with family ties to the Habsburgs. [21] In Spain, centre of the Counter-Reformation, religious motifs

Anthonis Mor van Dashorst (Antonio Moro), *Mary Tudor, Queen of England and later second wife of Philip II of Spain*, 1554.

Marcus Gheeraerts, *Anna van Buren, first wife of William I of Orange-Nassau*,
1533–1558.

such as crosses, images of the Madonna and saints once again appeared in the jewellery repertoire. The Dutch jewellery makers were keener on maritime motifs, further reinforcing the diversity of themes. Thus Erasmus Hornick (c. 1543–1583) of Antwerp presented figurative pendants representing fish, sea-horses and dragons in Nuremberg in 1562.[22] while, again in Nuremberg in 1581, Hans Collaert the Elder (1530–1581) created small figures riding sea monsters. Many Dutch artisans were obliged for political or religious reasons to move to England, Scandinavia, Germany, Prague or Florence, contributing to the internationalization of jewellery in the late Renaissance. The Dutch gold and silversmiths also played an important part in changing the form of pendants, which were the most popular form of jewellery.

Pendants were miniature, individual works of art that could be hung on a chain or attached to a garment. They were made to be seen from either side: the front usually showed a design in relief, while the back would be enamelled with moresque or grotesque motifs. Initially, pendants were circular or oval in shape and made of cut stones or cast and enamelled metal set into mounts whose style ranged from extreme simplicity to extreme sophistication. Over time, medallions were more often pear-shaped and elongated with baroque pearls. For purely ornamental reasons they might be set with stones, either cabochons or cut with facets. Sometimes the stones were set in the form of a monogram. Erasmus Hornick further expanded the repertoire by making pendants in the shape of a tabernacle decorated with small figures. These motifs were sometimes in openwork, a technique refined around 1600, when the small figurines became increasingly delicate. Many copies of the basic structure of the pendant would be cast, but the decoration and colouring would always be done on an individual basis, with a choice of portraits, religious or profane themes, allegories, virtues, models of boats or fantastical human figures or animals. The creatures' bodies, set in gold or enamelled mounts, were made of irregular pearls, with baroque pearls completing the composition. Some pendants were also used as decorations for toothpicks, ear-cleaners and pipes. Rings were another much appreciated form of jewellery at the time and were worn on all the fingers. They would be set with precious stones and richly enamelled.

Though there are few surviving pieces of Renaissance jewellery in either private or public collections, the many portraits from the period give us a representative idea of the astonishing range and diversity of such pieces, which were regarded as works of art in their own right.

1. For a selection of inventories including descriptions of jewellery, see Hackenbroch 1979, pp. 385ff.

2. There is not space in a short essay to develop the issues raised by Renaissance jewellery, so this can only serve as an introduction.

3. See Evans 1970, pp. 88ff.

4. See Boucher 1996, pp. 213ff.

5. In the Middle Ages only men wore earrings, since women's ears were hidden by their headdresses and hair.

6. Bönsch 2001, p. 128.

7. The first manuscript version of the treatise on working gold and silver was a wedding gift from Cellini to Francis I and Joan of Austria. It was finished in 1565 and has not been preserved until the present day. In 1567, when the treatise on architecture was finished, both essays, dedicated to Cardinal Francis de' Medici, the groom's brother, were published in 1568 (Firenze e Peri). See Brepohl 2005, pp. 22–3.

8. Hackenbroch 1979, p. 15.

9. Comparison with enamelled gold mounts for cut stones confirms that these pendants and medallions were indeed made in Milan.

10. Somers Cocks 1980, p. 3. The French crown jewels were preserved until the eighteenth century, but were dispersed following the French Revolution.

11. Emperor Maximilian I pawned an extremely valuable 'fleur-de-lis' diamond from the dowry of his first wife, Mary of Burgundy. The stone then passed into the possession of Henry VII of England, and then of Henry VIII, who in turn sold it to Francis I of France for 44,444 gold crowns. The diamond enabled the French king to buy the freedom of his son, Henry II, who was a hostage of Charles V. Thus the stone made its roundabout way back to the Habsburgs (Hackenbroch 1979, p. 114).

12. Hackenbroch 1996.

13. Distelberger 2002, pp. 219ff.

14. For example, Ferdinand I sent a counsellor to Augsburg and Nuremberg to buy jewellery to a value of between 12,200 and 16,000 florins, which he gave to his daughter Eleonora (1534–1594) as dowry when she married Duke Guillermo of Mantua (1538–1587) in 1561 (Hackenbroch 1979, p. 143).

15. The *Codex Monacensis*, icon 429 (53 miniatures on parchment) is preserved in the Bayerische Staatsbibliothek, Munich.

16. Hackenbroch 1967, no. 664, pp. 74ff.

17. Dates of birth and death unknown.

18. Prague, c. 1600. See Vienna 1988

19. Since 1860 the sketches have been preserved at the British Museum, London.

20. At this time Lisbon was the main port for the trade in spices, fabrics and precious stones from India.

21. When Johann VII Khevenhüller served as ambassador to Emperor Maximilian II and Rudolf II in Madrid, he also brought paintings and jewellery to the Habsburg courts at Innsbruck and Graz.

22. Evans 1970, pp. 110ff.

70

Portrait of Emperor Charles V

< Period copy after Christoffel Amberger (1500/1510–1562), 1532
(original painting)
Oil on panel, transposed to canvas, 67 x 51 cm
Lille, Musée des Beaux-Arts (inv. P 755)

Emperor Charles V (1500–1558) is seated at a table and appears to be in conversation, his gloved right hand opening a book as if to substantiate his arguments. On his left hand he wears a ring with a point-cut diamond that appears to be almost untouched. Like many of the Habsburgs, the emperor was superstitious and viewed the diamond – the hardest substance in nature – as a means of protecting himself against evil; he believed that cutting a diamond diminished its magical powers. He wears the insignia of the Order of the Golden Fleece, suspended from a decorative chain whose pattern features the Burgundian standard. The emperor's crest can be seen above his head, topped by the imperial crown and flanked by the Pillars of Hercules, which in turn are flanked by Charles V's motto '*Plus oultre*' (to the utmost). The emperor's age – thirty-two – is given just below.

Charles V was one of the great defenders of a European policy of alliances through marriage, which allowed him to extend his territory, or at least to exert his influence abroad. He was king of Aragon and Castile through his grandparents, and from his father he inherited the title of Holy Roman Emperor and ruler of the Burgundian Netherlands. The matrimonial politics practised by his grandfather Maximilian I made him the ruler of a vast territory that extended not only across Europe, but also as far as the newly discovered American continent. JW

Parure with portrait of Emperor Charles V

Parure: Reinhold Vasters (1827–1909), Aix-la-Chapelle, c. 1870;
cameo: 16th century
Gold, enamel, pearls, diamonds and onyx cameo,
cameo pendant: 90 x 55 mm; small pendant: 40 x 35 mm;
earrings: 95 x 50 mm; small ornaments: 40 x 35 mm
Tokyo, Albion Art Collection

The chain, or collar, from this parure has twenty-three links of different sizes terminating in a pendant set with a cameo portrait of Charles V (1500–1558), Holy Roman Emperor and King of Spain, wearing contemporary dress. Two other pairs of ornaments make up the parure, one attached to a larger element, the second independent. The links of the collar are composed of asymmetrical foliate scrolls, each enamelled in a white 'blackwork' pattern. The tendrils are highlighted with touches of red and white dots, and are set with pearls and diamonds. Similarly, the two pairs of ornaments are of scrolled design, enamelled in

red and white, and set with pearls and table-cut diamonds. The ensemble is a late-nineteenth-century imitation of important sixteenth-century jewellery depicted in portraits and described in royal and noble inventories but nearly always broken up. A rare survival is in the Munich Residenz (Hackenbroch 1979, p. 145, fig. 369) where a portrait of Duchess Magdalena (Hackenbroch 1979, p. 187, fig. 508) shows how such collars were worn across the shoulders below the ruff with the extra ornaments pinned to the sleeves and on the tab at the shoulder. All the links could be separated and sewn on to the fabric of the dress when required. DSC

BIBLIOGRAPHY : Krautwurst 2003, pp. 204–7.

Medallion with portrait of Emperor Charles V

Medal : Leone Leoni (1509–1590), 1550 ;

frame : Vienna, late 19th century

Gold, diamond, ruby, lapis lazuli and enamel, 86 mm

Thyssen-Bornemisza Collection (inv. DEC 0696)

Charles V (1500–1558) is shown in profile, a flat cap on his head and wearing the insignia of the Order of the Golden Fleece. He is depicted at the age of fifty and appears tired having failed to achieve many of his ambitions. He had neither managed to secure a lasting peace with France, nor to bring the Protestant German princes under his sway, nor establish good relations with the Pope.

The Renaissance played an important role in the various neo-styles of the nineteenth century, and it is inescapable when it comes to medallion portraits. The creator of this piece of jewellery has used a medallion from 1550 made by Leone Leoni. We know of several copies of this medallion : sovereigns commissioned such pieces in a series – made from gold, silver or even bronze – and distributed them as a form of introduction. Those cast in gold were given to the most distinguished persons. The profile portrait is mounted on a plate of lapis lazuli and set in a typical frame, whose white enamel has been distressed in order to give the piece a more 'authentic' appearance. JW

BIBLIOGRAPHY : Somers Cocks/Truman 1984, pp. 158–9.

Medallion with portrait of Emperor Charles V

Flanders (?), 1550–70

Gold, diamonds, rubies, cameo in agate, enamel, 44 x 41 mm

Aalst, Fabrique de l'Église Saint-Martin (inv. LR 650)

This nearly frontal portrait of Charles V (1500–1558) has been carved in an oval agate cameo. The sovereign is depicted wearing the insignia of the Order of the Golden Fleece. The openwork setting features four table-cut diamonds arranged crosswise and interspersed with table-cut rubies. On the back, the oval is deco-

rated with engraved floral patterns; the undersides of the diamond settings are square, while those for the rubies are round. There are traces of wear, particularly a missing piece from the bottom of the frame – no doubt the spot from which a pearl was hung – offering proof that this piece was often worn. It has sometimes been suggested that the portrait is not of Charles v, but that of his son Philip ii of Spain. JW

BIBLIOGRAPHY : Robijns 1980b, no. 650 ;
Kockelbergh/Vleeschdrager/Walgrave 1992, p. 32.

Pendant with cameo of Philip II

Cameo : Circle of Jacopo da Trezzo (1515–1589), Italy ;
setting : Spain, c. 1560
Gold, enamel, diamond, pearl and onyx cameo, 47 x 31 mm
Private collection, courtesy Albion Art Jewellery Institute, Tokyo

The black enamel frame, set with eight table-cut diamonds alternating with gold and black quatrefoils, encloses an onyx cameo portrait bust of Philip ii (1527–1598). The border is inscribed PHILIPPUS REX HISPANIA (Philip King of Spain). The king is depicted with short curly hair and a beard, wearing a small frilled ruff, gorget, cuirass and cloak, facing in profile towards the right. His armour is echoed by the black military trophy enamelled on the back of the cameo, in which gun, halberd, sword, helmet, powder flask and drum are combined. A pearl hangs beneath the pendant.

This cameo, unusual for its contemporary jewelled setting, is one of a small number of portrait cameos commissioned by Philip from a group of Italian artists led by Jacopo da Trezzo to give to those he particularly wished to favour. It stems from the tradition for hardstone official portraiture established by Alexander the Great in the fourth century BC and adopted by the Roman emperors, which was revived by the kings and queens of the Renaissance. However, whereas other monarchs such as Francis i and Henry ii of France are recorded in very few such images, Philip ii ordered several, now in the Palazzo Pitti, Florence, the Hermitage Museum, St Petersburg, the Bibliothèque Nationale, Paris, The British Museum, London and the collection of Queen Elizabeth ii at Windsor Castle. These majestic portraits, in which Philip personifies the ideal monarch in all his grandeur, must have inspired his sister-in-law, Elizabeth i, to commission similar images of herself later in the century. DSC

Ring of Queen Isabella of Hungary

Mid-16th century
Gold, enamel and diamonds, 32 mm
Private collection

This gold ring is chased with strapwork scrolls and moresques. The shoulders are set with four table-cut diamonds, supporting the bezel set with a point-cut diamond surrounded by four triangular-faceted diamonds. The outside of the hoop is chased with the initials s[IC] F[ATA] V[OLUNT] in roundels, and the inside is engraved with the name YSAB–R–UG (Isabella, Queen of Hungary). Isabella (1519–1559) was the daughter of Sigismund i of Poland and his wife, the Milanese Bona Sforza. In 1539 she married John Zápola, King of Hungary (1487–1540). The ring bears her name but the initials SFV are those of the Zápolya family motto, which translates 'As the Fates Wish'. For sixteenth-century monarchs, diamond rings symbolized the virtues of endurance and invincibil-

74

ity with which they wished to be associated. They were subsequently a favourite choice for royal marriage ceremonies. DSC

Ring with table-cut diamond

Italy (?), c. 1500
Gold and diamond, 18 x 13 mm; diam. 24 mm
Pforzheim, Schmuckmuseum (inv. 1963/59)

This solid, cast-gold ring is set with a table-cut, lozenge-shaped diamond in a bezel with four rounded sides.

Rings of this type often appeared in Italian paintings such as the *Portrait of Agnolo Doni* by Raphael (c. 1506, Palazzo Pitti in Florence). This ring shows how diamond cutting had become progressively more sophisticated – the table is quite large in comparison with the full octahedron. JW

BIBLIOGRAPHY: Antwerp 1968, no. 227; Tokyo 2003b, no. I–2.

'Ring of Queen Mary of Hungary'

Central Europe (?), c. 1560
Gold, diamonds and enamel, 22 mm
Budapest, Magyar Nemzeti Múzeum (inv. Ann. Jank. 300)

This cast golden ring has a small Gothic M set with diamonds on the bezel. The shoulder is enamelled with ronde bosse and *champlevé* enamel and embellished with nine hog-back cut diamonds in closed settings. The renowned collector Miklós Jankovich (1772–1846) bought this ring at an auction of items from the treasury of Mariazell monastery in Steiermark, Austria. According to the original inventory of Jankovich's collec-

tion, the ring was a votive donation to Mariazell by Mary of Hungary, the widow of King Louis II of Hungary. The Miklós Jankovich collection became part of the collections of the National Museum of Hungary in 1836.

Richly moulded ornamentation, cast and enamelled in ronde bosse, is a characteristic feature of jewellery from the Habsburg and Wittelsbach courts of Central Europe in the 1560s. The fashion for setting diamonds in the form of a puzzle was also popular in the earlier decades of the century. In some portraits, for example those now in Coburg (1519) and Vienna (1522), Mary of Hungary wears a pendant and an enseigne of similar size and decoration to this jewel. However, the association of this ring to her is without doubt a later attribution. Mary left Hungary for the Netherlands after the disastrous battle of Mohács in 1526, in which the Louis and other key figures were killed. She remained there until her death and had no further association with Hungary. ERK

BIBLIOGRAPHY: Domanovszky 1939, p. 302; Hlatky 1939, p. 79; Bois-le-Duc 1993, no. 38; Budapest 2004, no. III–2; Budapest 2005, no. II–17.

Casket of Archduchess Anna Dorothea of Austria

First half of the 17th century

Silver and enamel, 210 x 185 x 160 mm

Madrid, Monasterio de las Descalzas Reales, Patrimonio Nacional (inv. 00610933)

An inscription on the lid tells us that the relic contained in this silver casket belonged to Sister Anna Dorothea, Archduchess of Austria and daughter of Rudolf II, Holy Roman Emperor. The reliquary probably entered the Descalzas Reales Monastery in Madrid in 1628, the same year that Anna Dorothea took her vows. The relic itself should be distinguished from the case. Like other relics in this cloister, this piece may have been created by the emperor himself. We know that he was a skilled silversmith and that he gave the relic to his daughter before she entered the monastery. The case was probably a later addition. Designed to display its contents, the case features openwork that allows one to see inside and to address prayers to the relic.

The pattern of multicoloured enamel rosettes, the garlands and rock-crystal vase are reminiscent of other pieces from the Austrian court, such as the one in the Augustinian monastery at Salamanca. FMG

BIBLIOGRAPHY : Palma 1995, no. 18, p. 45.

> Casket

Workshop of Wenzel Jamnitzer (?), Nuremberg, last third of the 16th century

Ebony, silver, cameos and semi-precious stones

270 x 360 x 280 mm

Madrid, Monasterio de las Descalzas Reales, Patrimonio Nacional (inv. 00612589)

This little casket is clearly not a religious object, and was probably used to hold jewellery or coins. It tells the story of Tereus, King of Thrace, who was married to Procne, the daughter of King Pandion of Athens. Tereus raped his sister-in-law Philo-

mela, and then cut out her tongue and held her captive. However, Philomela managed to alert her sister by weaving a message into a tapestry. To avenge her, Procne killed her son and served the flesh to his father. In punishment, the gods changed Tereus into a hoopoe, Philomela into a nightingale and Procne into a swallow. This is the Latin version of the myth; some Greek authors switch Philomela and Procne's metamorphoses.

The scenes are depicted on small rectangular plates, and the gods that intervene at the end of the story are shown in the semi-circular niches between the plates. The rest of the surface of the piece – which has been restored in several places – is decorated with cartouches of cameos and stones. The depictions of the gods were clearly inspired by engravings on the same theme by Giovanni Jacopo Caraglio (1504–1565), an Italian engraver who worked in Rome and Krakow, and whose work was highly sought after in Central Europe. The meticulously chased plates, like the placement and workmanship of the gods suggest that the casket originated in the workshop of Wenzel Jamnitzer (1508–1585), who excelled at working with semi-precious stones.

The casket, along with other pieces from Central Europe, was probably presented to the Descalzas Reales Monastery either by Queen Anna of Austria – daughter of Holy Roman Emperor Maximilian II and fourth wife of Philip II of Spain – or by her mother, Maria of Austria (1528–1603). **FMG**

BIBLIOGRAPHY : Madrid 1998b, no. 256, p. 518.

Portrait of Maria of Austria

< Period copy after Anthonis Mor van Dashorst (Antonio Moro)
(1519–1576), 1550 (original painting)
Oil on canvas, 99 x 81 cm
Brussels, Musées Royaux des Beaux-Arts de Belgique (inv. 1297)

In 1548, Maria of Austria (1528–1603), daughter of Charles v, married Maximilian, the future Holy Roman Emperor (1527–1576). The marriage was one in a long series of matrimonial alliances by the Habsburgs. Maria wears a headdress consisting of a chain of gold, enamel, diamonds and pearls. She has a pearl earring and wears a large cross, decorated with three *en tremblant* pearls ; the chain is set with table-cut diamonds and faceted stones. Her chatelaine (belt) consists of alternating round and square links set with diamonds and rubies, culminating in a brooch set with a table-cut diamond. Her dark dress is fastened in the front with a gold buckle and the ribbons on the sleeves are trimmed with gold and crystal *tressons*. The empress is wearing a ring with a single large diamond. One can just make out the slits placed in the fingers of her gloves at ring level.

This distinguished portrait of a lady of quality combines simplicity and splendour. The imperial couple had sixteen children, of whom only seven survived infancy. JW

BIBLIOGRAPHY : Antwerp 1968, no. 306 ; Tokyo 2003b, no. I–17.

Pendant cross

Spain, c. 1560
Gold, diamonds, pearl and enamel, 88 x 53 mm
Paris, Musée du Louvre, Département des Objets d'Art
(inv. OA 5603)

The borders of this Latin cross are decorated with small scrolls and flowers in multi-coloured enamel set with *dos d'âne* diamonds that form, in Gothic lettering, the Latin phrase IN CROCE SALUS ('Salvation is in the Cross'). The enamelled back of the cross features the Instruments of the Passion : the cock that crows at the moment that Peter betrays Christ, the pillar with the whip and scourge, the high priest's mitre, the pitcher that Pilate used to wash his hands, the sword that cut off Malchus's ear, the nails from the Cross, the sponge set on a reed that was used to offer vinegar to Christ, and the spear used to confirm that he was dead. At the bottom, the piece ends in a winding line of black enamel and a suspended pearl.

For two thousand years, the cross has been the ultimate Christian symbol. Women are frequently depicted in portraits wearing a cross suspended from a chain. Some of these chains, particularly in the sixteenth century, were very richly decorated, like this magnificent example from a profoundly Catholic country.

The *dos d'âne* diamonds – oblong and with a triangular shape – are produced by cutting a rough octahedron diamond on one face only, thereby barely cutting the stone. Oblong stones such as these lend themselves better to forming letter shapes. JW

BIBLIOGRAPHY : Molinier 1902, no. 53 ; Tokyo 2003b, no. I–14.

< **Pendant depicting the Annunciation**

Germany (?), second half of the 16th century

Gold, diamonds, rubies, pearls and enamel, 134 x 58 mm

Paris, Musée du Louvre, Département des Objets d'Art

(inv. OA 5630)

This pendant comprises a semicircular platform flanked by two columns : the scene is a miniature sculpture in multicoloured enamel. Mary kneels as the archangel Gabriel speaks to her. Overhead, two cherubs blow a horn. The pendant is richly decorated with rows of rubies and table-cut diamonds, and the entire piece is attached to an openwork cartouche whose base is wider than its top. Three pearls hang from the base, while at the top the three chains with pearls terminate in a clasp in the shape of a cross, which is also adorned with enamel and a diamond.

The Annunciation is one of the great moments in the Gospel : it announces the coming of the Messiah, and emphasizes both the divinity of Christ and Mary's virginity. In the troubled period of the wars of religion, a piece of jewellery with such a scene was a declaration of faith by its princely owner. JW

Pendant

Father Juan Poch (?), Vienna, 1580–7

Gold, diamonds, rubies, pearls and enamel, 111 x 72 mm

Pforzheim, Schmuckmuseum (inv. 2000/18)

Coloured enamel has been laid over a French-style gold frame, in the manner of the jeweller Daniel Mignot. At the centre of this piece is a square, raised setting holding a faceted diamond. Around it, rubies and table-cut diamonds form a square, with the rubies at the corners of the square and the diamonds on the sides. Three pendant baroque pearls enrich this piece, whose bail is placed front-to-back. This lavish yet elegant piece of jewellery is typical of the intricate Spanish style that dominated the European courts in the last decade of the sixteenth century. JW

BIBLIOGRAPHY : Schmuckmuseum 2006, no. 31.

> **Chain and pendant with Jupiter and Juno**
Four small welded plaques with the initials GK
Southern Germany (?), c. 1600
Gold, pearls and enamel, chain : 412 mm ; pendant : 29 mm ;
rosettes : 15–29 mm
Thyssen-Bornemisza Collection (inv. DEC 0690)

The chain consists of eleven openwork rosettes that have been chased using filigree and granulation techniques, interspersed with a gold pattern and a central blue motif. Short chains with pointed leaves in white enamel link the rosettes. The oval medallion displays two standing figures : Jupiter with his eagle and Juno accompanied by her peacock. This remarkable piece – a symbol of power via its Roman deities – is completed with pearls and probably belonged to a king.

There are similar rosettes in the collections of the Museum für Kunsthandwerk in Vienna, which were given by the arch-duchesses Leonora and Maria Christina to the imperial convent. This allows us to date this piece with a high degree of certainty. JW

BIBLIOGRAPHY : Somers Cocks/Truman, pp. 110–13.

Rosette for clothing
Dresden (?), c. 1600
Gold, diamond and enamel, 48 mm
Pforzheim, Schmuckmuseum (inv. 1998/9)

In an open cartouche, a table-cut diamond rests in a raised setting decorated with bands. The gold is decorated with polychrome enamel. This type of rosette would have been sewn on to a piece of clothing, such as a cloak or the brim of a hat. JW

BIBLIOGRAPHY : Tokyo 2003b, no. I–10.

>> **Four rosettes for clothing**
c. 1610–15
Gold, diamonds, enamel and pearls, large rosette : 36 x 26 mm ;
small rosettes : 31 x 21 mm
Budapest, Magyar Nemzeti Múzeum, (inv. öL/88.2–5)

Made in a fluid style, the S shapes on these rosettes swirl around a central setting on which is mounted a table-cut diamond flanked by two pearls. Arching out from the central element are stylized branches in green and white enamel with hints of blue, ending in red calyces. Rings placed above and below allow the rosettes to be sewn onto clothing. The backs of the pieces are plain.

Depending on the desired effect, rosettes of this type could be attached to a dress, bodice, coat, collar or hat. The S-shape

was very popular and several examples that feature a diamond or ruby as the central element have come down to us, particularly at MAK (Museum für Angewandte Kunst) in Vienna and the Walters Art Gallery in Baltimore. Rosettes are quite often seen in royal portraits, notably on the *ropa* (Spanish gown) of the Duchess Magdalena of Bavaria in the painting by Pieter Candid of about 1613 in the Munich Alte Pinakothek. JW

BIBLIOGRAPHY : Muller 1972, p. 98 ; Feuchtmüller 1974, no. 5 ; Somers Cocks 1980, no. 72 ; Antwerp 1993, no. 64-5.

Chain

Hungary or Poland, last quarter of the 16th century
Gold, enamel and sweetwater pearls, 1546 mm
Budapest, Magyar Nemzeti Múzeum (inv. Pig. Jank. 6)

The closest parallel to this fine chain is a similar example dating from the mid-sixteenth century, part of the Krakow burial treasure of Constance of Austria (1588–1631), the second wife of King Sigismund III of Poland. The design, materials, techniques and enamel colour of this chain suggest that it is likely to have originated from the same source. Some Polish authors date the Krakow chain to the middle of the sixteenth century.

This date might be challenged by a group of jewels, including dress ornaments and fragments of chains, found mainly in graves from the Carpathian Basin (Hall in Austria ; Csenger and Szolnok in Hungary ; Dolné Strhar in Slovakia ; Cetatea de Baltă and Buzău in Romania). The funeral dates indicate that the owners died in the first decades of the seventeenth century. A further comparison can be made to another chain in the collection of the National Museum of Hungary (inv. Pig. Jank. 238.) This example bears similar soldered maker's marks to many of the above mentioned dress ornaments.

Based on this evidence, the present chain is likely to date from the end the sixteenth century. According to the original inventory of the collection, Jankovich's agent purchased the chain in Transylvania and Jankovich that believed it originally belonged to Isabella Jagiello (1519–1559), wife of the Hungarian king John Zápolya (1487–1540). ERK

BIBLIOGRAPHY : Kiss 1994, p. 159 ; Budapest 2002, no. 163 ; Pforzheim 2003, no. 35 ; Letkiewicz (forthcoming).

< Lucas van Valkenborch, *Portrait of Archduke Matthias of Austria*, 1580.

< Pomander

Southern Germany, c. 1600

Gold and enamel, 83 x 42 mm

Thyssen-Bornemisza Collection (inv. DEC 0695)

This elaborately enamelled object illustrates the popularity of the pomander in the sixteenth century. Like other accessories – such as bells for summoning servants, mirrors, perfume flasks, toothpicks and ear-picks shaped like raptors' claws – it would have been hung from a bracelet, a belt or, more commonly, from a finely-worked chain that could be easily handled. Whenever it was needed, it could be shaken or held up to the nose in order to prevent infections or to spare delicate nostrils from disagreeable odours. Its openwork body held aromatic mixtures of cloves, cinnamon, nutmeg, civet and musk. Sometimes, a piece of ambergris would be inserted, or bezoar – a concretion found in the stomach and intestines of ruminants such as the antelope, camel, goat and deer. The word 'pomander' comes from the Persian *padzehr*, meaning antidote, which no doubt explains its widespread use in the courts of Europe. Elizabeth I and Eric XIV of Sweden both wore pieces of jewellery set with bezoar. Pomanders in silver filigree or in enamelled gold set with precious stones and pearls were made in a wide variety of forms; most often they were spherical, but they were also shaped like books, birds and pears. One of the oldest pomanders appears to have been commissioned by the Duke of Buckingham in 1520. Finally, according to an inventory from 1607, Anne of Denmark, the queen consort of James VI, owned no fewer than fourteen chains with pomanders. CV

BIBLIOGRAPHY : Scarisbrick 1998, pp. 98–101 ; Meininghaus 2001, pp. 2220–1.

>> Marten's head

France, 1560–70

Gold, enamel, rubies and crystal, 66 x 30 mm

Thyssen-Bornemisza Collection (inv. DEC 0731)

The fashion for sculpting martens' heads goes back to fifteenth-century Italy. Milan was a major centre for rock-crystal cutting, and it is possible that this piece from the Thyssen Collection came from a Lombard workshop. However, the Moorish details in the enamel work suggest it is more closely linked to French enamelled objects in the collections of the Kunsthistorisches Museum in Vienna. Whatever the case, this precious example gives us a glimpse of the little-known practice of wearing the skin of a marten, stone marten or sable in order to trap fleas, with the idea that the undesirable creatures would be attracted to such a cosy, warm spot. To hold the protective fur in place, ladies hung extremely realistic marten's heads from sumptuous and elaborate chains. Inventories tell us that Mary Stuart had several such pieces when she returned to Scotland in 1561. In the same period, the Duchess of Savoy – sister of Henry II, King of France – Elizabeth I and Catherine of Poland all owned marten's heads. Several paintings and support research into these peculiar objects, including Sofonisba Anguissola's *Young Woman*, a work from 1557 in the Gemäldegalerie, Berlin, Hans Mielich's 1556 portrait of Anna of Bavaria, in the Kunsthistorisches Museum, Vienna, and the portrait of countess Maria zu Oettingen, dated 1550, in the collections of the princes of Oettingen-Wallerstein. As well as the drawing of Anna of Bavaria's marten, also by Mielich (Bayerisches Nationalmuseum, Munich), other marten's heads have come down to us. One, in gilt copper and fitted with real teeth, is on display at the Musée de Cluny in Paris. Another, in repoussé gold, enamel, pearls and rubies, was part of the collections of Philip II, now in the Walters Art Gallery in Baltimore. The frequent use of rubies for eyes recalls the bloodthirsty nature of these small carnivores. The use of rock crystal is not without meaning. According to various works from the period on the symbolism of stones and precious materials, rock crystal was used to soothe the pain of burns and bites – a useful property when dealing with fleas. The Museo Lázaro Galdiano in Madrid and the Germanisches Nationalmuseum in Nuremberg both have rock-crystal marten's heads in their collections, all of them dating from the sixteenth century. CV

BIBLIOGRAPHY : Hunt 1963 ; Biedermann ; Schiedlausky 1987.

> **Portrait of an Infanta of Spain, possibly one of the daughters of King Philip II**
>
> Spanish School, Pantoja de la Cruz (1553–1608) (?), c. 1585
> Oil on canvas, 204 x 125 cm
> Brussels, Musées Royaux des Beaux-Arts de Belgique (inv. 418)

The princess is dressed in the Spanish style, with upswept hair, a tall narrow-brimmed hat, and a small ruff with 'figure-of-eight' lace. The corsage compresses her chest. The skirt forms a cone over a farthingale – a stiff petticoat made with young branches – and her outer garment, or *ropa*, lays heavily over the tight-fitting dress. Ladies of the high nobility could barely move in such outfits, and this was often the point: their role was to be seen as symbols of a dominant society rather than as real human beings.

The garment is further stiffened by gems and embroidered brocade. The consummate skill and sense of detail of the mannerist goldsmiths are on full display. The hat – decorated with vertical twin rows of pearls – features a diamond and pearl rosette, and is topped by an ostrich feather crowned with an aigrette. Beneath the hat we can see the edge of a cap, with a chain of alternating diamonds and pearls, as well as a pear-shaped pearl. The princess is wearing a choker of table-cut diamonds in raised settings, at the centre of which is a cartouche of enamel cherubs containing a faceted large triangular stone.

Beneath this is a piece of jewellery that features an exceptional diamond – the Estanque, which was purchased by Philip II from the Italian merchant Giovanni Francesco Affaitadi in Antwerp around 1551 – and the pearl known as the Peregrina. This was one of the most famous pieces of jewellery of its time, among those that were worn by the women in the Spanish royal family. Like the necklace, the chatelaine consists of large gold links, enamel and table-cut diamonds, with a large faceted stone at the centre. Rosettes of table-cut diamonds can be seen at the centre of the corsage and on the sleeve ties, while *tressons* of gold and diamonds adorn the lacing on the skirt. The princess wears diamond rings, and one hand rests on the pelt of a stone marten, whose head and paws are made of gold, enamel and precious stones. This remarkable object, which was popular throughout Europe, was designed in Italy and was known as a *zibellino*, or flea-fur.

The identity of the woman has not been established. She does not resemble either of Philip II's two daughters, who were often depicted, but it must have been someone very close to the king to be allowed to wear the Estanque. JW

BIBLIOGRAPHY : Deurne 1977, pp. 59–60;
Hansmann/Kriss-Rettenbeck 1977, pp. 130, 154–7;
Hackenbroch 1979, pp. 29–31; Tokyo 2003b, no. II–31.

88

89

Amulet pendant in the shape of a hand

Spain, second half of the 15th century
Gold, silver, amber, wood and precious stones, 71 mm
Stuttgart, Landesmuseum Württemberg (inv. KK Grün 59)

This amulet pendant topped with a bail consists of a hand made from amber and wood; gold rings set with precious stones appear on the hand's little and ring fingers. A stiff, pleated cuff encircles the wrist and a sleeve is made of gold, enamels and emeralds. The time of the Great Discoveries brought Europe into contact with new animals, such as the sperm whale, which produces ambergris in its intestines. When first exposed to air, ambergris gives off a very disagreeable odour, but over time it takes on a scent that is highly prized in cosmetology. Notably, the sperm whale was reputed to increase sexual potency, as the spermaceti, a white substance contained within its enormous head, was at the time mistaken for sperm. The *manu cornuta* – a hand with thumb and index finger joined – was a sign exchanged by lovers when they wanted to make love. Sometimes the gesture was made more innocent by placing a carnation between the two fingers. The link between fertility and marriage is, in any case, clear. But it was also not uncommon for young princes to wear a black *manu cornuta* as an amulet to protect themselves from evil. JW

BIBLIOGRAPHY : Muller 1972, pp. 69–70 ; Grzimek 1973-7, no. XI, p. 541 ; Hansmann/Kriss-Rettenbeck 1977, pp. 256, 318–19 ; Hackenbroch 1979, p. 332 ; Karlsruhe 1986, no. L 127 ; Antwerp 1995, no. 80.

> Portrait of King Francis I

After Joos van Cleve (c. 1464–1540), c. 1530
Oil on panel, 44.1 x 34.9 cm
Scotland, Drumlanrig Castle, Collection of the Duke of Buccleuch and Queensberry

A cousin of Louis XII, Francis I (1494–1547) was the son of Charles of Valois and Louise of Savoy. By marrying Princess Claude, who had however been promised to Charles V after France's defeats in Italy, he became son-in-law to the sovereign he would succeed in 1515. The young king, with his imposing bearing, soon demonstrated a certain taste for luxury and elegance that further increased the prestige of his reign, already strengthened by a succession of victories and peace treaties favourable to France. But this period of calm was to last only a short while – the struggle against the Habsburg empire started up again with renewed vigour in 1522. Francis had a brilliant mind and a keen intellectual curiosity, and although absorbed by the vicissitudes of his responsibility, he demonstrated a marked interest in all forms of art. More than anyone else, Francis I embodies the spirit of the Renaissance. His influence was considerable but his patronage took a heavy toll on state finances. Although he protected the humanities, founded the Collège de France and acquired a number of manuscripts for the royal library, his role was greatest in painting and architecture. He initiated construction of the chateaux of Chambord, Saint-Germain, Villers-Cotterêts and Madrid in the Bois de Boulogne, Paris, and began renovating the chateaux of Blois and Fontainebleau, attracting a number of Italian artists including Leonardo da Vinci, Andrea del Sarto, Benvenuto Cellini, Il Rosso Fiorentino and Francesco Primaticcio, who founded the famous Fontainebleau school. Although in the portraits by Jean Clouet and Titian, Francis I is depicted as a conquering sovereign in opulent dress, the portraits painted after the work by Joos van Cleve show a sovereign, certainly, but also a man with marked physical particularities such as a hooked nose, almond-shaped eyes and a beard. The king wears an insignia on his feathered hat and his garments are opulently embroidered. The Flemish painter is one of only a few to have been called to the court of Francis I, who favoured French and Italian artists. But we know that the sovereign bought paintings and tapestries from Flanders through the merchant Joris Vezeleer. Joos van Cleve also painted the portrait of Queen Eleanora, a sister of Charles V who became the second wife of Francis I in 1530. Several versions of Joos van Cleve's portrait of Francis I can be found in the following collections and museums: the Philadelphia Museum of Art, the Muzeum Narodowe de Varsovie, the Musée Carnavalet in Paris, the Musée du Château de Fontainebleau, the City Art Museum of Saint Louis, the Royal Collections in London, the Fine Arts Museum of San Francisco, the Metropolitan Museum of Art in New York, the Cincinnati Art Museum, the Wallace Collection in London and the Arthur Houghton Collection in New York. CV

BIBLIOGRAPHY : Hand 2004, pp. 101–2, 166–8.

Pendant in the shape of a lizard

Spain, c. 1600

Gold, diamonds, rubies and enamel, 67 x 21 mm ; with chain : 56 mm

Private collection

A table-cut diamond and two diamond-shaped table-cut rubies are set into the lizard's flat and slender body. Small table-cut diamonds are used in the corners and in the joints of all four legs. The animal's long tail is set with table-cut diamonds and two small, faceted point-cut stones represent its eyes. The body in light green enamel with a black scale pattern is rendered in a very realistic fashion.

Most of the jewellery in the form of reptiles that has survived dates from around 1580. Both Hackenbroch and Muller see in these pendants of exotic animals the astonishing virtuosity of Central-American silversmiths, whose creations were imported into Spain where they caused a sensation. This is not to say, however, that every piece of jewellery in the shape of a reptile or a parrot came from Mexico. Either the Moroccan rock lizard or the eyed lizard could have served as a model for this piece : the former is found in North Africa and Minorca, the latter in Spain. It is thus unlikely that this example was created in Mexico.

Lizards and salamanders are symbols of death because, like the dead, they live beneath stones, but they also symbolize fire, because of their ability to spend hours sitting in direct sun. The king of France, Francis I (1494–1547), used the salamander as his emblem. JW

BIBLIOGRAPHY : Muller 1972, pp. 31–4 ; Hackenbroch 1979, pp. 322, 326 ; Antwerp 1993, no. 57 ; Antwerp 2002, no. 5 ; Tokyo 2003b, no. I–3.

Pendant in the shape of a gecko

First quarter of the 17th century
Gold, diamonds, rubies, pearls and enamel, 69 x 35 mm;
with chain : 80 mm
Private collection

This gecko forms an S-shape, with its feet drawn up to its sides and its winding tail. It is designed around a baroque pearl, with a rose diamond at the neck and two more diamonds, older than the first, at the rear of the body. The head, which houses a small case with a tightly fitting lid, is set with a red ruby. Like the rest of the piece, it is decorated in green enamel to represent the skin, on which scales have been engraved. The chain – attached at the level of the mouth, and the lower part of the body – features a clasp encircled by a crown and twin decorative chains set with pearls and enamel imitation stones. The back of the piece is also decorated in green enamel and shows signs of normal wear. The head may have contained spices, but perhaps also poison.

There are several species of gecko, found particularly in Madagascar, with shimmering, colourful bodies. It is thus conceivable that they could have served as models for jewellery set with precious stones, as was the case in Madrid (Instituto de Valencia de don Juan) and in the treasury of Santo Domingo Cathedral. ˌJW

BIBLIOGRAPHY : Brussels 1992, no. 110 twice ; Antwerp 1993, no. 58 ; Tokyo 2003b, no. 1–4.

Hat enseigne with David and Goliath pendant

France, mid-16th century ; frame added later
Gold, enamel, bloodstones and pearl, 54 mm
Private collection

The narrow raised border encloses a relief of the youthful hero, David, nude and triumphantly wearing the helmet and holding up the severed head and scimitar of the Philistine giant, Goliath, before the walls of a city. The four attachment loops for sewing the enseigne, or badge, on to the hat are concealed by a bloodstone frame, added so that the relief could be worn as a pendant. The episode that brought renown to the young shepherd David and led to his long reign over Israel is from the Bible (Samuel 1 : 18). Yvonne Hackenbroch suggests that the badge may be French since Henry II (1519–1559), was often compared to David, and attributes its design to the court artist Etienne Delaune (1518–1583). **DSC**
BIBLIOGRAPHY : Hackenbroch 1996, pl. 54

> ## Hat enseigne with Mettius Curtius pendant

Relief : Italy (?), c. 1540 ; frame : France, c. 1880
Gold, enamel, pearls, ruby and emerald, 90 x 48 mm
Tokyo, Albion Art Collection

This oval gold relief depicts the death of Mettius Curtius, fully armed and seated on a horse wearing a cabochon ruby collar. He plunges into the abyss watched by a group of women and soldiers gathered outside the city of Rome. The episode from Roman history occurred in 362 BC after a huge abyss appeared at the Forum in the city centre. The soothsayers declared that only the sacrifice of the city's greatest treasure could save it from destruction. The young patrician, Mettius Curtius, declaring that Rome possessed no treasure greater than the life of a brave citizen, rode into the abyss. The earth closed over him and the city was saved. Ever since, this act of patriotic self-sacrifice has been regarded as a model for all those in positions of power and responsibility. During the sixteenth century the Emperor Maximilian owned a similar jewel, listed in his inventory of 1544. **DSC**
BIBLIOGRAPHY : Hackenbroch 1996, pl. 53, p. 50.

94

Pendant with cameo of Cosimo de' Medici the Elder

Florence, second half of the 15th century

Metal and shell, 20 x 25 mm

Florence, Museo degli Argenti, Palazzo Pitti (inv. Gemme 1921 n. 211)

The oblong metal frame encloses a shell cameo portrait bust of Cosimo de' Medici the Elder (1389–1464), facing in profile towards the left and wearing contemporary dress and hat. Using shell rather than hardstone as his medium, the engraver has represented the *'Pater Patriae'* as he must have looked in real life: a shrewd, intelligent banker and citizen of the Republic of Florence. This is the man who, on his return from exile in 1434, used his vast wealth to employ Ghiberti, Brunelleschi, Donatello and Luca della Robbia to fill palaces and churches with works of art. For three centuries after his death the whole history of Florence was connected with the house of Medici, and his descendants who ruled the city continued the great artistic tradition he initiated. DSC

BIBLIOGRAPHY : Mosco/Casazza 2004, no. 1, p. 17.

Pendant with portrait of a Florentine princess (?)

Miniature : Florence (?), c. 1570 ; frame : Spain, early 17th century

Gold, enamel, green 'double' stones, oil on silver, 84 x 62 x 52 mm

Thyssen-Bornemisza Collection (inv. DEC 0620)

The obverse of this oval miniature features the portrait of a young princess. The reverse shows the Greek goddess Juno standing between allegorical figures. Cesare de Ripa's *Iconologia* of 1593 identifies these as nymphs associated with celestial and atmospheric phenomena such as comets, rain, dew and so on. In the foreground stands the lightly-clad figure of Pudicitia, the personification of Chastity. The small portrait could be that of a princess of the Medici family, either Lucrezia – the daughter of Cosimo I, Grand Duke of Tuscany, who married Alfonso d'Este – or Virginia, the half-sister of Grand Duke Francesco I, who married Cesare d'Este in 1586. There is no conclusive evidence for either of these theories ; consequently the princess of the pendant has never been identified with certainty. However, the goddess Juno and the figure of Chastity lead one to surmise that this miniature was painted on the occasion of a princely marriage. The frame, which consists of adjoining settings of green stones surrounded by volutes, does not completely match the oval of the miniature. It probably replaced the original frame several decades later. JW

BIBLIOGRAPHY : Somers Cocks/Truman 1984, pp. 76–7 ; Ripa 1603.

Pendant with double portrait of Cosimo II de' Medici, Grand Duke of Tuscany, and Magdalena of Austria

Florence, first half of the 17th century

Gold, enamel, pearl and cornelian cameo, 18 x 23 mm

Florence, Museo degli Argenti, Palazzo Pitti

(inv. Gemme 1921 n. 120)

The fluted and enamelled frame of this oval gold pendant encloses a double portrait cameo in cornelian, facing in profile towards the right, of Cosimo II de' Medici (1590–1621) and his wife, Magdalena of Austria (1589–1631). The back of the pendant is enamelled with scrolls flanking the Medici coat of arms, which is surmounted by a crown with ten points. The suspension loop is designed after the Medici symbol of a ring set with a point-cut diamond and there is a hanging pearl below. Monochrome cameo portraits are rare and this example is exceptional on account of the meticulously detailed dress and jewellery of the imperious and grand ducal couple, rulers of a rich and prosperous state. DSC

BIBLIOGRAPHY : Sframeli 2003, no. 73, p. 144.

Ring with portrait of Grand Duchess Christina of Tuscany

Florence, c. 1592

Gold and cornelian, ring : 22 mm ; portrait : 10 x 12 mm

Florence, Museo degli Argenti, Palazzo Pitti

(inv. Gemme 1921 n. 333)

The plain gold hoop supports a round bezel set with a cornelian intaglio portrait bust of Christina of Tuscany (1565–1637). The duchess is shown in profile facing right, wearing court dress with a high ruff, jewelled collar, two rows of pearls and jewels in her piled up hair. Christina of Tuscany, granddaughter of Catherine de' Medici and Henry II of France, married Grand Duke Ferdinand of Tuscany (1549–1609). Her status as a royal princess and consort of the ruler of Tuscany is affirmed by her elaborate dress and jewellery, which are also depicted in the medallic portrait by Michele Mazzafirri (1530–1597). DSC

BIBLIOGRAPHY : Sframeli 2003, no. 49, 55.

Pendant with cameo bust of a Moor

Milan, c. 1530–40
Onyx cameo, gold setting, pearls and emerald, 49 mm
Vienna, Kunsthistorisches Museum, Kunstkammer (inv. KK 1588)

At the centre of this round gold medallion is the bust of a young Moor in black onyx, a very valuable stone. The figure, partially sculpted in the round, is mounted in a gold setting that is reminiscent of a garment. His chest is decorated with an emerald, accenting in striking fashion the elegance of this set of colours. The gold plate in delicate repoussé serves as a support for the bust and is bordered in a wreath of spiralling branches and vine leaves. The vertical and horizontal axes of this frame have been highlighted with rosettes, while the diagonal axes are decorated with pearl rings.

The five suspended pearls – originally there were six – were probably added to the frame when this piece, once a hat medallion, was converted into a pendant. At first, the medallion had only four rings placed at right angles in the frame, which were used to sew the piece onto a bonnet or a cap. A hat ornament of very similar design and use can be seen in the portrait of a knight of the Order of Saint John, in the collection of the Niedersächsischen Landesmuseum in Hanover. The work is thought to be by the painter Parmigianino dating from 1526–7. FK

BIBLIOGRAPHY : Munich 2002, pp. 291ff., no. 68 ; Vienna 2003, pp. 400ff., no. III.3.16.

> Brooch with cameo of Cleopatra

Cameo : attributed to Ottavio Miseroni, Prague,
early 17th century ;
Gold, enamel and agate, 62 x 53 mm
Tokyo, Albion Art Collection

The frame, enamelled with trails of flowers and leaves in white, sky blue and dark blue, encloses a bust of Cleopatra. Her head and torso are in agate, a blue snake coiled round her white arm and hand. The queen is shown facing towards the front within an inner border of fruit and flowers. The combination of enamelled goldsmiths' work with hardstone cameos – illustrated in this bust – was a Renaissance innovation. Cleopatra, who took her own life rather than face the dishonour of captivity by her Roman enemies, was admired at the time as a model of majestic dignity. Her decision to kill herself by the bite of a snake is significant in itself, for the snake was one of the symbols of Egyptian royalty. DSC

Pendant with cameo of Johann Frederick, Duke of Württemberg

Attributed to Hans Kobenhaupt, Stuttgart, c. 1620

Gold, diamonds, rubies, enamel and cameo in topaz, 64 x 57 mm

Stuttgart, Landesmuseum Württemberg (inv. KK Grün 79)

Johann Frederick, Duke of Württemberg (1608–1628), is depicted in left profile on this octagonal topaz cameo. The cameo is mounted on gold and surrounded by individually set table-cut diamonds arranged in a cross. The diamond-shaped perimeter features two rows of rubies and small diamonds, all of them table-cut, with the exception of a point-cut diamond set at the top. The reverse consists of an eight-lobed plaited openwork with green, black and white enamel, which can also be seen on the edges of the front face. The bail is also covered in black enamel.

From the sixteenth century, sovereigns would commission cameos like this and present them to members of their family, dignitaries and deserving members of the court. They were often attached to a chain or ribbon and suspended in the middle of the chest. The black enamel on the obverse clearly shows the engraved bean pattern that began to appear around 1630 on other pieces. JW

BIBLIOGRAPHY : Fleischhauer 1970, pp. 287ff. ; Egger 1984, no. 54 ; Karlsruhe 1986, pp. 690 ff. ; Antwerp 1993, no. 29.

Urn-shaped pendant belonging to the Grand Dauphin

France or Italy, 17th century

Gold, enamel and lapis lazuli, 70 x 40 mm

Paris, Musée du Louvre, Département des Objets d'Art

(inv. MR 272)

A small lapis-lazuli jar is suspended from a three-part gold chain by its two delicate handles. One part of the chain holds the urn's lid, which is embellished with a border of small enamel balls.

The piece is described in the 1791 inventory of the French crown jewels. It is believed to have belonged to the Grand Dauphin – the son of Louis XIV – who died in 1711, four years before his father whom he was to have succeeded. The urn is designed to contain a valuable perfume. JW

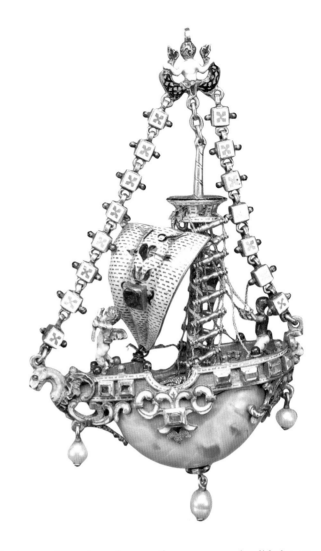

Pendant in the shape of a pelican

<< Pendant in the shape of a pelican

Transylvania (?), mid-17th century

Gold, rubies, pearls and enamel, 100 x 78 mm

Budapest, Iparmvészeti Múzeum (inv. 13.697)

The chased oval cartouche with scrollwork and asymmetrical foliage is richly adorned with white enamel and rubies. In the centre of the pendant, in gold-flecked white enamel, is a pelican with its wings spread. Its breast is set with a large ruby and it is accompanied by three of its young. Three pearls are attached to the pendant.

A pelican feeds its young by sliding its prey, usually fish, into their open beaks. The oldest observers of the pelican, who were obviously not equipped with binoculars, thought they perceived a wound in the bird's throat and pouch – which sometimes turns red during egg-laying season – leading them to believe that the pelican nourished her young by tearing open her breast and feeding them with her blood. This explains the importance of this animal in Christian symbolism as a representation of maternal love and sacrifice, and also of Christ's crucifixion. Pendants in the shape of pelicans were worn in the seventeenth century as a sign of motherhood, or of the wish to have children, and were often given as engagement and wedding gifts. JW

BIBLIOGRAPHY : Grzimek 1973, VII, p. 185 ; Szilágyi 1991, no. 5.54 ; Timmers 1993, no. 97.

Gondola pendant

< Gondola pendant

Southern Germany, c.1570

Gold, diamonds, pearls, enamel and precious stones, 75 x 73 mm

Florence, Museo degli Argenti, Palazzo Pitti

(inv. Gemme 1921 n. 2500)

The pendant is in the shape of a gondola, the hull enamelled with white and black details. It is set with rubies and diamonds between forget-me-nots on tall stems, enclosing the figures of two men rowing. Two musicians serenade a pair of lovers seated under a canopy set with rubies and surmounted by two pearls. The two extremities of the gondola are marked by table-cut rubies supporting enamelled dragons, each with a pearl, and there is another ruby in the water below between fishes. Three chains interspersed with pearls between alternate diamonds and rubies hang from an enamelled diamond and pearl cartouche. Although inspired by the gondolas of Venice, the courtly amusement represented by this pendant took place elsewhere, in pleasure boats on the calm rivers and lakes near the residences of the European rulers. The rhythmic movements of the rowers and the sound of the music would have contributed to the harmonious atmosphere as the amorous pair glided over the water. It is an image of the leisure hours of kings and queens, associating their rule with happiness and love.

The pendant was recorded as no. 231 in the 1743 inventory of Anna Maria de' Medici, Electress Palatine. DSC

BIBLIOGRAPHY : Sframeli 2003, no. 46, pp. 103–4.

'Ship of Love' pendant

Copy by Henrik Egger, c. 1880, of the original in the

Esterházy Treasury

Gold, diamonds, rubies, pearls, mother-of-pearl and enamel, 105 mm

Budapest, Iparmvészeti Múzeum (inv. 15.912)

This little ship is made of mother-of-pearl bordered with gold and rubies. In the centre, a cartouche set with a table-cut diamond is linked to two ruby-linked chains attached to a double-tailed mermaid. The mast has a crow's nest and the sail is decorated with symbols of the sorrows of love. Cupid stands at the prow, bow and arrows in hand, while at the stern, the figure of a sailor in red enamel pulls on the sail while another climbs the rigging. Three pearls are suspended from the pendant.

The symbolism of this piece of jewellery is fairly clear: the ship (of marriage), Cupid, the entrancing mermaid and the images on the sail. This object is most certainly an engagement present. Pieces in the shape of boats were very popular during the mannerist period. They generally did not have the same symbolic association with marriage as the small ships peopled with figurines from the Italian popular theatre, found at the Château d'Ecouen (Musée National de la Renaissance) and in Florence (Museo degli Argenti).

The figure of Cupid has disappeared from the original, but it is mentioned in the 1685 inventory of Grand Palatine Paul Esterházy. JW

BIBLIOGRAPHY: Szilágyi 2006, no. 95.

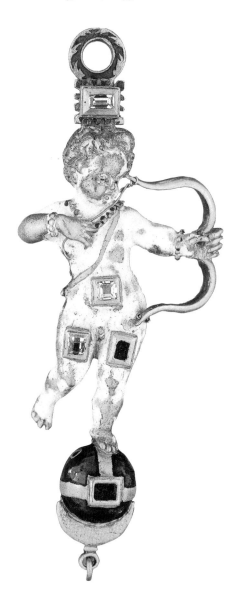

Pendant with Cupid

Netherlands or Southern Germany, c. 1600
Gold, diamonds and enamel, 56 mm
Stuttgart, Landesmuseum, Württemberg (inv. KK Hellblau 72)

This piece of jewellery features a standing Cupid made of gold covered in white enamel with one foot resting on a blue enamelled globe and the other raised behind him. Although his quiver and arrows have disappeared, Cupid – who wears jewels around his neck and at his wrists – still has his bow, which he aims to his left. The table-cut diamonds over the head and on the stomach and Cupid's right thigh have survived, those set in the globe and on his left thigh have been lost. In addition, a loop is missing from the half-moon beneath the globe, probably a pearl. The enamel on the body of the Cupid is damaged, suggesting that the piece was worn frequently. A similar figure, which can be seen atop an astronomical watch made by François Laffille in Paris around 1600 (Musée de l'Horlogerie et de l'Emaillerie, Geneva), gives an idea of how this Cupid might have looked in its complete state.

Duchess Barbara Sophia von Württemberg purchased this piece in 1609 from the jeweller and merchant Cohorst in Stuttgart. However, it is not impossible that the piece is of Dutch origin. Figurines representing popular mythological figures – such as this Cupid – were very much in fashion around 1600. JW

BIBLIOGRAPHY: Fleischhauer 1970, p. 113; Geneva 1983, no. 6; Karlsruhe 1986, pp. 689ff.; Antwerp 1993, no. 50.

Pendant with sea monster and naiade

Spain, after a drawing by Hans Collaert the Elder of Antwerp
(1582), first quarter of the 17th century
Gold, diamonds, pearls and enamel, without chain : 118 mm ;
with chain : 165 mm
Pforzheim, Schmuckmuseum (inv. 1959/8)

A sea monster with pinions, wings, a pair of fins, scales and a raised, winding tail carries a white enamel naiad on its back. The naiad turns as she leans with her right arm on a ewer. Beneath the monster with its open jaws, three *en tremblant* pendants are attached to six bails by scrollwork, masks and a shell pattern, in which three table-cut diamonds have been set. Two chains, attached to the creature's tail and mane, meet beneath a winged setting with a table-cut diamond topped by a bail. Orange enamel can be seen on the tail and green enamel has been used for the monster's wings as well as the scrollwork. The back of the piece is also decorated with scales. The pendant makes clear references to a drawing by Hans Collaert the Elder of Antwerp (1530–1581), published in Antwerp in 1582 by his son, Hans Collaert the Younger (1566–1628), helped by the engraver Philip Galle (1537–1612). In the drawing, there is also a male figure with his foot on the monster's head and a mast in his hands while the nymph is depicted with an oar in her raised hand. Yvonne Hackenbroch places this remarkable and rather heavy piece of jewellery within the context of the influence of Flemish artists or Spanish goldsmiths in the first decade of the seventeenth century. Had it been the work of a Flemish goldsmith, however, this piece would have been more elegant and created with more virtuosity. Other specialists date the piece to the nineteenth century. This pendant displays a mannerist taste for fantastical representations, inspired by mariners' tall tales about journeys to undiscovered shores. JW

BIBLIOGRAPHY : Bott 1972 ; Walgrave 1973, p. 37 ;
Hackenbroch 1979, pp. 334-5 ; Schmuckmuseum 1981, no. 130 ;
Antwerp 1993, no. 49.

Pendant in the shape of a parrot

Augsburg (?), 1560–70

Gold, diamonds, rubies, pearls and enamel, 82 x 52 mm

Private collection, on loan to the Schmuckmuseum,

Pforzheim (inv. KJ1)

A multicoloured parrot sits on a bough between two stylized branches, facing right. The entire piece is decorated in coloured enamel. Arranged around the parrot are a snail, a rabbit and a bee. The bough is set with six table-cut diamonds, and the bird is decorated with eight rubies. The small chains are partly made from pearls and meet in a clasp set with a facet-cut diamond.

In his text *Defensorium Immaculatae Virginitatis*, the Dominican monk Franciscus de Retza (d. 1425) compares the parrot and the snail to the Virgin Mary. The parrot, since it chooses a partner for life, is the symbol of conjugal fidelity. The snail symbolizes domesticity, the rabbit fertility and the bee is the symbol of zeal – all seen to be virtues in a married woman. The young noblewoman to whom this piece was given would be in no doubt as to what was expected of her. JW

BIBLIOGRAPHY : Timmers 1993, p. 145 ; Antwerp 1995, no. 138, 199 ; Stockholm 2000, no. 22 ; Antwerp 2002, p. 18.

> Portrait of Queen Elizabeth I of England

George Peter Alexander Healy (1808–1894), after a painting attributed to Marcus Gheeraerts the Younger, 1844

Oil on canvas, 128 x 99 cm

Versailles, Châteaux de Versailles and Trianon, (inv. MV4116)

This copy of the *Rainbow Portrait* of Elizabeth I (1533–1603), at Hatfield House, was made in 1844, during the reign of Louis Philippe, by George Peter Alexander Healy for the Musée Historique, Versailles. The portrait's iconography makes it one of the most fascinating of all the symbolic depictions of the queen and is today quite difficult to decipher, despite many attempts at interpretation. Attributed to Marcus Gheeraerts the Younger (1561/62–1636), it is thought to have been painted for the queen's Prime Minister, Sir Robert Cecil, in the first decade of the seventeenth century, doubtless on the occasion of a court performance. The queen is thought to be depicted as Astraea, goddess of the Golden Age and eternal spring.

Adorned in magnificent jewellery, she holds a rainbow in her right hand. The accompanying phrase 'Non sine Sole Iris' (no rainbow without the sun) associates her with the sun, which creates the rainbow and brings peace to humanity, in an image of good governance.

The jewellery cannot be dissociated from the motifs that cover the queen's clothes and which symbolize her power while also referring to precise events. Although the dress embroidered with spring flowers signifies Astraea, the coat of gold sewn with eyes and ears is thought to represent the queen's advisors, who are also her discreetly observant informers. On the coat's sleeve a snake – possibly embroidered, possibly a piece of jewellery – holding a heart-shaped jewel in its mouth, its head surmounted by a celestial sphere, is thought to symbolize Prudence, mistress of the passions, who inspires wise decisions. Meanwhile the gauntlet attached to the lace collar recalls the glove given by the queen to her champion at the tournament celebrating the anniversary of her accession to the throne, and the crescent-shaped piece surmounting her headdress may recall Cynthia, goddess of the moon and empress of the seas, to whom Sir Walter Raleigh used to compare his queen in the 1580s.

Did these pieces of jewellery ever exist ? Where they created for a fleeting occasion or are they simply props in a highly literary image of the imposing, ageless Virgin Queen ? They are shown in combination with a long string of pearls and a pendant of precious stones, which frequently appear in portraits of Elizabeth I.

BIBLIOGRAPHY : Constant 1995, no. 2561.

NON SINE SOLE
IRIS

The Jewel of Sir Francis Drake

Miniature : Nicholas Hilliard (1547–1619), England, 1575
Gold, diamonds, rubies, pearls, enamel,
sardonyx cameo and miniature, 117 mm
Sir George Meyrick, on loan to the Victoria & Albert Museum,
London

Enamelled scrolls and forget-me-nots interspersed with rubies and diamonds form the border of this oval gold locket and frame a sardonyx cameo of a black man and a white woman, crowned with a tiara, with a cluster of pearls hanging beneath. The reverse, which is enamelled blue, opens to reveal a fine portrait miniature of Elizabeth I painted by Nicholas Hilliard within a border of table-cut rubies.

The parchment lining of the cover is painted with a phoenix (now damaged) and is inscribed : ANO DM 1575 [formerly 1586] REGNI 20. Whereas the miniature and the device of a phoenix are personal to Elizabeth, the significance of the sardonyx cameo is more elusive. The theme of the black man was adopted by the gem cutters of the Renaissance as a means of utilizing the contrasting dark and light layers of the sardonyx, and was perhaps inspired by depictions of the black king, Balthazar, in paintings of the Adoration of the Magi. These cameo busts of emperors, kings or princes wear jewellery, draped necklines and Roman armour, indicative of their rank. Recent scholarship suggests that Elizabeth chose this cameo to express her imperial ambitions, and that the man represents Saturn and the woman Astraea, the virgin goddess. According to this interpretation the message of the cameo is therefore that under the rule of Queen Elizabeth her country would return to the legendary Golden Age, when Saturn ruled over a period of peace and prosperity and Astraea distributed blessings (Dalton 2000, pp. 180–214).

Sir Francis Drake (c. 1543–1596) is considered the most famous of the heroes and navigators of British maritime history. He was the first Englishman to sail around the world and he fought the Spanish navy on many occasions, culminating in the defeat of the Armada in 1588. Queen Elizabeth recognized his courage, patriotism and achievements by conferring a knighthood on him and decreeing that his ship, the *Golden Hind*, should be preserved as a national monument. Elizabeth gave this jewel to Sir Francis Drake in 1586 and he is depicted wearing it in the portrait of 1591 by Marcus Gheeraerts the Younger. The jewel passed by descent to Lady Seaton. DSC

Marcus Gheeraerts the Younger, *Portrait of Sir Francis Drake*, 1591.

> > The sun jewel of Sir Francis Drake

England, second half of the 16th century
Gold, diamonds, rubies, opals and enamel, 50 x 14 mm
Sir George Meyrick, on loan to the National Maritime Museum,
London

The sun jewel has at its centre a ruby engraved with an intaglio orb, surrounded by opals within a diamond and opal border. This is framed by straight and curved rays alternately enamelled red and set with rubies. On the back of this engraved hat jewel is a miniature of Elizabeth I of England (1533–1603). The orb, which is emblematic of sovereignty, may allude to Elizabeth, or to Sir Francis Drake's (c. 1543–1596) historic circumnavigations of the globe. The jewel has four loops for attachment to a hat. DSC

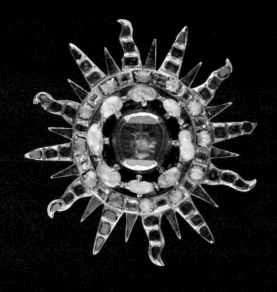

Miniature of Queen Elizabeth I of England

Nicholas Hilliard (1547–1619), c. 1595

Oil on vellum on a playing card and rubies (?), 53 x 47 mm

London, Phillip Mould Ltd.

The queen is seated before a red background in a traditional pose, her torso turned slightly to the left. She wears a dress sewn with precious stones. The small red stones mounted on the miniature may be real rubies. She is wearing a double necklace, the lower element decorated with three double pendants. The stiff lace collar is also mounted with precious stones.

In 1595 the queen was sixty-two years old, but she is portrayed looking much younger. Either the painter was trying excessively hard to flatter her or it was painted far earlier. However, we know that Elizabeth was obsessed with her appearance, constantly experimenting with creams and powders of her own making, sometimes with unfortunate results, including the loss of her hair. When she was nearly seventy she bought six large wigs, a dozen even larger, and around a hundred small hairpieces. Before appearing in public she would put small pieces of fabric inside her cheeks to improve their shape and hide her lack of teeth.

The miniature belonged to Francis Denis Lycett Green (1893–1959) and was passed on to his niece Ursula, Duchess of Glasgow. JW

BIBLIOGRAPHY : Antwerp 1998, pp. 106–9.

Cameo of Queen Elizabeth I of England

France, 1575–1603

Gold and sardonyx with three layers (brown, blue, red), 60 x 46 mm

Paris, Bibliothèque Nationale de France, Cabinet des

Monnaies, Médailles et Antiques (inv. BAB 967)

The oval gold frame encloses a sardonyx cameo portrait bust of Elizabeth I (1533–1603). Facing towards the right in profile, the queen is crowned and wears an embroidered dress with a high ruff, jewelled collar and gold chains with a cameo representing Saint George (Knight of the Order of the Garter). The three layers of the sardonyx have been used to differentiate between the hair, face, details of dress and jewellery, the dark background, and the pale border. This is one of the most important of the group of thirty surviving cameo portraits of Queen Elizabeth. All were made in the period 1575–1603, according to established patterns, size and style, presumably in a specialist workshop, which supplied the court jewellers with cameos for setting into rings, brooches and pendants. Following the example of the emperors and empresses of ancient Rome, Renaissance monarchs commissioned these cameo portraits of themselves to award as marks of royal favour. The lucky beneficiaries wore them with pride. DSC

BIBLIOGRAPHY : Babelon 1897, no. 967, pl. LXXI.

The Aberdeen pendant

England, 16th century ; reliquary added later
Gold, enamel, diamonds, opals, rubies and pearls
The Marquess of Aberdeen and Temair

The pendant consists of a hand holding a laurel crown of victory, flanked by dragons with diamond necks, each head crowned with a point-cut diamond emerging from ruby cornucopiae. Diamond scrolls in the shape of the letter C link the dragons to the top of the pendant, which is marked by a line of rubies surmounted by opals. The reverse is enamelled. Within the laurel crown is a reliquary enclosing hair under glass, said to belong to Mary Queen of Scots (1542–1587). Three round pearls hang beneath. The jewel was presented by Mary to her loyal supporter, James Gordon of Methlick and Haddo (1531–1582) and was inherited by the Marquess of Aberdeen in about 1560. It remains in the family to this day. The reliquary is a later addition. DSC

> Chain of Mary of Scotland

c. 1580
Gold, enamel, pearls and rubies, 275 x 176 x 5 mm
Private collection, on loan to the National Museums of Scotland, Edinburgh

This chain, now joined into a necklace, consists of links of green snakes coiled around twin pearls with a ruby to each side, alternating with white closed esses, studded with rubies. The back is enamelled in white and red. The snake and the closed letter s symbolize, respectively, wisdom and '*fermesse*' or steadfast loyalty, both virtues associated with exemplary rulers. Another section of this chain, formerly owned by the Earl of Eglington, is now in the collection of Queen Elizabeth II. Queen Mary I of Scotland (1542–1587) gave the part shown here to her faithful lady-in-waiting, Mary Seton, and it has descended to the present owners from Elizabeth Seton the wife of William Hay of Drummelzier. DSC

the centre of each knot is a black stone, no doubt a diamond. We can see a larger diamond in her curly hair – possibly a wig – and a red stone at her forehead. In addition, the queen is wearing two pins on her collar, each with three rhombus-shaped segments, a pair of earrings, a diamond choker and a pendant on a cord. She holds her right hand conspicuously in front of her chest, a gesture that surely has some meaning. The frame is narrow, with a diamond in a lozenge setting at top and bottom. The lid of the box is red and set with diamonds that form a crowned monogram: at the centre are the intertwined letters A, R and C; they are flanked left and right by a letter S, and at the base are two mirror-image C's. Four other diamonds in square settings are placed outside these letters.

This magnificent jewel was presented to the queen as a wedding present by a lady of the court, Ann Liviston, who had commissioned her portrait in 1612. JW

BIBLIOGRAPHY : Scarisbrick 1994, pp 136–8.

> ### Chain and pendant bearing the monogram FB(I)
England or Scotland, first half of the 17th century
Gold, diamonds, rubies, pearls and enamel, 442 mm
Thyssen-Bornemisza Collection (inv. DEC 0678)

The links in this light blue enamel chain consist of alternating double loops and back-to-back crescent moons set with rows of table-cut rubies. In between, rubies connect square links with pearls in the corners, to a table-cut diamond at the centre. The pendant itself consists of an anchor topped by a crown and the monogram FB, and perhaps also the letter I, unless it is the anchor shaft. A pearl is suspended from the pendant. The back of the chain is decorated in dark blue enamel and there is an inscription in Scots on the crossbar of the anchor HOUP.FEIDIS.ME (hope fills me). The text, which underscores the significance of the anchor as a symbol of hope, and the style of the piece, allows us to place it in England or Scotland in the first half of the seventeenth century. A portrait box from 1610–20 in the Fitzwilliam Museum in Cambridge (inv. 3863) displays the same sinuous lines of rubies.

In this troubled era, James VI of Scotland also ruled England as the Stuart king James I. He attempted to bring religious peace to Europe by strengthening Anglicanism in England, signing a treaty with the Protestant United Provinces and making peace with Catholic Spain. He also married his successor, Charles I, to Princess Henrietta Maria, a French Catholic. This commendable desire to create a unified Europe was rare for its time. JW

BIBLIOGRAPHY : Deurne 1977, no. 4 ; Somers Cocks/Truman 1984, pp. 136–7 ; Kenyon 1992, pp. 198–9.

Box with portrait of Queen Anne of England
Miniature : Nicholas Hilliard (1547–1619), England, c. 1610
Gold, diamonds and transparent enamel ;
miniature : watercolour on parchment, 54 x 43 mm
Cambridge, Fitzwilliam Museum (inv. 3855)

This oval miniature is a nearly frontal portrait of Anne, wife of James I, King of England. She is wearing a high lace collar and an extremely low-cut neckline decorated with three knots. At

The 'Naseby Jewel'

Germany, early 17th century

Gold, enamel, diamonds and rubies, 90 x 65 mm

London, The Trustees of Sir John Soane's Museum (inv. SDR 21.33)

This enamelled gold hat jewel is decorated with a trophy of arms surrounding the figure of a bearded man with long hair wearing a hat with upturned brim. He carries a shield on his arm and an unsheathed sword in his hand ; another sword, still in its scabbard, hangs from his belt. He is crowned with a ruby and diamond coronet. A lion lies at his feet and a white flag with ruby saltire cross is draped beside him. Acquired by Sir John Soane at the Mrs Barnes sale at Redland Hall, Bristol in 1833, the jewel was previously exhibited at the Society of Antiquaries in 1755, when it was fully described and recorded in a drawing. Unfortunately the name of the owner was not given.

Various arguments have been proposed regarding the origin of the jewel. It has been associated with Christian IV of Denmark, with James I of England and with his son, Charles I (1600–1649). The latter is said to have worn it in his hat at the Battle of Naseby in 1645 where his defeat effectively marked the end of the Civil War. The jewel takes its name from this episode. However, none of these speculations can be substantiated, though the style of the white blackwork enamelling and the cutting of the stones suggest an early seventeenth-century date. Moreover, the jewel is comparable to other military examples surviving at the Grünes Gewölbe, Dresden and in the Royal Palace, Stockholm, which may derive from the designs of Theodore de Bry (1528–1598), *Stamm und Wappenbuechlein* (Frankfurt 1593) or those of Hendrick Goltzius (1558–1617) engraved by his pupil, Jacob de Gheyn. The jewel may have symbolized the importance of military practices in the training of a future king so that he could defend his country and safeguard his throne. DSC

BIBLIOGRAPHY : Tait 1986, pp. 94–6.

Military hat jewels

Flanders, late 16th century

Gold, diamonds, pearls, enamel and rubies, 42 x 38 mm each

Florence, Museo degli Argenti, Palazzo Pitti

(inv. Gemme 1921 n. 2503–2505)

These three ornaments with figures come from a set of nine or ten jewels, apparently designed to encircle the brim of a hat attached to a velvet ribbon. Each represents an armed soldier or military musician, in different poses and parade uniforms, standing amidst flowers and leaves and ornamented with rubies, pearls and table-cut diamonds. The significance of this theme

117

in royal jewellery is clear, for mastery of military skills was the sign of a good ruler, enabling him to keep the peace. The figures derive from woodcuts by Hendrick Goltzius, (Haarlem about 1587) adapted by Theodore de Bry (1528–1598) in his *Stamm und Wappenbuechlein* (Frankfurt 1593). DSC

BIBLIOGRAPHY : Sframeli 2003, no. 99, pp. 170–1.

< Pendant with helmet motif

Germany (?), c. 1605

Gold, diamonds, rubies or almandines, pearls and enamel

100 x 71 mm

Budapest, Iparmvészeti Múzeum (inv. 13.698)

An openwork helmet striped with rows of rubies rests on a framework of sinuous curves. At the top, a bail is decorated in white enamel and a pattern reminiscent of a small, elongated crown with points. The lines of the frame are ornamented with red and white enamel balls that show some signs of wear. Around the helmet, there are two table-cut rubies in square settings, and three faceted diamonds in triangular settings. Below, three pearls hang from the pendant.

Jewellery shaped like a trophy of war was very popular in the early seventeenth century. The Treasure Chamber in Munich's Residenz has a very large trophy brooch by Hans Georg Beuerl (Augsburg, 1603). These pieces were naturally intended for the nobility, from whose midst came the highest-ranking officers. JW

BIBLIOGRAPHY : Gregorietti 1970, pp. 206–7.

The seventeenth century: the reign of the diamond

JAN WALGRAVE

The transition from the sixteenth to the seventeenth century was not a good period from the political point of view. Two powerful monarchs, Philip II of Spain (1527–1598) and Elizabeth I of England (1558–1603), left the stage in 1598 and 1603 respectively, while Henry IV of France was assassinated in 1610. Henry's son, the future Louis XIII, was only nine years old and his mother, Marie de' Medici, governed without flair. Meanwhile the weak emperor of Germany, Rudolf II (1552–1612), was living in retirement at his palace in Prague, surrounded by his art treasures. However, across the continent the arts and crafts were flourishing, with jewellery-making encouraged by the royal courts, whose displays of dazzling wealth were used as a sign of power. This was particularly true on grand occasions, from the preparations and celebrations of royal weddings to the birth or baptism of an heir and visits by ambassadors or foreign monarchs. There are countless eyewitness accounts of such events, while biographies endlessly relate the ruling class's occasionally excessive fondness for pieces of great value. Whereas today jewellery is largely the preserve of women, at that time the men too had their parures and members of the court nobility would try to outdo each other in their splendour. Such unhealthy rivalry, source of many scandals and bankruptcies, led kings such as Louis XIII in France – vainly – to issue sumptuary decrees restricting the wearing of jewellery and the almost equally costly lace.[1]

SOVEREIGNS AND PARURES
IN THE SEVENTEENTH CENTURY

Where the relationship between seventeenth-century sovereigns and jewellery is concerned, we shall confine ourselves to citing a few examples. The symbolic importance of royal jewels is illustrated by the fact that in 1603, shortly after his coronation, James I of England added some large jewels to the crown and declared them to be inalienable, so that the royal family could never sell them or give them away. In 1604 he told Parliament that these jewels were emblems of the divine right to rule.[2] In the same year he bought another of the most celebrated gems in history, the famous Sancy diamond, weighing 53.8 carats and now preserved in the Louvre. When James sent his son, the future Charles I, to Madrid to negotiate his betrothal to a Spanish princess, he gave him many extremely valuable jewels and, to add weight to his proposal, had him accompanied by the flamboyant George Villiers, first Duke of Buckingham, a man who habitually appeared 'manacled, fettered and imprisoned with jewels'.[3] The prince himself wore the famous 'Three Brothers' brooch, stolen from the tent of Charles the Bold, Duke of Burgundy, after his retreat at the end of the lost battle of Grandson in 1476.[4] The betrothal did not go ahead and the jewels were elegantly returned.

Shortly after his accession to the throne in 1613, Charles married Henrietta Maria, daughter of Henry IV of France. On her marriage she received a veritable fortune in jewels and was also able to buy back the parures that her mother, Marie de' Medici, had taken into exile and pawned.[5] For the baptism of the Dauphin (the future Louis XIII) in 1606, Marie de' Medici had worn a gown sewn with 3,000 diamonds and 22,000 pearls.[6] It is hardly surprising that the documents of the period regularly describe queens and princesses as unable to take a step unaided: on the contrary, they had to be supported, and sometimes even carried, in order to go anywhere at all.[7]

Louis XIV of France was not known as the 'Sun King' for nothing. Not content to attend a ball dressed as the sun, he gleamed and glittered every time he appeared. He ran life at court like one great theatrical performance, in which he was the sole leading actor. Even the morning *'lever du roi'* ('king's rising') unfolded as a solemn ceremony attended by a select few. When he received the ambassador of Turkey in 1669, he was wearing a gown laden with diamonds valued at 14 million florins.[8] It is possible that these were diamonds borrowed by the king from his prime minister, Cardinal de Mazarin, who had bought them that same year from Jean-Baptiste Tavernier,

< Peter Candid, *Duchess Magdalena of Bavaria*, 1613.

121

Pierre Mignard, *Maria Theresa of Austria and her son,*
'The Grand Dauphin', c. 1665.

the famous traveller to the Indies and dealer in precious stones. These sixteen diamonds, known as 'Mazarins', were bequeathed by the cardinal to the French crown, along with the Sancy diamond and the 'Mirror of Portugal'.[9] They were later worn by all the kings and emperors of France and their wives. Some are now on display in the Galerie d'Apollon in the Louvre.

Between 20 May 1684 and 24 April 1686, Louis xiv had ten recorded deliveries of diamonds, for a total sum of 4,932,796 florins.[10] When, shortly before his death in 1715, he received the ambassador of Persia, he was wearing diamonds with a total value of 12,500,000 florins. Saint-Simon observed that 'the king was bent over under the weight', and indeed he was quick to change his dress after dinner.[11] Such unprecedented splendour made a great impression on the other European sovereigns, who took their lead from Versailles. When, in 1687, the seventeen-year-old Prince Frederick Augustus of Saxony – Augustus the Strong – was making the obligatory *Kavalierstour* and visiting most of the European courts, he was received with the greatest courtesy by Louis xiv. The young man perfectly understood the power and persuasive force of such a dazzling display of wealth.[12] In 1697 he went to Poland to stand for election as the new king and, in order to make the right impression, took with him an extensive suite and almost all the treasures he owned. The transportation of the *Silberkammer* – precious metals, jewels and precious stones – alone required twenty-two horses.[13] On 23 July Frederick Augustus was crowned king in Krakow. His entire dress was studded with diamonds, right down to the buttonholes of his magnificent blue gown; his hat was decorated with an aigrette and there were diamonds on his buttons, shoe buckles and garters. His dagger, too, was inlaid with diamonds. His jewellery was valued at an estimated one million *thaler*.[14] In commissioning a whole series of 'trimmings' and parures in precious stones, Augustus the Strong displayed the even greater fondness for splendour that was to characterize the sovereigns of the eighteenth century, and still more their wives.

THE EVOLUTION OF JEWELLERY
IN THE SEVENTEENTH CENTURY[15]

In the early seventeenth century jewellery had a certain unity of style, resulting from the 'migration' of the many princesses who were married to foreign princes as a form of political exchange currency. They would be accompanied by a suite of servants and often also craftsmen, and by a dowry consisting largely of gold, silver and precious stones. In this way local trends spread from one nation to another. But there was also a second reason for this uniformity: increased demand encouraged the finest jewellers to produce books of designs, which were widely distributed. In the sixteenth century this

122

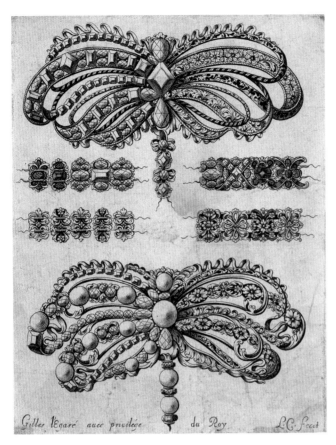

Gilles Légaré, *Flowers and jewellery*, 17th century.

Balthasar Lemercier, *Design for a brooch in the 'peapod' style*, Paris, 1626.

practice was largely confined to the Dutch artists; in the seventeenth century it was the French, including François Lefèbre, Etienne Canteron, Gilles Légaré and Jean Toutin, who set the tone. Around 1600 mannerist jewellery was still in fashion. The sumptuous, yet severe, Spanish style was dominant and aristocrats – particularly women – were confined by opulent cuirasses. Their heavy brocades were sewn with a multitude of rosettes in precious stones and a great variety of jewellery was worn. The first decade of the seventeenth century saw a gradual change of atmosphere. There were various reasons for this: in 1624 Cardinal de Richelieu launched his brilliant career and the centre of gravity of European politics shifted to France, arousing new interest in the French culture and art of living; courtly attitudes became much freer and imbued with a gleeful gallantry; in fashion corsets were replaced by lighter, more fluid garments giving greater freedom of movement, and décolletés and bouffant sleeves made their appearance.

Jewellery followed these developments. The new fabrics could no longer support the weight of rows of rosettes, and figurative brooches and pendants were replaced by parures with symmetrical designs of stylized scrolls by French designers. The new pieces reflected a taste for the natural world and drew on floral sprays and seed pods, while the term *cosse-de-pois* ('peapod') began to be seen in descriptions of parures. The splendid hues of coloured stones gave way to the brilliance of diamonds, particularly since the many-faceted rose cut was starting to replace table-cut stones.

So the diamond parure was born. Without miniature enamelled sculptures and coloured stones these parures provided less opportunity for the symbolism of earlier pieces. However the portrait boxes, crosses, *memento mori* rings and betrothal jewellery remained popular. Diamonds and pearls could be combined to marvellous effect and were used to create brooches, earrings and aigrettes. Many diamond parures were worn with pearl necklaces and bracelets. The new fashion did not completely supplant enamel, but the latter took on a different role, decorating the backs of freely hanging pendant jewellery such as chains, watches and pendants. Around 1630 in Châteaudun, Jean Toutin (1578–1644) invented a new technique that made enamel more adherent and its colours richer. His little pictures on religious, mythological or pastoral themes, miniature portraits and heraldic emblems are masterpieces of virtuosity.

124

Around 1650 a number of German jewellers – among them Heinrich Raab and Johannes Hellek – published designs for floral jewellery which proved very popular. Raab set roses, marguerites or tulips on a black ground. As, by definition, these pieces did not include any large stones, members of the royal families seldom wore them on grand occasions. Nevertheless they are among the most charming trinkets produced by the jewellers of the day. They were inspired by a new interest in the art and flora of gardens, of which the tulip craze of the 1630s is the best-known and most excessive example: a moral fable on the theme of pride and its fall.[16] This was also the period in which artists such as Jan Breughel the Elder, Daniel Seghers and Hans Boulenger were creating their matchless flower paintings.

By the mid-century it was no longer fashionable to have jewels sewn all over a garment, but their disappearance was compensated for by the placement here and there of larger, more costly stones. Rosettes, too, were a thing of the past; brooches and clasps were decorated with sometimes impressive diamonds. This trend can be observed as early as 1629, in designs by the alderman of The Hague, jeweller Thomas Cletscher, notably for two pendants each decorated with two rose-cut diamonds of around 15 carats. The fashion for parures sometimes encouraged the rich and powerful to resort to a little artifice, such as setting several diamonds into the same mount to create the impression of a larger stone. On 24 March 1641 the Antwerp diamond merchant Gaspar Duarte wrote to Constantin Huygens that he had sold a piece of this type to William II of Orange, who wanted to give it to his young wife Princess Mary Stuart of England: 'the four diamonds joined together have the appearance of a single diamond with a value of one million florins.' Yet the four stones had cost 'only' 80,000 florins.[17] It seems reasonable to suppose that this technique was used more than once.

In addition to floral themes, a great deal of jewellery used the knot motif, a symbol of attachment and fidelity. The usual silk knot was reproduced in precious metal, with the largest stone in the centre, and worn as a corsage, a coat-fastening or as earrings. Knots were also used to crown a rosette or a miniature portrait. From this time they remained a constant feature of classic parures. When, around 1700, it was fashionable for ladies to wear their hair caught up in a bun, there was a renewed interest in aigrettes. These were a borrowing from the Spanish fashion of the early seventeenth century, when they had adorned the little bonnets that ladies were expected to wear at that time.

In his book *Merveilles des Indes Occidentales et Orientales* of 1661, the Paris jeweller Robert de Berquen accuses wealthy ladies of reducing the value of fine diamonds that they regarded as outmoded by having them cut with new facets. They were jealous of the new rose-cut diamonds, which shone so brilliantly at nocturnal festivities and concerts in the light of the hundreds of candles that all eyes were drawn to their owners. It was just a fad, he decided, that would soon pass. Berquen was very wrong, for this trend marked the birth of the brilliant, which appears more and more frequently in descriptions from this period onwards. By the eighteenth century brilliants had become common currency among jewellers and their clients. Towards the end of the seventeenth century diamonds were increasingly mounted not in gold but in silver, which was thought to set off the brilliance of the new cuts more effectively. The art of jewellery was now prepared for the unimaginable passion for diamonds that was to seize the royal courts in the eighteenth century.

1. Antwerp 1977, p. 45.
2. Scarisbrick 1994, p. 69.
3. Scarisbrick 1994, p. 72.
4. In fact, the 'Three Brothers' seems to have been one of the pieces in the Burgundian booty following the defeat at Grandson in 1476.
5. Scarisbrick 1998, p. 153.
6. Franklin 1885–6, vol. I, p. 184.
7. Antwerp 1995, p. 96; Franklin 1885–6, vol. I, p. 178.
8. Franklin 1885–6, vol. I, p. 225.
9. Morel 1988, pp. 149–58.
10. Franklin 1885–6, vol. II, pp. 221–3.
11. Franklin 1885–6, vol. II, p. 223.
12. Arnold 2001, p. 13.
13. Bäumel 1997, p. 20.
14. Bäumel 1997, p. 37.
15. For this chapter see Antwerp 1993.
16. For the gardens of the period see Hamm 2001.
17. Gans 1961, p. 98.

< Anthony van Dyck, *William of Orange and his wife Mary Stuart, Princess of England*, 1641.

Portrait of the Infanta Isabella, daughter of King Philip II of Spain

After Frans Pourbus the Younger (1569–1622), probably c. 1597 (original painting)

Oil on canvas, 235 x 125 cm

Brussels, Musées Royaux des Beaux-Arts de Belgique (inv. 320)

The Infanta Isabella, a grown woman, stands before a raised curtain, her hand resting on a table. She is certainly wealthy, but is not excessively adorned for someone of her era and rank. Her dress and robe are embroidered in brocade, with embroidered double rings and fleurs-de-lis on white satin. The fleurs-de-lis are a reference to her mother, Elisabeth of Valois, the daughter of Henry II, King of France. In her upswept hair she wears a bandeau of coral, pearls and a diamond. Coral was thought to protect young women and children from misfortune. On her chest is a gold cross set with table-cut diamonds and pearls, and around her shoulders is a long rope of pearls. The high starched collar and the bands encircling her wrists are of extremely fine reticella lace.

The portrait was probably painted on the occasion of Isabella's engagement to Albert VII, Archduke of Austria, as indicated by the rings on the robe. Isabella Clara Eugenia (1566–1633) was the oldest daughter of Philip II of Spain and Philip's third wife, Elisabeth of Valois, who died two years after Isabella's birth. Don Carlos, Isabella's older half-brother, also died that same year, leaving her heir to the vast kingdom of Spain, and making her a coveted prize on the European diplomatic scene. Plans to marry her to the future Holy Roman Emperor, Rudolf II – which would have resulted in the reconstitution of the kingdom of Charles V – led to nothing. When Henry III of France was assassinated in 1589, Philip claimed, without success, the French throne for his daughter in the name of her French origins via her mother. In 1599, at the age of thirty-three, she married her cousin Albert VII, who was staying at the Spanish court. He was cardinal of Toledo and viceroy of Portugal, and was named Governor General of the Habsburg Netherlands. The couple reigned over the Habsburg Netherlands as though it were a separate kingdom, a situation that could only be maintained provided the couple had children, which was not the case.

Albert and Isabella's reign, though short-lived, was considered to be a time of peace and calm and they were responsible for signing the Twelve Years' Truce (1609–21) with the United Provinces, although this did not entirely put an end to hostilities. Both sovereigns were very devout and staunch defenders of the Counter-Reformation. They were also active culturally and supported the arts, being responsible in large part for Peter Paul Rubens's (1577–1640) artistic and diplomatic career. By force of circumstance, Isabella also took the art of war very much to heart; the infantry corps that she recruited in great numbers takes its name from her. JW

BIBLIOGRAPHY : Hamann 1988, pp. 168–9 ; Brussels 1998, no. 6.

< Corsage ornament with two-headed eagle

Spain, c. 1630

Gold, enamel and diamonds, 175 x 115 mm

Madrid, Museo Nacional de Artes Decorativas (inv. 18.699)

This large and prestigious piece of jewellery has two parts: an eagle with two crowned heads – the symbol of the Habsburg

dynasty – and, in the centre, the Virgin with a crown of sunbeams and the moon, representing the Immaculate Conception. A dove flapping its wings, symbol of the Holy Spirit, appears above her head. Beneath the moon is a lily, the symbol of purity. The eagle is upright with outstretched wings, and its large black enamelled tail is set with table-cut diamonds. The imperial crown features table- and facet-cut diamonds, as well as red, green and white enamel, much of it showing signs of wear. Both of the eagle's talons are also set with a table-cut diamond. The Virgin Mary is surrounded by symbols from the Litany of Loreto, in particular, at the centre top, the Morning Star. To the right are the Gate of Heaven, the Sealed Spring, the Ark of the Covenant and the Tree of Life, while to the left we can see Jacob's Ladder, the Enclosed Garden, the Tower of Ivory and the Throne of Solomon. As in the famous corsage in the collections of the Victoria & Albert Museum in London (inv. M 143-1975), both the crown and the decoration surrounding Mary have settings in the shape of tulips, a fashionable motif in the 1630s.

This remarkable piece clearly belonged to a member of one of the great families in the immediate entourage of the Habsburgs of Spain. JW

BIBLIOGRAPHY : Madrid 1998, no. 122.

Marianum pendant

Spain, c. 1600
Gold, enamel, baroque pearls, 80 mm
Brussels, Musées Royaux d'Art et d'Histoire (inv. BJ17)

The Virgin, dressed in red with a blue mantle, with neither a crown nor the Baby Jesus, her hands joined in prayer, stands atop a reversed crescent moon within a halo of red flames, each of which terminates with a small pearl. Eight large pearls in fleuron settings encircle the design, which is also topped by a crown composed of floral elements and three pearls. An empty setting testifies to the loss of one pearl.

The Marianum pendant is a type of religious ornament that was very common in the sixteenth and early seventeenth centuries and often appears in portraits of Catholic sovereigns such as Isabella Clara Eugenia. The rays represent the sun – both the sun and the moon are attributes of the Virgin Mary, according to a description by John the Evangelist : 'A woman clothed with the sun, and the moon under her feet.' (Revelations 12 : 1). This type of image of Mary represents the Immaculate Conception, a teaching that gave rise to a very popular Spanish name for girls : Concepción. JW

BIBLIOGRAPHY : Ferguson 1966, p. 45.

Pendant with the letter A

Central Europe, late 16th to early 17th century
Gold, diamonds, enamel, rubies, sapphire and pearls,
57 x 47 x 16 mm
Budapest, Magyar Nemzeti Múzeum (inv. Orn. Jank. 129)

This symmetrical openwork pendant is richly decorated on both sides with multicoloured enamel. It consists of two levels laid over a base that is designed in a late sixteenth- or early seventeenth-century style. This style was developed in Augsburg, either by the Huguenot refugee Daniel Mignot or the Altenstetter workshop; it is also found in various western European centres in France and the Netherlands. The pendant is decorated with a letter A made of table-cut and *dos d'âne* diamonds. It is surrounded by two allegorical female figures in white enamel, a sapphire in a raised setting and three rubies set in rosettes (one precious stone at the top of the A is missing). The figure on the left, holding a chalice and a cross, is that of Faith; the identification of the other figure is more difficult to establish. According to Yvonne Hackenbroch, this is Hope (or Charity), but it might also be other virtues such as Steadfastness, in which case the woman would be holding a torch in her right hand and would be linked to Penelope. The letter A was quite popular on jewellery, and the nineteenth-century owner of this pendant, Count Marczibányi, wrongly believed that it had once belonged to Queen Anna, the third wife of Ladislaus II of Bohemia and Hungary. The *dos d'âne* diamond-cutting technique was no longer in widespread use in the late sixteenth century, but it was still used in decorative letters. This jewel with an innovative design but consisting of traditional, somewhat old-fashioned elements is a noteworthy example of a style that was popular in central Europe around 1600. **EK**

BIBLIOGRAPHY : Hackenbroch 1979, p. 201 ; Brussels 1998, no. 36 ; Pforzheim 2003, no. 7.

Reliquary pendant in the shape of a cross

<
Germany, partially late 16th century, partially c. 1620
Gold, diamonds, pearls and enamel,
crucifix with pearls : 89 x 62 mm ;
fastening chain : 45 mm ;
chain joining the two ends : 173 x 12 mm
Private collection

Cross with table- and rose-cut diamonds

Netherlands (?), first half of the 17th century
Gold and diamonds, 53 x 39 mm
Aalst, Fabrique de l'Église Saint-Martin (inv. Rob. 639)

The arms of this flat gold cross are fitted with five raised qua-trefoil compartments. Each is set with two table-cut diamonds arranged horizontally at the ends of the cross, and vertically in the middle of the central bar. At the centre of the cross, in a very low-relief setting, there is an interesting ensemble consisting of two diagonal shapes that form an x set with facet-cut and triangular table-cut diamonds. In all cases, the settings are divided lengthwise into two lobes corresponding to the placement of the diamonds. Each of the four ends of the cross features a curved pattern reminiscent of a fleur-de-lis. The back of the cross, surrounded by a fluted border, forms the cover of an empty case. Three hanging pearls complete this unusual gem. It is decorated on the front and sides with black enamel, much of it worn away, and on the back, graceful spirals in green, black, orange-yellow and red enamel swirl around satyrs, dolphins and dragonflies. The decorative motifs are similar to sixteenth-century designs for engravings published by Adriaen Collaert (d. 1618). Part of the chain appears to be original and features seven baroque pearls, four small hearts in red enamel and four appearances of the letter H, which also show traces of black enamel. The twinned diamonds never repeat the same colour and the table-cut diamond at the top right is comple-mented by a flat rose-cut stone towards the base. This is an as-tonishing combination which, considering the abundant use of diamonds in an extravagant decor, suggests a date of around 1620. There are no known similar examples surviving.

Apart from the cross shape and the container for relics, the richly elaborate finish and decoration of this piece are hardly those of an object of devotion. The letter H on the chain is not a known religious monogram and its association with the hearts suggests that it had a personal, sentimental significance. JW

BIBLIOGRAPHY : Christie's 1988, no. 112 ; Antwerp 1993, no. 2 ; Tokyo 2003, no. I–13.

The cross is made up of six large table-cut diamonds, five of them oblong. Three small diamonds are set at each extremity : table-cut at the top and bottom, and rose-cut to the left and right. Around the edges are four oblong rose-cut diamonds and close to the bail a rose-cut diamond and two small faceted stones to either side of the shaft. The settings of the large stones are fairly open, and the base of each setting is serrated. The back of the cross is plain and bears the inscription : DO. DT. DNUS. EMM.DE HERT. F.S. DNI. JUDO/JUDOCUS PHIL. CL EMM : LIS. This refers to the gift of the piece to a church, and to the identity of the donor, Emmanuel de Hert. An inventory of 1909 mentions the date 1755 inscribed on a twenty-five-diamond cross. The count is correct, but the inscription is not to be seen. Whatever the case, this table- and rose-cut diamond dates to the first half of the seventeenth century. Both the finishing on the back, which is rather unusual for the period, and the in-scription, are probably later additions. JW

BIBLIOGRAPHY : Robijns 1980, no. 639 ; Aalst 1980, p. 77 ; Antwerp 1993, no. 4.

Instruments of the Passion cross

c. 1660

Gold, enamel and diamonds, 90 x 68 mm

Private collection, courtesy Albion Art Jewellery Institute, Tokyo

This substantial, gold Latin cross is richly set with diamonds of various sizes, in rose and other cuts. The diamonds are clustered together in groups, emphasizing the top and base of the upright and the ends of the arms, and set within a frame of black and white acanthus leaves. On the back of the cross the twenty-three Instruments of the Passion are enamelled in black, white and pink. They are represented in the following order, from top to bottom :

1. The three nails used to fix Christ's arms and legs to the Cross.

2. The scroll inscribed INRI, the abbreviated form of the Latin JESUS OF NAZARETH KING OF THE JEWS, which was nailed at the top of the Cross, mocking Christ's claim to kingship.

3. The cock that crowed each time Saint Peter denied being one of the followers of Christ.

4. The column to which Christ was bound when the soldiers whipped him.

5. The Crown of Thorns placed on Christ's head, mocking his claim to kingship.

6. The lance used to pierce his side to ensure that he was dead.

7. The sponge dipped in vinegar given to torment him when he asked for water.

8. The whip used by the soldiers when Christ was bound to the column.

9. The hammer used to nail Christ to the Cross.

10. The ewer containing the water in which Pontius Pilate washed his hands, signifying that he wanted no further part in the trial of Christ and was innocent of 'the blood of this just person'.

11. The sword with which Saint Peter cut off the ear of Malchus, servant of the High Priest.

12. The palm of victory waved by one of the crowd as Christ rode into Jerusalem on Palm Sunday, before the Passion.

13. The ladder used by the soldiers to fix Christ to the Cross and to remove him from it.

14. The chalice used to consecrate the wine at the Last Supper, with the Host, or consecrated wafer, distributed at Holy Communion.

15.The pincers used to extract the nails when Christ was brought down from the Cross.

16. The image has been rubbed out, but presumably representing the bag containing the thirty pieces of silver given to Judas Iscariot for his betrayal of Christ.

17. The lantern held by a soldier when Christ was arrested at night in the Garden of Gethsemane.

18. The tunic worn by Christ and taken from him so that the soldiers could have it.

19. The dice thrown by the soldiers to decide which one of them would have Christ's tunic.

20. The veil with which Saint Veronica wiped the face of Christ as he carried his Cross, and which bore the imprint of his face.

21. The torch held by one of the men who came to arrest Christ in the Garden of Gethsemane at his betrayal.

22. The reed placed in Christ's hand as a sceptre to mock his claim to kingship.

23. The ear of Malchus which Saint Peter cut off with his sword and which Christ put back.

Finally, there also appears the hand of Christ pierced by a nail. Between the ear and the hand, below the veil of Saint Veronica, are the initials IHS, an abbreviation for the name of Jesus.

The symbols represent the last events of Christ's earthly life, from his entry into Jerusalem on a donkey to his burial after being taken down from the Cross. They are known as the Instruments of the Passion for each represents a particular aspect of his suffering. The front of the cross is richly embellished, but the Instruments of the Passion are to be found on the back. Therefore, only the wearer would be aware of their presence and their constant reminder of Christ's suffering to inspire perseverance against the challenges of a Christian life. Although the Instruments of the Passion appear on earlier devotional jewellery – particularly on crosses – the technique of opaque enamelling used here, by which a wide variety of colours could be applied directly onto the white ground making it possible to paint a far greater range than before, suggests a date of around 1660. The variety of cuts used shows how far the seventeenth-century diamond cutters had progressed from the limitations of the primitive point and table cuts of Renaissance jewellery. The acanthus-leaf ornament and flowers and the use of gold for the settings, which was later replaced by silver to avoid yellow reflections from the diamonds, also indicate this date. The significant size and quality of this magnificent cross suggest that it was made for a person of high rank of the Roman Catholic faith, whether French, Spanish or Austrian is impossible to tell without documentary evidence. Portraits show that crosses of this importance were worn over the heart, suspended from ribbons or ropes of pearls. DSC

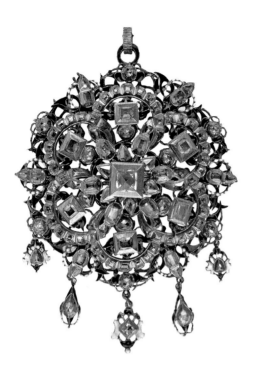

Rosette pendant

c. 1630

Gold, diamonds and enamel, 99 x 72 x 29 mm

Budapest, Magyar Nemzeti Múzeum (inv. Pig. Jank. 241)

This pendant is made entirely of openwork; it consists of six foils surrounding a point-cut diamond in a setting. Six large table-cut diamonds, both square and rectangular, are placed in a circle of eight small table- and facet-cut stones. Six table-cut diamonds, six facet-cut stones and six rose-cut stones surround the central point-cut gem. Around the outside, one table-cut and one facet-cut diamond appear between each foil, and a rose-cut diamond is set at the centre of each lobe's arc. The five teardrop pendants hold stones of various cuts. On the frame between the settings, one can make out white enamel dots, black enamel leaves and traces of green enamel around the central point-cut stone. The abundance of diamonds is supported by a clever construction and the plain background frame is both practical and elegant.

This piece has more similarities to the famous pendant in the Victoria & Albert Museum in London than the one worn by Hélène Fourment in the portrait painted by her husband Peter Paul Rubens around 1630–1 (Munich, Alte Pinakothek, inv. 340). Similar pieces of jewellery may also be seen in other portraits from the period, mainly those of sovereigns. These constitute some of the most famous creations of the great jewellery designers such as Daniel Mignot, Peter Symony, Paul Birkenholz and Wendel Dietterlin, all of whom were active in the first decade of the seventeenth century. Although of a similar type, these pieces, like the London example, were created along a central axis and consequently have a more refined appearance. However, the pendant from Budapest conveys a greater sense of opulence and unyielding power. JW

BIBLIOGRAPHY : Antwerp 1993, no. 37 ; Antwerp 2002, no. 6.

> Corsage piece

Iberian peninsula (probably Spain), 1650–1700

Yellow gold, diamonds (table-, brilliant- and baguette-cut),

closed settings

Later mounted as a brooch

Antwerp, Diamond Museum Province of Antwerp (inv. CMD 96/1)

This yellow gold corsage piece consists of a large curved motif, a crown and five pendants. One hundred table-cut diamonds form a pierced floral motif, with the later addition of a single brilliant. The largest diamonds are higher-set in a rosette, bringing three dimensions to the piece. The back is engraved with vine motifs.

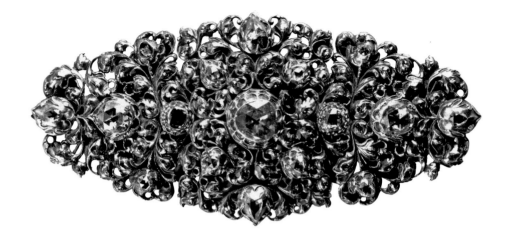

The ornament reflects the style of the Iberian peninsula, and more specifically Spain, in the late seventeenth century. In both Spain and Portugal the working of precious metals had an importance equal to that of precious stones, and this is reflected in the settings of the diamonds. Mounts were far more than just a way of holding a precious stone in place. They would be made with particular care and much larger than strictly necessary. Some contemporary scholars wrongly regard this as revealing a lack of skill on the part of the diamond-setters of the period.

Corsage jewellery had a symbolism of its own and, from the sixteenth to the eighteenth centuries, particularly alluded to what was then regarded as a woman's primary function: reproduction. Corsage pieces, whether large or small, in one section or two, emphasized the inverted triangle of the torso formed by breasts, belly and pubis. The female trunk was an object of veneration – primarily for men. Meanwhile the lower part of the body would disappear under the voluminous skirts typical of Spanish fashions.

It is not known whether this diamond piece was part of a larger parure. Its crown suggests that it was part of a wedding parure, since crowns, forerunners of the tiara, were often worn by brides. WL

Brandenburg-style corsage jewel
Portugal, third quarter of the 17th century
Silver, silver gilt and diamonds, 60 x 130 mm
Lisbon, Museu Nacional de Arte Antiga (inv. 1 Joa)

This magnificent oval ornament with flower and leaf motifs is composed of three separate elements for sewing horizontally onto a garment. When fastened together, the pieces serve as a clasp. The piece is set with rose-cut diamonds and the central axes are accentuated with seven large stones. The silver-gilt backs of each of the three parts are engraved with an identical plant motif and feature four vertical hooks that can be used to attach the brooch to clothing.

This type of ornament is reminiscent of the decorative stripes denoting rank worn on Brandenburg soldiers' uniforms. It was only later that they became popular as items of jewellery for women. Several Brandenburg-style corsage jewels in decreasing sizes were sometimes worn together in a vertical arrangement.

According to legend, this particular jewel was found in the tomb of Queen Louisa de Guzman (1613–1666), wife of the Portuguese king, John IV (1603–1656). This is highly likely, since it is a superb example of seventeenth-century jewellery with a particularly high degree of sophistication and great intrinsic value. LO

BIBLIOGRAPHY : Evans 1951 ; Brussels 1991, no. 52 ;
Copenhagen 1992, no. 52 ; Antwerp 1993, no. 104 ; Orey 1995 ;
Antwerp 2002, no. 14.

Corsage ornament

c. 1680
Gold, enamel and diamonds, 70 mm
Private collection

This corsage ornament is composed of a large rosette set with
a faceted diamond framed by a double border of smaller table-
cut stones. A garland of eight flowers with white enamel petals
accented with blue and black details, each centred on a table-
cut diamond, encompasses the border. Two similar flowers flank
the rosette in the upper section. The back is entirely enamelled
with flowers around rosettes enamelled in black and white. DSC
    BIBLIOGRAPHY : Walgrave 1995, p. 205.

Bracelet slide

Mid-17th century
Gold, enamel, diamonds and chrysolite, 41 mm
Private collection

The front of this bracelet is set with a square chrysolite framed
by a double border of table-cut diamonds. The back, with two
loops for a ribbon to be threaded through allowing the slide to
be worn either on the wrist or neck, is enamelled with flowers
of different colours on a white ground. The detachable pendant
is decorated with diamonds. DSC

Pendant in the shape of a bow
Hungary (?), mid-17th century
Gold, enamel, almandines and sweetwater pearls, 72 mm
Budapest, Magyar Nemzeti Múzeum
(inv. 60. 305 / Orn. Jank. 436)

Pendant in the shape of a bow
Signed JOH. SISM. CORO. FECIT, Hungary,
mid-17th century
Gold, rubies and enamel, 85 x 63 mm
Private collection

Made popular by French courtly fashion of the mid-seventeenth century, jewellery ornamented with bows was also taken up by the Hungarian nobility. Unlike in western Europe, these were exclusively used as ornaments for women's clothing, generally amongst western Hungarian aristocracy. Bowknots were less favoured among the Transylvanian elite. This kind of ornament was sometimes imported, with rather stiff, formal bows being more characteristic of local Central-European production. There are several examples of this type of pendant in the collection of the Hungarian National Museum, of comparable design, make and colour but of lesser quality, suggesting that they were made in different locations and workshops to the present example. According to his inventory, Jankovich purchased this pendant in Vienna. EK

BIBLIOGRAPHY : Pforzheim 2003, no. 13.

This double bow is surrounded by looped ribbons and has a rosette at the centre. Further down, a second, smaller knot with a teardrop pendant is set with a central ruby surrounded by smaller rubies. Four other teardrops are attached to the bow's lower loops. The jewel is decorated in white, black and light blue enamel, with pink enamel on the back and numerous rubies on the front. It is a magnificent piece of ceremonial jewellery that was used as an amulet. The ruby was thought to protect the wearer against blood infections and poison. It is also a symbol of love and lasting friendship. The National Museum of Hungary in Budapest has several bow-shaped jewels of this type. JW

BIBLIOGRAPHY : Falkiner 1968, p. 79 ; Hanau 1991, no. 131 ; Antwerp 1995, no. 33 ; Schiffer 1998, pp. 153–4 ; Pforzheim 2003, no. 13, 17.

Wedding pendant

Hungary, 1626

Gold, enamel, garnet and rock crystal, 97 x 75 x 30 mm

Brussels, Musées Royaux d'Art et d'Histoire, Musée du Cœur

Boyadjian (inv. 400)

Above the central red enamel heart, supported by two hands, is an anchor with a green enamel rope, signifying that marriage is like casting anchor. Two doves perch on the top and the flames of love spiral outwards near the anchor. This multicoloured piece is enamelled and encrusted with red and clear table-cut stones. It also features three *en tremblant* drops. The entire piece is attached to a frame with a fastener and the back is engraved with scrollwork. This example of wedding jewellery was a gift from the future king of Transylvania, Gabor (Gabriel) Bethlen (1580–1629), to his wife on the occasion of their marriage in 1626. Its symbolism, which is clear, is found on a number of other pieces of jewellery from this period. JW

BIBLIOGRAPHY : Boyadjian 1980, p. 24 ; Antwerp 1993, no. 24 ; Antwerp 1995, no. 200.

Aigrette for a hat

Transylvania (now Romania), mid-17th century

Gold, diamonds and enamel, 97 x 45 mm

Budapest, Iparmvészeti Múzeum (inv. 53.4927)

The lower part of this piece consists of a quadruple knot surrounding a rosette. Each loop of the knot is set with a table-cut and a facet-cut diamond, while the rosette features six three-faceted diamonds surrounded by twelve small table-cut stones.

The upper section of this hat ornament consists of a tripartite feather. Each part is set with lozenge-shaped, point-cut stones surrounded by small table-cut diamonds and surmounted by a point-cut stone between rose-cut stones. At the top, only the central section is set with diamonds – three-faceted stones and diamond chips.

The beauty and brilliance of the enamel colours are striking. At the front, the black enamel is visible on the multicoloured flowers on the knot. To the rear, various types of flowers stand out against a predominantly blue background. The rosette has the appearance of a small container, whose white enamel cover is decorated with green stems and pink, yellow and blue flowers.

This exceptionally beautiful piece is enriched by the presence of diamonds with various cuts. It is astonishing that a jewel from this period of such quality contains so many facet-cut stones, in particular a point-cut diamond – rather old-fashioned for the times – and that only four of the stones feature rose cuts, confirming that the diamonds used here were most likely taken from older pieces that had been disassembled. The black enamel knots with their profusion of multicoloured floral patterns are reminiscent of pieces by Heinrich Raab of around 1650. This allows us to date this piece to the mid-seventeenth century, a time when aigrettes were as likely to be worn by men as by women. JW

BIBLIOGRAPHY : Budapest 1965, no. 36 ; Budapest 1988, no. 5.57 ; Antwerp 1993, no. 46 ; Tokyo 2003b, no. II–18.

Aigrette with three feathers

Brasov (now Romania), second half of the 17th century

Gold, enamel, pearls and rubies, 158 x 69 mm

Budapest, Magyar Nemzeti Múzeum (inv. Pig. Jank. 242)

This aigrette is composed of three feathers. Two of the feathers – one in white enamel and one in black – lean to the left; a third, smaller feather, encrusted with a line of rubies, bends to the right as if to balance the composition. A few pearls appear between the feathers, which meet in a central knot adorned with four rubies and a pearl. The pin is lightly enamelled.

The charm of this magnificent hat ornament stems from the realism of its feathers, which have been painted using the enamelling technique that was typical for the region. Both men and women would have worn these types of multicoloured aigrettes. There are several examples in the collections of Hungarian museums and further designs can be found in the anthologies of seventeenth-century jewellery in the Esterházy family archives. JW

BIBLIOGRAPHY: Guide Budapest 2005, II, no. 64; Szilágyi 2006, p. 8.

Bouquet of flowers brooch

Paul Birckenholtz (?), Germany, 1620–30

Gold, diamonds, emeralds and enamel, 85 x 64 mm

Pforzheim, Schmuckmuseum (inv. Sch 1550)

Several small stems rise out of a small basket of finely enamelled gold. Six of the stems are slightly thicker and decorated with fully opened flowers, the largest with a decoration of multicoloured enamel – reminiscent of fruit tarts – and a table-cut or old style rose-cut diamond at their centre. The central flower has a slightly larger table-cut emerald. All the stones are mounted in round, raised settings. Small balls of coloured enamel can be seen in the basket. The backs of the flowers and green leaves have been finished in white enamel.

Although there is an example of this kind of piece in the Museum für Kunst und Gewerbe, Hamburg, they remain extremely rare. Most are attributed to Paul Birckenholtz of Frankfurt (1561–1634), some of whose copper engravings showing similar pieces are still in existence. The charm of this bouquet lies in the success of its composition, the virtuosity of its execution and the choice of strong, warm colours, which imitate natural flowers to wonderful effect. Pieces of this kind were quite popular and would sometimes be worn by high ranking aristocrats, as seen in a childhood portrait of Elisabeth de Valois (1545–1568), later the third wife of Philip II of Spain (Galleria Palatina, Florence, inv. 1602), and in particular the portrait of the beautiful Marchesa Brigida Spinola Doria, painted by Rubens in 1606 (S.H. Kress Collection, National Gallery of Art, Washington). Her hair is held in place by a series of coloured pins in the same style, proof, not so much of her wealth, as of the lively, open mind of a natural beauty. JW

BIBLIOGRAPHY: Steingräber 1956, p. 138; Antwerp 1977, pp. 22–3; Schmuckmuseum 1981, pp. 142–3; Stockholm 2000, no. 54; Antwerp 2002, no. 10.

> Statue of King Louis XIV on horseback

Copy after François Girardon (1628–1715)

Bronze, 108 x 36 x 64.5 cm

Brussels, Musée de la Ville de Bruxelles – Hôtel de Ville (inv. B.1905/2)

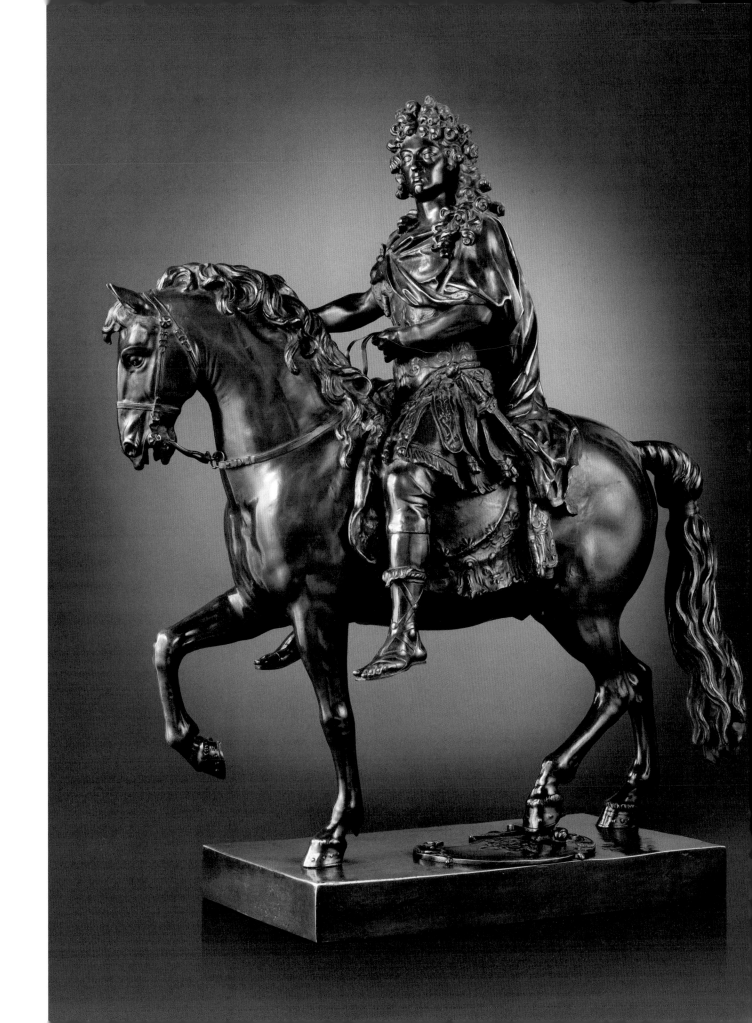

The king, whose hand is raised in an imperious manner, sports a tall, French-style wig, but is wearing a military tunic, cloak, sandals and a Roman double-edged sword: Renaissance and Baroque sovereigns liked to pose wearing a Roman general's garb. *Grimpant* griffons may be seen on the king's breastplate, while the saddle covering is adorned with fleurs-de-lis. The stallion is in motion, and beneath its hooves it is trampling a shield with the head of Medusa – symbolizing the enemy in general, and Protestantism in particular. Following the revocation of the Edict of Nantes in 1685, Protestant-Catholic relations remained a burning issue for decades thereafter.

This statue is a faithful copy of an immense statue, the initial models for which appeared in 1687. It was inaugurated on 13 August 1699 at the Place Louis le Grand in Paris, which today is known as the Place Vendome. When it was being installed, twenty workmen would sit in the horse's belly to eat their lunch. The statue, which was destroyed during the French Revolution, was inspired by the statue of Marcus Aurelius in Rome, and was itself an inspiration for dozens of statues of European sovereigns on horseback, all of whom wanted to identify themselves with the Sun King. JW

BIBLIOGRAPHY : Burke 1992, pp. 93, 115–19 ; Antwerp 1999, no. 16.

Medallion pendant with portrait of King Louis XIV

Miniature : Jean Petitot the Elder (1607–1691),
Pierre le Tessier de Montarsy, Paris, 1683
Silver gilt, miniature and enamel, 93 x 57 mm
The Hague, Collectie Gemeentemuseum (inv. 1009956,
ODI-1929-0001.1)

The medallion is surrounded by silver settings from which the diamonds have been removed, and is surmounted by a royal crown whose gems have suffered the same fate. The back is decorated with stylized floral motifs in white, black and pink enamel. In the centre of the back, on a blue background, are two letters L positioned back to back. This piece was originally set with thirteen large and forty-seven small rose-cut diamonds.

Medallions were highly prized at the beginning of the sixteenth century. They might be worn like pieces of jewellery in memory of the dead or of close friends, or exchanged as tokens of love when couples became engaged. However, most pieces of this type that have come down to us were given to faithful followers for services rendered, or as gifts within the framework of diplomatic relations. On 6 November 1683, Louis XIV gave this particular medallion to Grand Pensionary Anthony Heinsius from the United Provinces. At that time the Provinces were at the height of their power, mainly as a result of their good relations with England. In 1641 William II, Prince of Orange, married

142

Mary, the eldest daughter of Charles I of England, and in 1677, Stadtholder William III married the daughter of James, Duke of York (the future James II of England), who was also named Mary. From 1689, the couple reigned over England, Scotland and Ireland (something that Louis XIV could not possibly have foreseen in 1683).

Nearly forty miniatures of Louis XIV have come down to us. According to Frits Scholten, they were all meant for a 'portrait box' and were thus part of a propaganda campaign carried out by the French king. JW

BIBLIOGRAPHY : Antwerp 1993, no. 95 and (F. Scholten) pp. 55–62 ; Paris 2001, p. 247.

Bourbon to rule over Spain. The King of France had, in effect, married the daughter of Philip IV of Spain, and thus felt that a member of the French royal family could lay claim to the Spanish throne. His actions led to the War of Spanish Succession, which was ended by the Treaty of Utrecht in 1713. The armour indicates that the king is ready for war. It was common in the European courts to give medallions like these to members of one's entourage. Such gifts enabled bellicose sovereigns to secure the support of both diplomats and generals. JW

BIBLIOGRAPHY : Pforzheim 1990, no. 13/6 ; Antwerp 1995, no. 26 ; Tokyo 2003b, no. II–26.

< ### Medallion with portrait of King Philip V of Spain

France (miniature) and Netherlands (?), 1701 (?)

Silver, diamonds and miniature on copper, 92 x 50 mm

Pforzheim, Schmuckmuseum (inv. 18990/25)

The king wears armour and a chain, and we can make out a fragment of the royal crown in red with white pearls. The openwork silver frame with its royal crown is set with seven large diamonds and a series of smaller stones, all of them rose-cut. After the death in 1700 of Charles II, the last of the line of Spanish Habsburgs, Louis XIV sent his grandson Philip de

Monogram pendant

Spain (?), second half of the 17th century

Gold, silver, enamel, emeralds, diamonds and pearl, 155 mm

Private collection

The central section of this pendant encloses the diamond monogram AOTL – the initials, perhaps, of a motto or of the owner. It is set within a frame of emeralds in petal-shaped collets and diamond scrolling foliage. The pendant is linked to an emerald and diamond crown surmounted by an orb and cross, and a pearl is suspended below. The back is enamelled with pink and black acanthus leaves and flowers on a white ground. DSC

Ring with portrait of King Louis XIII

France, c. 1610

Gold, enamel and intaglio in green jasper bloodstone,

intaglio 19 x 15 mm ; ring : 22 mm

Paris, Bibliothèque Nationale de France, Département des

Monnaies, Médailles et Antiques (inv. Chab 2494)

The hoop, shoulders and sides of the octagonal bezel of this ring are decorated with trails of leaves in lilac enamel. The ring is set with a bloodstone intaglio portrait of Louis XIII (1601–1643) facing in profile towards the left. On the assassination of his father in 1610 the young heir became king, with his mother, Marie de' Medici acting with full powers as Regent. This pair of rings marks his accession and her rule on his behalf. DSC

BIBLIOGRAPHY : Chabouillet 1858, no. 2495.

Ring with portrait of Marie de' Medici

France, c. 1610

Gold, enamel and intaglio in green jasper bloodstone, intaglio

19 x 15 mm ; ring : 22 mm

Paris, Bibliothèque Nationale de France, Département des

Monnaies, Médailles et Antiques (inv. Chab 2493)

The hoop, shoulders and sides of the octagonal bezel of this ring are decorated with trails of leaves in lilac enamel. The ring is set with a bloodstone intaglio portrait bust of Marie de' Medici (1573–1642), facing in profile towards the left. Marie de' Medici became Queen of France through her marriage to Henry IV and acted as Regent on behalf of their son, Louis XIII, after Henry's assassination in 1610. DSC

BIBLIOGRAPHY : Chabouillet 1858, no. 2495.

Fleur-de-lis ring

France (?), second half of the 17th century

Gold, diamonds and enamel, setting : 17 x 14 mm ; ring : 22 mm

Private collection

This ring features a compartmentalized setting with five different-sized table-cut diamonds. Together they form a stylized fleur-de-lis, which was associated with the French royal family. The setting is placed between two decorative studs, on which a coat of arms may be seen – an azure shield with a vertical band of argent. The studs have been extended to form a narrow ring.

Since antiquity, the lily has been a powerful symbol, representing both virginity and fecundity. But it is also the emblem of several royal families, first among them the French royal

house. This ring either belonged to a member of that house or to a staunch defender of the French throne. JW

BIBLIOGRAPHY: London 1988, pp. 8–9; Antwerp 1995, no. 235; Antwerp 2002, no. 8; Tokyo 2003b, no. II–8; Scarisbrick 1993, p. 96.

Enamelled ring with diamond solitaire

Portugal (?), early 17th century

Gold, diamond and enamel, solitaire 7 x 8 mm

Lisbon, Museu Nacional de Arte Antiga (inv. 765 Joa)

This type of enamelled ring set with a solitaire diamond is very characteristic of the period between the end of the sixteenth and the beginning of the seventeenth centuries. It appears frequently in European paintings of the time, for example in *Portrait of a Woman* by Geldorp Gortzius (Dutch School, Museu Nacional de Arte Antiga, inv 1492 P). The centre of this example with its square mount features a truncated pyramid shape set with a table-cut diamond. The ring is also embellished with spirals engraved in black enamel. LD

BIBLIOGRAPHY: Brussels 1991, no. 15; Copenhagen 1992, no. 15; Orey 1995.

Ring with four table-cut diamonds

c. 1620

Gold, diamonds and enamel, 25 x 20 mm

Budapest, Magyar Nemzeti Múzeum (inv. Ann. Jank. 309)

The shoulders of this ring feature blue and white floral patterns, ending in an open-backed bezel held by four corner claws in black and white enamel. The points of the claws extend to the edge of the bezel, which holds four table-cut diamonds; the stones have the same diameter but the table cuts are unequal. The sides of the setting are in black and white enamel, as is part of the shank. The back is covered in blue enamel. This piece of jewellery, which appears both sturdy and elegant, is remarkable

for the four diamonds set together. From around 1620, engravings for templates show multiple diamonds in settings, but in one row only, with bezels set entirely in stones. Here, the jeweller has wisely combined the brilliance of the diamonds with the vivid colours of the enamel. The claw motif, which evokes the popular sport of falcon hunting, suggests a dating of around 1600, but the unusual placement of the diamonds puts this lovely piece rather later in the seventeenth century. JW

BIBLIOGRAPHY: Antwerp 1993, no. 18.

Ring with fifteen table-cut diamonds

Second half of the 17th century

Gold, diamonds and enamel, ring: 24 x 20 mm; setting: 19 x 12 mm

Private collection

The shoulders of this ring are chased and enamelled in black and white; they end in a raised, three-part setting that resembles one large and two small interlocking squares. Fifteen table-cut diamonds are set diagonally with the larger, central stone raised slightly above the others. Both the side and back of the bezel are decorated in black and white enamel floral patterns.

This magnificent ring is a simple attestation to the status of its owner, rather than representing any other symbolic value. This is a later variation of the round and oval rosettes that appeared in the first half of the seventeenth century. JW

BIBLIOGRAPHY: London 1988, p. 17, C–D; Kockelbergh/Vleeschdrager/Walgrave 1992, p. 85; Antwerp 1993, no. 67; Tokyo 2003b, no. II–1.

> ## Polish eagle of Louis XIV
> 17th century
> Gold, enamel, pearl, emerald and hessonite garnet, 111 mm
> Paris, Musée du Louvre, Département des Objets d'Art
> (inv. MR 418)

This enamelled gold eagle with outstretched wings, carrying a sceptre and orb in its talons and surmounted with the royal crown, was originally part of a sword mentioned in an inventory from 1791 of which only the cross-pieces remain. It is set with 149 rubies and an impressive hessonite garnet with triangular facets, which forms the eagle's body. The garnet may have been cut in Germany, although some of the palmettes are similar to those on pieces created in Paris in the seventeenth century. With the exception of the heart-shaped stones in the tail, the rubies adorning the talons, head and wings are all table-cut. For a long time, it was thought that the central stone was a ruby : in times past it was difficult to distinguish rubies from spinels, almandines and hessonite garnets. It is certain that this piece belonged to Louis XIV and was thus part of the French crown jewels. At one stage it hung from the chain of a porcelain teapot from Japan.

The eagle entered the royal collections prior to 1673 and it is generally acknowledged that it came from the estate of Marie Louise Gonzaga (1611–1667), daughter of Charles I, Duke of Mantua. In 1646, Marie Louise married Ladislaus IV (1595–1648), King of Poland. After his death, she married the king's half-brother John II Casimir (1609–1672), who acceded to the throne. He was deposed in 1668 and sought exile in Paris. After the death of Marie Louise in 1667, Louis XIV charged his jeweller Nicolas Pitau with acquiring her jewellery, silver plate and precious objects. It is not impossible that the eagle was part of the long list of items that were purchased, which also included 9,795 pearls, a diamond aigrette, earrings, eight chains set with diamonds, rubies and emeralds, rings, a coral necklace with two crosses and a host of other pieces of jewellery that sold for 170,000 *livres*. It is also possible that John II Casimir sold the eagle upon his arrival in Paris. Whatever the case, this piece is depicted in two paintings. One, in the collections of the museum in Neuburg an der Donau in Germany, shows Constance of Austria, the second wife of King Sigismund III and mother of John II Casimir. Nevertheless, it appears that this example, which hangs from a chain, is set with diamonds. The other painting, in Vienna's Kunsthistorisches Museum, depicts Queen Cecilia Renata (1611–1644), daughter of Ferdinand II, Holy Roman Emperor, and the first wife of Ladislaus IV. The queen has pinned the eagle to her corsage, which proves that the piece, with its strong heraldic connotations, was not exclusively reserved for men.

The eagle has long been associated with the exercise of power. According to Xenophon, it was the emblem of the Persian army. It was taken up by Gaius Marius under the Consulate, and was finally replaced by the labarum under Constantine. Later, the Holy Roman emperors, who saw themselves as the heirs to Rome, used the eagle in their coats of arms. It was particularly associated with the Prussian and Russian blazons, but also with the First Empire, since Napoleon also appropriated this highly symbolic bird of prey. In Poland, it was chosen to represent the country's highest chivalric order, the Order of the White Eagle, which was created in the fourteenth century. The order later disappeared from view, but was re-established under Augustus II in 1705 and continued until it was abolished in 1795. It was reinstated in 1807 under the Duchy of Warsaw, before being modified to more closely resemble a Russian imperial order from 1831–1917. Its quality and artistry make this ruby-covered eagle, sometimes called the 'Chimaera', unique. No similar pieces are known in any collection of a European museum, apart from the two-headed eagle of the Holy Roman Empire in the Treasury of Munich's Residenz. **CV**

BIBLIOGRAPHY : Twining 1960 ; Morel 1988, p. 230 ; Alcouffe 2001, pp. 430–1.

Chain, cross and pendant of the Order of Saint Michael

France, 1651

Gold, enamel and pearls, chain : 650 mm ; cross : 78 x 78 mm ;

pendant : 54.9 x 40.8 mm

Apeldoorn, Paleis Het Loo Nationaal Museum (inv. E 262), on

loan from the Foundation for the Preservation of the Chancery

of the Dutch Orders of Knighthood. Acquired by Mrs J.A.

Nanninga-Thomassen a Thuessink van der Hoop van Slochteren,

Groningue (inv. E 326).

Between the arms of this gold Maltese cross – with its white enamel border and gold-tipped points – are fleurs-de-lis and the chain of the order. In the centre of the cross, Saint Michael pierces the conquered dragon with his sword. The cross hangs from a chain consisting of twenty-nine links : fourteen in the form of a golden braid encircled by black and white enamel, and fifteen double shells in white enamel. The oval openwork pendant also depicts Saint Michael, slaying the devil with his lance. The image is surrounded by the order's chain : a braided cord decorated with six shells. A bail connects a large pearl to the lower shell, and two smaller pearls, one above the other, are attached to either side.

Louis XI founded the Order of Saint Michael in 1469. Initially, there were thirty-six knights, but their numbers increased to such a point that the order began to lose its prestige. Louis XIV reformed the order on 12 January 1665, reducing the number of knights to one hundred.

The chain and cross belonged to Hendrick de Sandra (1619–1707), a merchant who later became a soldier and commander of the town of Deventer, and had been made a knight several years earlier in 1657. The origin of the pendant is unknown. It is interesting to note, however, that it was the Maltese cross that hung from de Sandra's chain, not the pendant. Hendrick de Sandra was not the only Dutchman admitted to this French order. His distinguished compatriots included Johan Van Oldenbarnevelt, Pieter Hooft and Constantijn Huygens, as well as the admirals Michiel De Ruyter, Maarten Tromp and Witte De With. GS

BIBLIOGRAPHY : Van Zelm 1988, pp. 25–7 ; Ploos van Amstel 1990, pp. 205, 213–14, 263–6 ; Edinburgh 1992 ; Collignon 2004, pp. 22–31.

Insignia of the Order of the Elephant with the monogram of King Frederick VI of Denmark, made for King Louis XVIII

Early 19th century

Gold, silver, diamonds, rubies and enamel, 80 x 70 mm

Paris, Musée du Louvre (inv. MV 1022)

This white-enamelled gold elephant, with highlights of gold on his feet, trunk and tusks, carries a red and white brick tower on its back, with a row of old European-cut diamonds at top and bottom interspersed with rubies. The tower is placed on a blue saddle flanked on either side by a Maltese cross between laurel branches, also sprinkled with diamonds. A black mahout with a goad in his hand sits at the elephant's head.

The Order of the Elephant was a very exclusive order of Danish knighthood founded by Christian I in 1458. Its origins are little known and the presence of the elephant is not easily explained. The Danish monarchy only bestowed the illustrious insignia on members of the high Protestant nobility and it was never granted to more than thirty people at once, apart from members of the royal family, explaining why this supreme honour is depicted in portraits much less frequently than, for example, the Order of the Golden Fleece. JW

BIBLIOGRAPHY : Ackermann 1855, pp. 170–2.

<< *Gnadenpfennig* (favour medal)
Saxony, c. 1630
Gold, enamel and medal, 128 x 48 mm
Private collection

This gold pendant is set with an oval medallic portrait of Duke Ernest of Sachsen-Weimar (1605–1640) on one side and that of his wife, Elizabeth Sophia, daughter of Duke Johann Philipp of Sachsen-Altenburg, on the other. Their names and titles are inscribed around the edge and both are portrayed in profile. The portraits are set in an openwork gold frame composed of an enamelled wreath of flowers with blue ribbons above and below.

Favour medals, or *gnadenpfennig*, were widely used by the rulers of Austria and the various states of Germany as a means of publicly conferring a mark of distinction on their most loyal supporters. The high quality of the enamelled setting of this example is a clear indication of the pride the owners took in these symbols of dynastic propaganda, which were worn suspended from massive gold chains. The floral frame reflects the contemporary passion for gardens and flowers. DSC

BIBLIOGRAPHY : Tenzel 1740, pl. 62 ; Borner 1981, no. 152b, fig. 73V.

> **Portrait of William III of Orange, Stadtholder of the Netherlands and King of England**
Caspar Netscher (1639–1684), 1675
Oil on canvas, 39.5 x 33 cm
Apeldoorn, Paleis Het Loo Nationaal Museum, on loan from the
Geschiedkundige Vereniging, Oranje-Nassau (inv. Sch. por A 5429)

The prince's pose is a comfortable one, and he is leaning on one arm. He is wearing the vestments of the Order of the Garter, which he had been awarded in 1653 at the tender age of three. He was not made a knight until 1671, in London, under the reign of his uncle Charles II. Around his shoulders is the Great George – a sumptuously decorated chain with a pendant of Saint George that is worn on important occasions. Most of the members of the order also own the Lesser George, a smaller and simpler piece of jewellery worn on a ribbon and destined for everyday use.

In 1677, William (1650–1702) married Mary, the daughter of the future James II of England. Eleven years later, seven eminent Protestant English politicians asked him to come to England to overthrow his stepfather, the Catholic James II. On 15 November, William landed at Torbay in Devon, while elsewhere along the English coast, James fled to France. Not a drop of blood was shed in what came to be known as the Glorious Revolution. On 13 February 1689, the English crown was offered to Mary, who accepted on the condition that her husband became king. William III had already acquired great renown in Europe by forcing Louis XIV's troops to leave the United Provinces. He was one of the fiercest enemies of the King of France, whose thirst for conquest threatened the European balance of power. JW

BIBLIOGRAPHY : Kenyon 1992, pp. 197, 362.

154

The jewellery of absolutism

DIANA SCARISBRICK

In the eighteenth century jewellery reached a peak of perfection that has never since been equalled. Realising that men are governed by their eyes rather than by their intellect, monarchs throughout Europe – from Lisbon to Dresden, Stockholm to Naples – used jewels to reinforce their aura of majesty. France took the lead, where, under Louis XIV, absolutism had given the monarchy a renewed lease of life, setting the pattern for the rest of Europe. The same went for the art of jewellery at which the French had always excelled but never more so than during the reigns of Louis XV and of his grandson Louis XVI. Both kings made major additions of diamonds to the crown jewels, including the 140-carat Regent and the Sancy. Other historic stones, like the ruby Côte de Bretagne, were remounted into more up-to-date designs and in 1784 all rose-cut diamonds remaining in the state treasury were sent to Amsterdam for re-cutting into sparkling brilliants.[1] Not only were there advances in faceting, foiling and tinting also brought colour as well as brilliance to diamond jewellery. The high standards of craftsmanship were raised to even greater heights by the revised statutes of the Corporation of Goldsmith Jewellers in 1734 and 1756 stipulating a seven-year apprenticeship and a further three years as a journeyman. Skilled as they were, these jewellers were driven to create masterpieces of elegance by French men and women customers of great taste who demanded nothing short of perfection and, above all, something new.

The effect of so many wonderfully bejewelled women added to the splendour of court life, with its balls, receptions and masquerades. The British ambassador, Lord Malmesbury, after attending the opera at Versailles in 1774, was impressed by 'the show which the French women always make above those of other nations'. Events like these kept the jewellers busy and after one of them, the court jeweller Aubert recorded that 'Arranging the diamonds on twelve outfits meant spending no less than three days and three nights in both Paris and at Versailles before the queen's ball'. On such occasions, first as dauphine and then as queen, Marie Antoinette's dress and jewels epitomized the Versailles style, combining grandeur with elegance. When Boehmer, Aubert's successor as court jeweller,

offered her the famous diamond necklace he must have believed there was every chance that Louis XVI would want to acquire it to ensure that his Queen outshone everyone at court.[2]

The patronage of Madame de Pompadour and Madame du Barry, the two mistresses of Louis XV, must also have simulated the creativity of the Parisian jewellers. By the king's side at the theatre or at the gaming table, they dazzled the aristocracy with the magnificence of their diamonds.[3] Madame de Pompadour went further in immortalizing the reign of her lover by commissioning hardstone cameos and intaglios on the theme of the French army, its heroes and conquests, which could be worn as jewellery.[4]

The international reputation of Parisian jewellery was maintained by the practice of giving expensive presents to other monarchs and diplomats, and on the occasion of royal marriages and christenings. Commissions for jewellery in the most fashionable styles were ordered at the time of the marriages of the princesses Maria Josepha of Saxony (1747), Marie Antoinette (1770), the Countess of Provence (1770–1) and the Countess of Artois (1773). Not only did the bride receive splendid jewels but others were also distributed to court dignitaries and Officers of Guard. In general, men received rings or gold snuffboxes, but there were exceptions: for instance, the Grand Aumonier of the king of Sardinia was given a cross with diamonds set against a royal blue ground. The same procedure was followed at baptisms.

The pattern books of the Parisian jewellers Mondon (1740), Augustin Duflos (1761) and Pouget (1761 and 1764) show how the seventeenth-century aigrette, bodkin, girandole earring and breast ornament were transformed into lighter, more graceful, asymmetrical ornaments epitomizing rococo taste. In addition to the floral, bowknot and ribbon motifs, new themes were introduced. Many of these took their inspiration from nature – flowers, leaves, bulrushes, birds, insects, shells, coral – and trophies were made celebrating gardening, agriculture and the arts. The leading exponents of the new rococo style were J.D.

< Louis de Silvestre, *Augustus II of Poland*, c. 1793.

Lempereur, A.L. Ronde, P.A. Jacquemin and J.M. Tiron. From the late 1760s, however, the neoclassical style became increasingly popular, taking its inspiration from the discoveries at Pompeii and Herculaneum and incorporating motifs such as ears of corn, palmettes, laurel, honeysuckle and Greek fret (an ornamental device incorporating straight lines and geometric shapes), whilst retaining the light and graceful character of rococo. As the 1770 designs of L. van der Cruycen illustrate, symmetry was now the rule, although the geometric shapes were softened by new decorative motifs of festoons, tassels and swags derived from upholstery and curtain trimmings. The principal jewellers of the neoclassical style were Aubert, Bapst, Boehmer, Bassange and Menière.

Due to improvements in the use of candles for lighting, grand events usually took place at night. The fashion for piled-up hair meant that hair ornaments were more important than ever before, with popular motifs including feathers, birds pecking at berries, fireworks exploding upwards and stars and crescents. To balance the height of the hair, earrings grew longer; the girandole three-drop style, now lightened with sprays of flowers and ribbons, remained a favourite, but the simpler top and drop styles were increasingly popular. Necklaces fashioned as garlands of flowers interspersed with ribbons, or hung with swags terminating in tassels, were some of the most beautiful ever made, challenging the supremacy of the pearl choker and the diamond rivière. An essential element of court dress was the huge breast jewel, worn *en suite* with shoulder knots, loops and buttons, and for a final touch of elegance, pearl bracelets with jewelled clasps emerging from lace-trimmed sleeves and diamond rings sparkling on the fingers.

Although ornaments for women were now 'the principal objective of the jeweller's art', men were by no means left out. On important occasions they carried a ceremonial sword, wore jewelled insignia of the Orders of Chivalry, a hat loop and button, buttons, buckles for shoes and knees, a cravat pin and rings set with rare and beautiful stones. Ungainly as he was, at his wedding Louis XVI looked splendid in a coat sparkling with 'most astonishingly rich buttons all of single diamonds, seams studded with diamonds, the rest embroidered with different coloured jewels'. These were the crown jewels which Louis XVI used again at the wedding of his brother the Count of Artois, when Aubert was informed that 'the King will be wearing the badge of the Order of the Holy Spirit, the epaulette, the loop and the hat button set with the Regent diamond.' [5]

Examples of the latest fashions were sent on approval to foreign courts and ambassadors were expected to acquire jewellery on behalf of their monarchs. It was through the Count of Creutz that Gustave III of Sweden ordered a parure for his queen on the birth of the Crown Prince in 1778, having already

Per Krafft the Elder, *Gustave III of Sweden*, 1779.

< Martin van Meytens, *Portrait of Empress Maria Theresa of Austria*, 1765.

acquired Parisian jewels for himself and as presents for his visit to Catherine II in Russia in 1777.[6] As Miss Stuart, lady-in-waiting to the Duchess of Brunswick explained to the writer Marmontel: 'at your court princes are trained to dominate.'[7]

Maria Theresa, Queen Empress of Austria (1717–1780) and mother of Queen Marie Antoinette, was emphatically absolutist and played a central role in the wars and politics of Europe. Not only was her accession in 1740 disputed, it also coincided with a low ebb in the fortunes of that country, yet through her courage, character and intelligence she succeeded in reforming the army and united the various states and races of the Habsburg dominions under her rule, proving to the people of Austria and Germany that a woman could be a great leader. Until her widowhood in 1765, and as the portraits by Martin van Meytens show, she was always beautifully dressed and bejewelled, and she dominated the brilliant court ceremonies at the Hofburg in Vienna and at Schönbrunn. Particularly dazzling was the great diamond parure, a wedding present from her mother-in-law who, in her turn, had received it from her own mother-in-law, the queen of Poland. A spectacularly large, yellow sapphire worn on the ribbon of her muff on ceremonial sleigh drives could be removed and set in the centre of another suite of brilliants. Matching earrings, necklace, bracelet and comb, inset with medallions of the crown of Hungary and surrounded by pearls, evoked the famous moment when, at the beginning of her reign, a new baby in her arms, she addressed the Hungarian Diet in their own language, appealing to their loyalty and patriotism and winning them over to her cause. She further demonstrated her regard for her Hungarian subjects with an aigrette and a parure with the cross of the Royal Order of Saint Stephen set with emeralds, diamonds and rubies representing the national colours. Her magnificent ancestral emeralds, pearls and diamonds demonstrated her right to rule as heir to the long line of Habsburgs. Recognizing their significance she decreed that the historic family pearls which Martin van Meytens depicted wound round her throat and across her shoulders should remain in the State Treasury for the use of the wives of her successors. The pearls – like so many of her jewels – have disappeared and it is alleged that the last Emperor Karl sold them to buy an aeroplane to take him on his ill-fated venture into Hungary in attempt to recapture the crown he had lost in 1918.[8]

Related to Maria Theresa by his marriage to her cousin Maria Josepha, Augustus III King of Poland and Elector of Saxony who in 1733 succeeded his father Augustus II the Strong, governed absolutely. Louis XIV and the court of Versailles had made such an impression on Augustus II, who visited France as a youth, that he too made a public spectacle of court life in the Dresden Residential Palace. He imitated the jewellery associated with Louis XIV by wearing sets of buttons for jackets and waistcoats, buckles for shoes and knees, the insignia of Orders of Chivalry, swords and scabbards, loops for the hat richly set with coloured stones as well as with diamonds. By the time of the marriage of his son and Maria Josepha in 1719 he had acquired no fewer than nine such sets or garnitures, displayed in the Jewel Room of the Grünes Gewölbe (Green Vault) from 1729. Augustus III added considerably to the collection. In 1742 he bought the famous Dresden green diamond at Leipzig fair and completed the unfinished topaz garniture. His grandson, Frederick Augustus III altered some pieces, and in 1782 donated the wonderful official set of diamond jewellery made for the Polish Saxon Queens. Of course, in addition to the important items of official jewellery given to the Treasury, these queens also had their own private collections, which remained their own property. It is thanks to the miraculous survival of seven of the garnitures from the Green Vault that it is possible to envisage the splendour of the Electors of Saxony, blazing with light and flashing colour at candlelit court ceremonies, prominent in their embodiment of royal power. Each takes the name of the predominant stone used – agate, cornelian, ruby, sapphire, diamond, both rose- and brilliant-cut – and are impressive not only on account of the rarity and cost of these stones but also through the quality of the settings.[9]

Despite being a thoroughly absolute ruler, none of this splendour seemed to interest Frederick II of Prussia (1712–1786), the military genius who is one of the few monarchs to have been awarded the title of 'Great'. During his reign Prussia emerged as one of the greatest powers on the continent, laying the foundations of a united Germany under her leadership, a policy finally completed in 1871 when William I, King of Prussia, became German Emperor. As a young man Frederick followed the French fashion for lavishly embroidered dress, but he soon adopted the uniform of his celebrated Foot Guard regiment, blue with red facings and a cocked hat, as if he was always on the battlefield commanding his troops. Not only were the uniforms torn, darned and patched at the elbows but they were also stained brown with snuff. It was in connection with his passion for tobacco that Frederick II demonstrated his sense of royal grandeur by supervising the design and execution of a particularly opulent type of snuffbox, made in the Fabrique Royale of Berlin, and which bears his name. These were richly encrusted with diamonds and coloured stones, which were applied to the hardstone body of the box. Frederick placed them everywhere in his palaces and he could not bear to be parted from them, even taking a box with him into battle at Kunersdorf in 1759, which is said to have saved his life by deflecting a bullet.[10]

> Pietro Antonio Rotari, *Princess Cunegonde*, 1755.

Anton Mengs, *Maria Louisa of Parma, future Queen of Spain*, 1764.

In England, although the powers of the Hanoverian monarchy were limited in comparison to continental absolutism, George II and George III understood the value of jewels in asserting their rank and that of their consorts. The quality was good, and as Huguenot immigrants such as Isaac Lacam, Peter Dutens and John Duval brought French standards of excellence and fashion to London it was no longer necessary to go over to Paris for fine jewellery. Widely admired, the jewels of Queen Charlotte, who married George III in 1760, were so numerous and magnificent that some doubted whether they were set with genuine stones. In fact, she did not have to resort to this pretence for some of her best diamonds were not bought from royal revenues but came to her from India as gifts from princes, such as the Nawab of Arcot, and from the wealthy English who had made fortunes there. As a result her collection became so famous that foreign visitors asked if they might view it. However it seems that she regarded her jewels as a statement of sovereignty, worn as a duty rather than for enjoyment, as she confessed to Fanny Burney, 'it is the pleasure of a week, a fortnight at the most to return no more. I thought at first I should always choose to wear them but with the fatigue and trouble of putting them on and the care they required and the fear of losing them, believe me, Ma'am in a fortnight's time I longed for my earlier dress.'[11]

Under the Bourbon king, Philip V, grandson of Louis XIV, his ambitious wife Elizabeth Farnese, and their son Charles III (1716–1788) who acceded to the throne in 1759, prosperity was restored to Spain and institutions reformed. Here, as elsewhere in Europe, jewellery played an important part in establishing the royal image, and Marie Amelia (d. 1760) daughter of Frederick Augustus II of Saxony, who married the future Charles III in 1738, was particularly aware of this. She invited the French jewellers Jean Duval and Augustin Duflos to Madrid, frequently calling on her ambassador Llovera to execute commissions from the Parisian trade on her behalf, and took immense trouble over all the details of court dress.[12] She was so pleased with a pair of bracelet clasps with enormous diamonds, 'of superb quality and beautifully set', given to her by Louis XV in 1759, that she wore them the very next day at a court reception.[13] This dependence on Paris for jewels continued during the reign of Charles IV (1748–1819) and his wife Maria Louisa of Parma, The demand from Spain for elegant jewelled insignia of the Orders of Chivalry, particularly the Order of the Golden Fleece, was also met by the leading French jewellers; J.H. Pouget, in his *Traité des Pierres Précieuses* of 1762, includes several designs for these. Coloured stones were as popular as blazing white diamonds, and the traditional preference for emeralds imported from South America continued to characterize Spanish jewellery.

The machinery of government in Portugal was comparable to those of other absolute monarchies in Europe, and from 1750–77, under the reforming minister Pombal, it became a model of efficient absolutism. The international style of court jewellery developed in France was adopted with spectacular results, due to the royal monopoly over diamonds mined in Brazil. For Portuguese men there were jewelled badges of the three Orders of Chivalry, the orders of Christ, Saint James and of Aviz, as well as diamond buttons, buckles and cloak clasps. Although each of the eighteenth-century queens of Portugal appeared in public with the magnificent jewels listed in their inventories, Queen Maria I was perhaps the most brilliant at her coronation in 1777, 'with a bodice and underdress adorned with diamond flowers, of excessive price and admirable skill, with the order of Christ hanging from a ribbon the colour of fire, the cross made of brilliant-cut diamonds of an extraordinary and astounding size, many ropes of diamonds of inestimable value: her headdress an imperial crown set with diamonds which appeared to be just one huge stone, two diamond clasps fastened her royal mantle.'[14] Again, from the correspondence between the Keeper of the Queen's jewels and the Portuguese ambassador in Paris, it is clear that she too preferred French designs, asking for 'sketches of the prettiest and most modern ornaments which are made there for the ears and the neck, for the breast and the head, all to be set with brilliant cut diamonds'.[15] Yet within a decade the absolutist system of government, inspired by that of Louis XIV and expressed by jewellery created in Paris, had received its death blow with the Revolution, which, ironically, also originated in France. French absolutism had sown the seeds of its own destruction.

1. Morel 1988.
2. Morel 1988, p. 205.
3. Denis/Klein 1992, pp. 142–4.
4. Stockholm 2000, pp. 20–3.
5. Archives Nationales, Paris, T* 299/3. *Letter from the jeweller Aubert 1773–85, to M. Couterot, à la Garde-robe du Roi, Versailles, 9 October 1773.*
6. Stockholm 1999, p. 558.
7. Renwick 1972, vol. I, p. 253.
8. Twining 1960, pp. 15–16, 18.
9. Jackson, Mississippi 2004, pp. 151–2.
10. Truman 1991, p. 204.
11. Scarisbrick 1994, pp. 226–9.
12. Huete 1993, pp. 33–9.
13. Bourget 1905, vol. XIX, pp. 441–7.
14. Orey 1995, p. 51.
15. *Dessins de bijoux commandés en France par Maria Ière en 1784*, Arquivo Nacional da Torre do Tombo, Lisbon.

Corsage jewellery of Elizabeth Augusta, Princess Palatine

Germany, probably the Palatinate, first half of the 18th century

Silver, silver gilt, diamonds and pearls, 408 x 285 mm

Munich, Bayerische Verwaltung der staatlichen Schlösser, Gärten und Seen, Residenz München, Schatzkammer

(inv. Res. Mü. Schk 1144 WL)

This two-part corsage piece has a symmetrical design, the two lines of the upper section fanning outwards and upwards from a 'spider' setting and the lower part having two overlapping and touching bean-shaped settings. Short, slightly curved floral elements decorated with rose-cut diamonds on silver leaf appear in closed settings. At the top centre a letter s in a lively rococo style helps to lessen the rigid symmetry of the whole. The piece is enhanced by no fewer than forty-five pendant pear-shaped pearls with one round pearl at the centre of the spider. Originally there were fifty pearls, but when the piece was restored in 1958, the craftsmen were unable to work out where four should be placed. Overall the piece reflects a naturalist style, resembling a shrub from which pearls hang like fruit.

This type of piece forms a triangle on a woman's body, between breasts and pubic bones, at the point where her pregnant belly expands. This part of the body enjoyed great veneration due to its reproductive function, while simultaneously being an object of male concupiscence. Although carefully covered, attention was nevertheless clearly drawn to it. Indeed it has been said that fashion is a perpetual struggle between two desires, the one to dress and the other to undress. This corsage, whose floral elements evoke fertility, can be seen as symbolizing this duality.

The piece was long dated to the period 1710–1720, although with no possibility of reference to archives or images. In *Lebenslust und Frömmigkeit*, Carl Ludwig Fuchs suggests that the use of silver settings and silver leaf in fact place it a little later. The use of detachable pearls was in any case particularly popular around 1740, as shown by many portraits reproduced in Fuchs's book.

This corsage probably belonged to the princess palatine of Bavaria Elizabeth Augusta (1693–1728). It has been in the Munich Schatzkammer since 1879. JW

BIBLIOGRAPHY : Munich 1970, no. 1144 ; Mannheim 1999, vol. 1.1, p. 127 ; Stockholm 2000, no. 63 ; Antwerp 2002, no. 18.

Triangular stomacher with three parts and pendant

Cordoba (?), first part of the 17th century

Gold, diamonds and pearl, 135 x 95 mm ; 80 x 30 mm

Madrid, Museo Nacional de Artes Decorativas

(inv. 2154 and 2126)

The three segments of this triangular stomacher are joined by pins. The flower at the centre of the largest, upper segment is surrounded by chased and pierced branches and interwoven festoons, set with table-cut diamonds and inlaid with very small diamonds. Branches also spread out from the button in the middle of the central segment, which is itself formed from a rose pattern of diamonds and ends in a bow. In the third, smaller part, leaves, also set with small diamonds, surround a half pearl. The back is engraved with a plant motif, which, as Letizia Arbeteta Mira has shown, strongly resembles a Cordoba mark.

On certain occasions, a cross in the form of a bow ending in a button would have been attached to the stomacher by a linking piece in the shape of a palm frond (inv. 2126). Like the other segments, the cross and palm are set with very small diamonds and table-cut diamonds. A similar drawing by Salvador Varivol in Barcelona in 1727 and preserved as no. 881 in the Passanties (collections of drawings by Spanish jewellers) suggests that the stomacher was made in the same year. A drawing in a manuscript from the Monastery of Guadalupe shows a similar

stomacher, with an emerald in the upper segment from which one could also hang a cross. The jewel was in fact attached to the statue of Our Lady of Guadalupe. Its old-fashioned design can be linked to a drawing by Francesch Cardo of 1701 (Passanties, no. 773) suggesting that the current example dates from the first third of the eighteenth century. FMG

BIBLIOGRAPHY : Madrid 1998, no. 118, p. 163.

< ### Pendant with cross in three parts

Cordoba, second half of the 18th century
Gold, diamond and green glass, 107 x 66 mm
Madrid, Museo Nacional de Artes Decorativas (inv. 2140)

The three parts of this pendant – a loop, an almond-shaped diamond and a Greek cross – are held together with pins. The plant-inspired loop comprises a small, finely pierced panel with, at its centre, a green glass stone in a bezel representing a flower bud, surrounded by eight smaller glass stones. Spirals, oblique lines and geometric shapes set with coloured glass stones surround the almond-shaped diamond in the central element. The arms of the cross are formed of round, closed settings with glass stones, ending in plant motifs. A rectangular chaton forms the centre of the cross.

According to Letizia Arbeteta Mira, the creator of this piece used techniques shown in designs published by Gilles Légaré in 1663 and later imitated in Spain, while adding elements from an earlier period, such as the high settings and chatons. Pieces of this kind were very popular and are still widely worn as decorations for the traditional costumes of Estremadura, the Valencia region and Catalonia. FMG

BIBLIOGRAPHY : Madrid 1998, no. 10, p. 86.

Stomacher of Queen Mariana Victoria of Portugal

Portugal, mid-18th century
Gold, silver, diamonds and rubies
Lisbon, Palácio Nacional da Ajuda (inv. 56593)

This stomacher is designed as a knotted bow fashioned from ribbons patterned with sprays of ruby and rose-cut diamond flowers and leaves. It is bordered by a line of diamond scrolls each with a ruby between and joined in the centre by a large ruby and diamond cluster. This is surmounted by a diamond knot entwined with ruby and diamond streamers passing beneath the cluster, enclosing the ruby and diamond pendant hanging below. In full court dress, a stomacher was the section of the bodice between the neck and waist, richly ornamented by jewels of the same name. Corsets were used to flatten the bust allowing the stomacher to lie flat across the stiff fabric of the dress. Designed for a royal or aristocratic lady, this stomacher derives from the engraving for a *Grand Noeud pour les robes de Cour* ('large bowknot for a court dress') included as one of a set published in Paris by the jeweller Mondon et Fils, and is indicative of his influence in the European courts. The motifs of ribbons, bow, flowers and leaves are quintessentially rococo in style. Queen Mariana Victoria, whose crowned cipher is on the leather box, was an Infanta of Spain who married Joseph I of Portugal and reigned with him from 1750–77. DSC

Floral spray

Portugal, c. 1760
Silver and pink topazes, 107 x 90 mm
Private collection

The stem, leaves, buds and open flowers of this decorative spray
are set with pink topazes of various shades. Perhaps originally
part of a stomacher, which covered the dress from neckline to
waist, this brooch illustrates the eighteenth-century passion for
floral motifs, soft colours and richly decorated bodice ornaments. DSC

> ## Choker

Spain (?), last third of the 18th century
Silver, topazes and imitation diamonds, 111 x 235 mm
Madrid, Museo Nacional de Artes Decorativas (inv. 5289)

This necklace comprises two semicircular parts linked by a central buckle, from which hangs an impressive pendant. The necklace is set with seven almond-shaped topazes surrounded by
leaves cut into the silver and set with imitation rose-cut diamonds. The pendant comprises a bow in the same style as the
necklace, also set with almond-shaped topazes, and ends in a
large table-cut topaz encircled by sixteen imitation diamonds
from which hangs a tassel. The bow is detachable so that the
necklace can be transformed into a stomacher and necklace.
Such a combination, generally known as a *'tour du cou'* ('round
the neck') was particularly popular during the Romantic period,
the last third of the eighteenth century. This type of jewellery
appears in portraits from this period of princesses and monarchs
from all the European courts. FMG

Necklace with pendant

Portugal, third quarter of the 18th century

Silver and chrysoberyls, necklace : 252 mm ;

pendant : 133 x 68 mm

Lisbon, Museu Nacional de Arte Antiga (inv. 391 Joa)

This elegant silver necklace set entirely with chrysoberyls is remarkable for its composition and finish compared with the European style of the period. Composed of a series of very delicate floral motifs, the necklace is fastened by a ribbon threaded through rings at each end. The large pendant is in the shape of a double bow and a dove is suspended from a set of three floral elements identical to those of the necklace.

Citron yellow chrysoberyls are characterized by spectacular effects of shape and colour, and were sometimes combined with precious stones of other hues. The richness and diversity of pieces such as this necklace attest to the popularity of these stones imported from Brazil. Reserved for women's jewellery, chrysoberyls were used in earrings, necklaces, brooches, buckles, rings and bracelets. These items reveal the immense richness of the shapes and styles used by Portuguese jewellers of the period. LO

BIBLIOGRAPHY : Brussels 1991, no. 237 ; Copenhagen 1992, no. 237 ; Washington 1993, no. 54 ; Orey 1995.

Brooch from the Spanish royal family

Spain (?), 1740–60

Gold, silver, emeralds, rubies and diamonds, 130 x 75 mm

London, S.J. Phillips

The brooch is designed as a shell outlined in diamonds. Further lines of diamonds run between emerald ribs, crowned by six cabochon emeralds to which sprays of ruby and diamond flowers are applied, highlighted by groups of small diamonds. An emerald drop, a small shell and emerald chains ending in diamond tassels hang beneath. Illustrating Spanish taste for deep green emeralds, this brooch unites three characteristic motifs of the rococo style – shells, flowers and tassels. Pinned to the corsage, the flowers bordering the low-cut neckline and the tassels falling down to the waist, this handsome brooch would have stood out against a stiff brocade court dress, drawing attention to the royal wearer. DSC

Stomacher and earrings

Portugal, last quarter of the 18th century

Silver and chrysoberyls, stomacher : 91 x 108 mm ;

earrings : 53 x 28 mm

Lisbon, Museu Nacional de Arte Antiga (inv. 615 Joa and 690 Joa)

This magnificent silver and chrysoberyl set is composed of an impressive corsage and a pair of earrings. The brooch features a very elegant design of symmetrical stylized leaves placed around a large round rosette. Three girandole drops, the largest placed in the centre, are suspended from the main part of the brooch. The earrings are composed of three jointed elements linked together : a rosette at the top followed by a bow and finally a girandole drop.

These decorative chrysoberyl pieces demonstrate the level of refinement Portuguese jewellery had attained by the eighteenth century. The elegance and variety of the design are matched by excellent craftsmanship and mounting. The size and density of the stones' settings give them the impression of being detached from their bezels. LO

BIBLIOGRAPHY : Brussels 1991, no. 237 ; Copenhagen 1992, no. 237 ; Washington 1993, no. 54 ; Orey 1995.

Top and drop earrings

England, c. 1790

Gold, silver and diamonds, 56 x 20 mm

London, S.J. Phillips

These earrings are designed in three sections : from the top solitaire of each hangs a cluster of small stones encircling a round cushion-cut diamond (about 8 carats) attached to a pear-shaped drop (about 20 carats) within a border of smaller stones. The length of the pendants would have balanced the towering hairstyles that were in fashion from the late 1760s. Since they framed the face, those who could afford to do so reserved their best stones for earrings. The swinging diamond frames further enhance the brilliance of these long pendant drops. For less formal events the round clusters could be detached and worn on their own. DSC

Portrait of King Frederick II of Prussia

Antoine Pesne (1683–1757) and workshop, Berlin, c. 1740

Oil on canvas, 78 x 63 cm

Château de Hohenzollern, HRH George Frederick,

Prince of Prussia (inv. GKI 9954)

This portrait was painted by the French artist Antoine Pesne, who was called to Berlin as court painter in 1711 and subsequently worked under three kings of Prussia. It shows Frederick the Great shortly before or after his accession to the throne in 1740. Although it does not have the same expressive force, it is reminiscent of another portrait of Frederick painted in the same period, which is today in the Gemäldegalerie, Berlin. Both paintings show the king from the waist up and turning to the left. In this picture he is dressed in a blue uniform jacket with silver braid and a three-cornered hat, and wears the cross and orange scarf of the Order of the Black Eagle, the supreme distinction of the Kingdom of Prussia, founded by his grandfather Frederick I in 1701. Only the bright, proud eyes of this round-faced young man recall the highly characteristic features of the mature king's portraits by which he is better remembered.

Frederick II's boyhood and youth were marked by conflict with his father, the severe 'Soldier King' Frederick William I (1688–1740). During Frederick II's reign, when he became known as 'Great', the three Silesian Wars enabled him to raise Prussia to the rank of a European power. In the fields of the arts and culture he was resolutely francophile, and Sans-Souci, the summer residence he had built near Potsdam, is a masterpiece of the rococo style. He loved to collect valuable snuffboxes and to give them as gifts and is thought to have commissioned between 300 and 400 examples. **UF**

BIBLIOGRAPHY : Börsch-Supan 1986 ; Michaelis 2003, pp. 14ff.

Snuffbox of King Frederick II of Prussia

Berlin, c. 1765–70

Gold, diamonds and enamel, 52 x 104 x 82 mm

Berlin, Stiftung Preussische Schlösser und Gärten Berlin-Brandenburg, HRH George Frederick, Prince of Prussia (inv. HZ 3580)

This cagework snuffbox, comprising six enamel panels placed in gold frames, is made particularly attractive by the contrast between the relative severity of its lines and the richness of its decoration. In addition to its ornamentation of brilliant-cut diamonds set in floral motifs on a partially coloured ground, the box is noteworthy for the *grisaille* representations on the lid, base and each of the four sides. These show Diana bathing, apparently pointing to Actaeon who is out of the picture, and other nymphs, naiads and Cupids. The female figure in the foreground, bottom left, clearly resembles a model used by François Boucher (1703–1770) who also appears in an engraving by Gilles Demarteau (1722–1776).

A sketch for the lid by Jean Guillaume George Krüger was once held at the Schlossmuseum, Berlin, but is now thought to be lost. The ground of pale blue, also known as *bleu mourant* or 'dying blue', reflects the king's personal taste: he chose the same colour for the wall hangings and porcelain that he commissioned. In the early twentieth century during the reign of Emperor William II (1859–1941), this box from the royal treasury and the other two snuffboxes on display were given to the Hohenzollern Museum housed in the Monbijou Palace, Berlin, which was destroyed during the Second World War. Today it can be admired, with four other ornamental boxes, in the collection of the House of Hohenzollern currently on loan to Charlottenburg Palace. UF

BIBLIOGRAPHY : Seidel 1901, pp. 74–86 (ill. 1, 1a, 1b) ; Munich 1992, pp. 270–2.

Cane of King Frederick II of Prussia

Isaak Jakob Clauce (1728–1803), Berlin, c. 1756
Gold, silver, enamel, diamonds and wood, 750 mm
The strap and lower quarter of the cane are missing.
Château de Hohenzollern, HRH George Frederick,
Prince of Prussia (inv. HZ 3564)

Among the favourite accessories of King Frederick II of Prussia, particularly towards the end of his life, were his canes, which he used to support himself as he walked and undoubtedly also to emphasize his words. A great many portraits of the king, mostly posthumous, show him leaning on one of his many canes

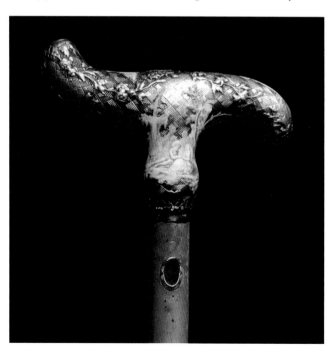

with their artfully worked handles. This example could have been made around 1756 by the painter on enamel Isaak Jakob Clauce who, although he worked mainly in Berlin, was living in Saxony at the time. The Malacca rattan cane is surmounted by a curving crow's beak, the body engraved with a chequered and layered design and decorated with branches and flowers in relief. On the top and broader parts of the handle the artist has shown pairs of lovers in landscapes in blue on a white ground.

Having undoubtedly been used during the king's funeral in 1786, it was preserved in the Potsdam Palace. In 1806 Napoleon took it to Paris as spoils of war and later gave it to Marshall Ney. It then passed from hand to hand, eventually coming into the possession of Lord Willoughby, who gave it to King William I of Prussia as a gift in 1870. In 1877 the cane finally arrived at the museum of the Hohenzollerns, in the Berlin Palace of Monbijou, which was later destroyed during the Second World War. It seems that the piece was removed in time to be taken to a safe place. After this it was transferred to Hohenzollern Castle. The cane bears the traces of its turbulent history. UF

BIBLIOGRAPHY : Munich 1992, pp. 364ff.

> Portrait of the Grand Elector Frederick Augustus II of Saxony, King of Poland, under the name Augustus III

Copy after Pietro Antonio Rotari (1707–1762), 1756
Oil on canvas, 108 x 86 cm
Dresden, Staatliche Kunstsammlungen Dresden,
Gemäldegalerie Alte Meister (inv. S 451)

Augustus III (1696–1763) is wearing armour under his blue coat. His left hand rests on a commander's baton. At this time relations between Saxony and its neighbours were strained. The war with Silesia began in 1756 and Frederick II of Prussia, known as Frederick the Great, tried to invade Saxony, though without success. The ermine-lined coat – a royal privilege – is spread before Augustus and he is wearing the insignia of the Order of the Golden Fleece, awarded by his wife's uncle, Emperor Charles VI, and, almost hidden, the Polish Order of the White Eagle on a blue ribbon. The insignia of the Golden Fleece is almost certainly the version in brilliants and Brazilian topazes (Grünes Gewölbe, inv. VIII 5) that the jeweller Jean-Jacques Pallard had delivered to the sovereign in the spring of 1756 and which he liked to wear in his portraits. Yellow topazes are so pale that they can easily be taken for diamonds. Augustus also wears a large diamond on his shirt button.

During his reign the Saxon capital, Dresden, enjoyed a period of prosperity and exceptional cultural influence. Augustus

176

III overcame the divisions within the Polish nobility but, on his death, the country was divided between the neighbouring powers of Russia, Prussia and Austria. **JW**

BIBLIOGRAPHY: Weber 1999, pp. 75–9; Arnold 2001, pp. 99–102.

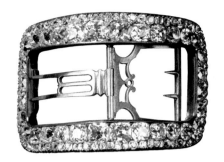

< Portrait of Archduchess Maria Josepha of Austria, Queen of Poland

Copy after Pietro Antonio Rotari (1707–1762), shortly after 1755

Oil on canvas, 108 x 86 cm

Dresden, Staatliche Kunstsammlungen Dresden,

Gemäldegalerie Alte Meister (inv. S 453)

Maria Josepha of Austria (1699–1757) is wearing the Russian Order of Catherine I on a red sash and the Austrian Order of the Star Cross (*Sternkreuz*) on her right breast, next to a heart-shaped red jewel hanging from a black bow. Her hair is adorned with glittering ornaments from the diamond parure of her father-in-law Augustus the Strong (Grünes Gewölbe, inv. VIII 21) and the famous hairpin showing an eagle in gilt enamel holding a large teardrop diamond (Grünes Gewölbe, inv. VIII 196). In her ears and around her neck the Queen of Poland has chosen to wear magnificent diamonds that no longer feature in this form in the present-day collection of the Grünes Gewölbe. This is not surprising, since it is known that the Electorate's archives are full of commissions and that jewellery was regularly modified and the stones reused. Magnificent sleeves in Spanish blonde lace and two diamond bracelets, one showing a miniature of her husband Frederick Augustus, complete her parure, while the royal crown also appears in the painting, placed on a red cushion. **JW**

BIBLIOGRAPHY: Arnold 1994, pp. 192–214, 231–2; Weber 1999, pp. 77–9.

Shoe buckles with brilliants

Christian August Globig, Dresden, 1782–9

Diamonds, silver, silver gilt and steel, 57 x 84 x 38 mm

Dresden, Staatliche Kunstsammlungen Dresden,

Grünes Gewölbe (inv. Nr. VIII 19)

Of all the Dresden shoe parures, the buckles from the diamond garniture, made between 1782 and 1789 by Christian August Globig, are the most opulent. Frederick Augustus III commissioned them to replace two rosettes created for Augustus III in the mid-eighteenth century. Unlike the parures that adorned the shoes of sovereigns during the first half of the eighteenth century, which were generally smaller, flat and rectangular, the buckles of this diamond garniture are curved. Similar buckles were made in the same period for the rose-cut diamond garniture. However, the baroque form was retained in the same series for the buckles fastening the breeches at the knee. The curved buckles of the diamond garniture follow the curve of the shoe and are unusual for the noble sobriety of their ornamentation, with four corners showing an absence of the traditional ostentation. They are nevertheless together studded with 64 large and tightly set brilliants, surrounded by 181 smaller diamonds. The larger stones are placed at the top, by the instep.

Like breech buckles and hat brim ornaments, in the baroque period shoe buckles were a compulsory item in any jewellery 'garniture' for persons of high rank. The other pieces in the set included many coat and jacket buttons, a cane with a decorative handle, hat decorations and jewels or insignia of orders, awarded by favour or for merit. The Dresden jewellery garnitures indicate that these pieces might also be supplemented by hunting knives, riding crops, snuffboxes, ornamental buttons and fob watches, depending on the identity of the eventual wearer.

The diamond garniture, dating back to Augustus the Strong (1670–1733), was the most prestigious ornamental ensemble in the royal ceremonial wardrobe. Sovereigns attached great importance to it until the early nineteenth century and made more changes to it than to any other set of jewellery in their possession. Even before 1719 Augustus the Strong had organized his diamond collections according to their type of cut, which in turn gave rise to the garnitures of rose-cut diamonds and brilliants. At a time when the size of the diamonds on buttons was more important than the shape into which they had been cut such discernment was remarkable. Although it was not until the late eighteenth century that they acquired the appearance we see today, these stones clearly date from the end of the baroque period. DS

BIBLIOGRAPHY : Arnold 2001, p. 210 ; Syndram 2006, pp. 166ff.

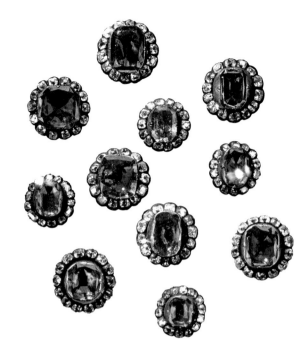

Buttons from the ruby garniture of King Augustus of Poland

Probably workshop of Johann Melchior Dinglinger (1664–1731), Dresden, before 1719

Additional buttons made by Johann Friedrich Dinglinger, Dresden, 1736

Gold, silver, spinels and brilliants, 21 and 17 mm

Dresden, Staatliche Kunstsammlungen Dresden, Grünes Gewölbe (inv. Nr. VIII 110–111)

Buttons decorated with diamonds were very fashionable in the later decades of the seventeenth century and first decades of the eighteenth. They were generally a part of sets with many pieces, which had already represented one of the most valuable garnitures in the king's collection in the reign of Louis XIV. As indicated by the inventory of 1719, most of Augustus the Strong's (1670–1733) jewellery garnitures comprised three-dozen coat buttons and as many smaller jacket buttons. Their primary role was as glittering prestige items, intended to display the wealth and splendour of the man who used them to adorn the sleeves, pockets and braid of his ceremonial dress, to which they would be sewn and later removed as circumstances dictated. The number and size of these precious jewels were intended to impress all those who were present at court ceremonies, even at a distance. In the late baroque and rococo periods, these buttons were regarded only secondarily as functional garment fastenings.

We have proof of the existence of a ruby garniture, almost certainly created by Johann Melchior Dinglinger for the coronation of Augustus the Strong as King of Poland in 1697. The red of the principal stones and the white of the brilliants that surrounded them evoked the national colours of the 'aristocratic republic' of Poland. However, we do not know when and to what extent those that we can admire today may have replaced these coat and jacket buttons. In any case, twelve additional buttons were made after 1719 to allow both the elector king and his son to use the set at the same time. Those that have come down to us – from which, it should be noted, twenty buttons were withdrawn from each series in 1924 – are among the oldest pieces in the ruby garniture.

The coat and jacket buttons differ in size, but not in form, and all have a surrounding crown of fourteen small brilliants.

To heighten the effect of their colour the 'rubies' on the buttons are set in gold, whereas the brilliants have the usual silver settings. At the centre of each button a spinel rests on a red leaf. Typically of buttons made in the early eighteenth century, the central stones vary in shape and size. The same is true of the vast and highly valuable collection of buttons belonging to Louis XIV. DS

BIBLIOGRAPHY : Arnold 2001, p. 129 ; Syndram 2006, pp. 96ff.

> Hat agrafe

Christian August and August Gotthelf Globig, Dresden, 1782–9

Gold, silver and diamonds, 220 x 70 mm

Dresden, Staatliche Kunstsammlungen Dresden, Grünes Gewölbe (inv. Nr. VIII 11)

During the eighteenth century monarchs gradually lost the habit of wearing a crown after their accession to the throne as a symbol of their majesty. They preferred to decorate their rich, formal clothing with magnificently jewelled parures, large and valuable hat ornaments could be worn as a substitute for the crown. Men's fashion in the seventeenth and eighteenth centuries was highly influenced by the French court and hat ornaments or agrafes set with precious stones became the favourite jewellery of monarchs. These fasteners in three sections could be unbelievably valuable. In practical terms, the agrafe ornament made it possible to attach the hat brim to its crown in an elegant fashion. As shown by this example in the Grünes Gewölbe, the ornament comprised a main or lower button fixed to the raised edge of the hat close to the face. This button was

178

usually decorated with a large and particularly fine precious stone, often mounted as a solitaire. In this case the diamond weighs almost 25 carats. Two flexible chains set with precious stones link the lower button to its upper counterpart fixed to the crown of the hat. The stones on the upper button protruded slightly from the felt of the hat so that they were visible, especially when the monarch's head was turned.

The hat agrafe with rose-cut diamond garnitures has its origins in the rose-cut jewellery created in the early eighteenth century for Augustus the Strong and set for a second time shortly before 1718. Between 1782 and 1789 Prince Elector Frederick Augustus III commissioned his jeweller to provide new mounts for the rose-cut diamonds from the diamond garniture that had been dispersed in the meantime. Clearly influenced by baroque ideas of the representation of royalty, while also containing elements of the early classical style, the current rose-cut diamond garniture almost certainly has fewer pieces than the original, but is of far higher quality. The exuberant decoration of ornaments with large and elegant diamonds reached its height in the late eighteenth century. DS

BIBLIOGRAPHY : Arnold 2001, pp. 185–7 ; Syndram 2006, pp. 162ff.

> ## Epaulette

António Gomes da Silva (?), Rio de Janeiro, 1811
Gold, silver and diamonds, 214 x 45 x 11 mm
Lisbon, Palácio Nacional da Ajuda (inv. 4795)

Suspended from a large oval diamond of around 10 carats are three diamond chains linked at the other end to three large diamonds : one of 9 carats in the centre flanked by two of 7 carats. These in turn are linked to a crosspiece from which hang eleven identical pendants set with diamonds. Epaulettes of this kind were much favoured by monarchs and members of the high nobility in the eighteenth century. They could usefully be worn as part of a parure including such elements as coat buttons, a hat badge, insignia and shoe buckles (see cat. 123, 124, 125). This piece was made in the reign of the Portuguese king John VI (1767–1826), who escaped Napoleon's army and continued to rule his country by moving to his Portuguese colony of Brazil for fourteen years (1807–1821). Indeed it was here that this epaulette appeared, a rather outmoded piece for the time. It may be that the latest trends had not yet made their way to Latin America, or that the court placed little importance on the canons of European fashion. In the portrait of the king attributed to Domingos António de Sequeira (1768–1837) (Palácio Nacional da Ajuda, inv. 4115), he wears an epaulette, which is probably the one under discussion here. Later, in the 1870s, Queen Maria Pia wore it as a bracelet, epaulettes having by then become completely outmoded. JW

BIBLIOGRAPHY : Lisbon 1992, pp. 46, 58–9, 183–4.

Decoration of the Polish Order of the White Eagle

Johann August Jordan, Dresden, 1746

Gold, silver, silver gilt, brilliants, emeralds and enamel,

insignia : 104 x 78 mm ; slide : 43 x 45 mm

Dresden, Staatliche Kunstsammlungen Dresden,

Grünes Gewölbe (inv. Nr. VIII 143)

On 1 November 1705, Augustus the Strong created the Polish chivalric Order of the White Eagle in Tykocin, Lithuania. A shrewd politician concerned to honour the Polish and Lithuanian nobility, the elector, king and future master of the order staged the event as the revival of an order founded in 1325 by King Ladislaus I the Short. The creation of the order was the culmination of a long-standing project in the tradition of the Order of Saint Andrew, founded in 1698 by Tsar Peter I, and the Order of the Black Eagle, created by Frederick I of Prussia in 1701. The order's insignia was the work of Johann Melchior Dinglinger, a gold and silversmith at the Saxon court. Under Augustus the Strong it took the form of a life-like eagle in white enamel turning its crowned head to the right. The heraldic symbol was placed on the background of an eight-pointed cross with interspersed flames and precious stones mounted as solitaires at the points. The whole was set in a broad strip of white enamel and the inner surfaces of the cross were filled with translucent red enamel. The original canonical form is attested in the decoration of the sapphire garniture, made around 1713 and preserved in the Grünes Gewölbe.

A generation later Augustus III was keen to improve the quality of the two diamond garnitures and commissioned ceremonial versions of the insignia of the Order of the Golden Fleece and the Polish Order of the White Eagle. The elector and king selected Johann August Jordan, a goldsmith from Dresden, as an artist capable of making decorations for the Polish order that would reflect both developments in parures and the desire of the royal Grand Master to have prestigious symbols at his disposal. In 1744 Jordan created a new decoration for the ruby garniture, followed, in 1746, by the decoration for the emerald garniture, which included no fewer than 16 emeralds and at least 342 brilliants. At the centre is an emerald of exceptional beauty. The Polish eagle, symbol of the order, has entirely lost its realistic character and seems to melt into a dense bed of brilliants, while between its sparkling wings the red enamel ground behind the star's six principal points is barely visible. The specific symbolism of the order's insignia is relegated to the reverse side and cannot be seen by the onlooker. The canonical image of the order's insignia as it had existed since 1714 is maintained here in a reduced form. DS

BIBLIOGRAPHY : Arnold 2001, pp. 121–3 ; Syndram 2006, pp. 61, 146ff.

Decoration of the Order of the Golden Fleece

Jean-Jacques Pallard (1701–1776), Geneva or Vienna, 1755–6

Gold, silver, brilliants and yellow topazes, 109 x 80 mm

Dresden, Staatliche Kunstsammlungen Dresden,

Grünes Gewölbe (inv. Nr. VIII 5)

After their official elevation to the Order of the Golden Fleece, Augustus the Strong and his son, the crown prince Frederick Augustus II of the House of Wettin, were authorized by the emperor to have ceremonial versions made of the order's insignia. As well as fleeces worked into the design of pieces of jewellery, the fleece was also depicted in separate pendants richly ornamented with precious stones. Seven of these garnitures are at the Grünes Gewölbe (Green Vault), the treasury museum built by Augustus the Strong. One of the most notable of these is the order's insignia in Brazilian topazes, made between 1755 and 1756 by the jeweller Jean-Jacques Pallard, who was active in Geneva and Vienna. Made ten years after the Dresden green diamond golden fleece, created for Augustus III and now lost, it is a true masterpiece of rococo gold jewellery making.

Three large octagonal topazes of sparkling yellow are set in the centre of the button, the flintstone and the flame. The various distinctive elements of the order are decorated with 369 densely set, small- and medium-sized brilliants. Pallard designed variations on diamond-shaped settings for the largest stones across the button and flintstone, evoking flowers. In addition to seven medium-sized, round brilliants, a large number of smaller rectangular diamonds are set all along the flames. Pallard placed the ram's hide very close to the flames. This golden fleece and the Dresden green diamond fleece were cast from the same mould. The highly decorative back of the golden fleece is made visible by means of an identical technique reflecting the highest art of the goldsmith.

In 1756 Augustus III owned sixteen ceremonial versions of the insignia of the Golden Fleece. Pallard's topaz fleece was the last to enter the Grünes Gewölbe. On 29 August 1756, the Prussian troops invaded Saxony. DS

BIBLIOGRAPHY : Arnold 1994, p. 283 ; Arnold 2001, pp. 101–3 ; Jackson, Mississippi 2004, p. 174 ; Syndram 2006, pp. 154ff.

Ceremonial sword and sheath

Probably Johann Melchior Dinglinger (1664–1731), Dresden, 1719–22

Gold, silver gilt, diamonds, rock crystal set on red leaf, silk velvet and wood, 937 mm

Dresden, Rüstkammer, Staatliche Kunstsammlungen Dresden (inv. VI 456)

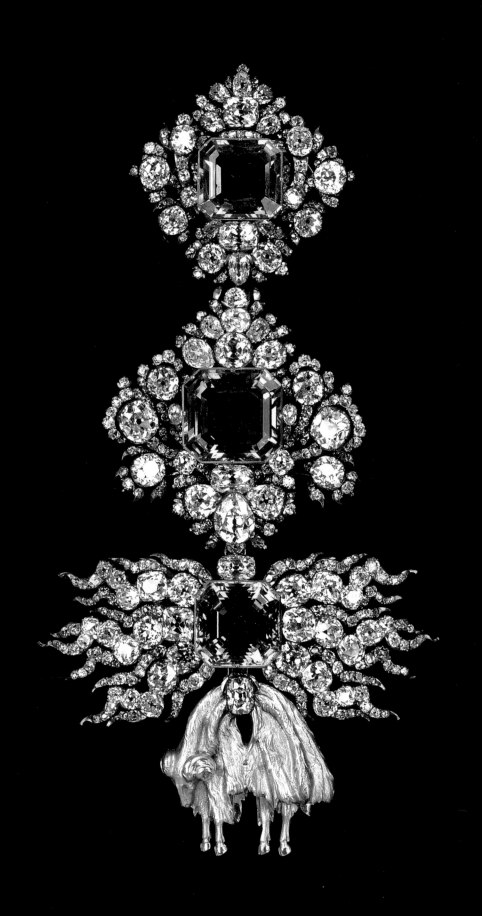

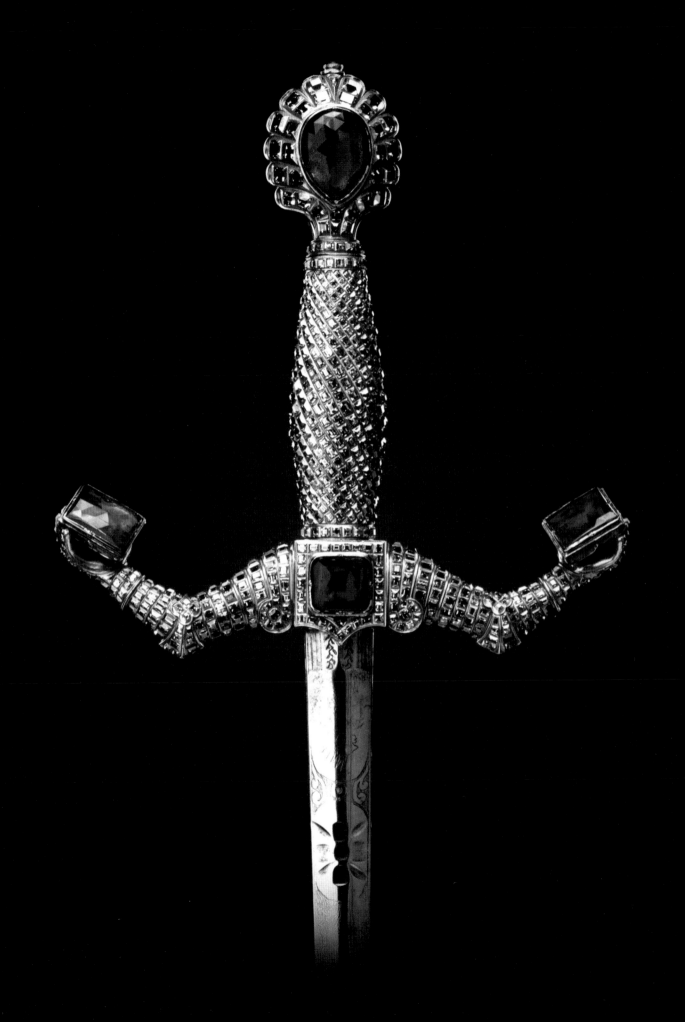

The armory (Rüstkammer) of the State Art Collections in Dresden contains a ceremonial sword that occupies a special place among the eighteenth-century weapons of war and ceremony. Its history is directly linked to the admission of Augustus the Strong and his son, the future Augustus III, into the Habsburg branch of the Order of the Golden Fleece. Augustus the Strong featured on the list of the Knights of the Order of the Golden Fleece from 1697, the year of his election as king, as second representative of the house of Wettin after Duke George (1531). However, it was not until 1722 that Emperor Charles VI awarded the collar and coat of the order to both him and his son. The ceremony took place on 9 April 1722. In accordance with the rules of the order, the future knight had to be dubbed a few weeks before his investiture. We do not know whether it was for this ceremony that this sword laden with symbols was hastily made by Johann Melchior Dinglinger, the court jeweller, or whether, as an illustration suggests, Augustus the Strong wore it in 1719 in his role as 'Master of Fire' at a carousel (tournament) of the four elements given for the wedding of the crown prince and an archduchess of Austria.

The sword appears as an almost sacred object. Like a monstrance in Catholic worship, the pommel, with its large blood-red stone, rises above the slightly oblique arms of the cross guard, which are also set with large red stones, as a sign of faith and fidelity. The silver gilt guard and brilliant profusion of 1,132 densely set diamonds ornamenting the hilt and guard give the sword its fiery brilliance. The large red stones dominating the decoration are not rubies or spinels but rock crystal set on red foil to give them their highly suggestive colour. DS

BIBLIOGRAPHY : Leipzig 1997, 655, pp. 339ff. ; Bäumel 2004, pp. 127ff.

> ## Grand Cross insignia of the Three Military Orders of Portugal

Ambrósio Gottlieb Pollet (1754–1822), Lisbon, 1789

Gold, silver, diamonds, rubies and emeralds, 129 x 122 x 22 mm

Lisbon, Palácio National da Ajuda (inv. 4777)

The insignia of the Grand Cross of the Three Military Orders of Portugal was created by the jeweller Ambrósio Gottlieb Pollet. A bill he issued for it on 14 November 1789 still exists today. This insignia belonged to King John VI as early as 1825 since it is included in an inventory of the sovereign's possessions prepared that year by his private secretary. This was the first time the emblems of the three orders appeared together. The insignia represents the Order of Saint Benedict of Aviz, founded in 1162, the Order of Saint James of the Sword, a branch that separated from the Spanish order established in 1175, and the Order of Christ, founded by King Denis in 1318 when the Order of the Templars was abolished. The first order's symbol is set with 66 emeralds, while rubies are featured in the crosses of the other two and in the emblem of the Sacred Heart of Jesus surmounting the insignia. The decision to unite the three grand orders of Portugal in a single decoration was taken by Queen Mary I of Portugal (1734–1816), who promulgated a decree to this effect in 1789. Almost all of the stones used in this insignia came from the royal treasury and the diamonds alone account for 119.5 carats. Pollet chose an openwork gold and silver setting to accentuate the density of the design and the great size of the stones. He incorporated over 600 diamonds into the piece, placing the 32 largest stones at the extremities of the rays extending out from the centre, while the three orders of Portugal are set off against a background of paved diamonds. With its extraordinary opulence, this insignia is a truly dazzling jewel. CV

BIBLIOGRAPHY : Estevens 1944 ; Rosas Junior 1954 ; Twining 1960, p. 489 ; Ajuda 1986, no. 6 ; Lisbon 1990, no. 120 ; Brussels 1991b, pp. 488, 493 ; Lisbon 1992, pp. 147, 149.

< Chaton rivière of Empress
Maria Theresa of Austria

1770

Gold, silver and diamonds

Private collection

According to tradition this splendid rivière of sixty-two old-cut diamonds was a gift from the Empress Maria Theresa (1717–1780) to her favourite daughter Archduchess Maria Christina (1742–1798), wife of Archduke Albert, Duke of Teschen. Maria Christina succeeded Charles of Lorraine as Governor of the Netherlands in 1781 and laid the first stone of the future Laeken palace. When not in Brussels, she sometimes stayed at Attre to enjoy the pleasures of country life. Maria Theresa and Albert oversaw the art collections that later founded the Albertina in Vienna, and also bequeathed jewellery and a considerable fortune to their nephew Archduke Charles (1771–1847), son of Emperor Leopold II, who also inherited the title of Duke of Teschen and this rivière. The piece then passed to Maria Caroline (1825–1915), a daughter of Archduke Charles, who died without children from her marriage to her cousin Archduke Rainier. The chaton rivière has long been part of the jewellery collections of the princesses and queens of the great monarchies. This example is of exceptional quality, set with diamonds ranging from 0.85 to 9 metric carats. **CV**

Portrait of Empress Maria Theresa of Austria

Martin van Meytens (1695–1770), 1765

Oil on canvas, 82 x 71 cm

Vienna, Bundesmobilienverwaltung–Hofmobiliendepot

Möbel Museum (inv. MD 072781)

At the service of the imperial court since 1730, painter Martin van Meytens was at an advanced age when he created this flattering portrait of forty-eight-year-old Maria Theresa. Although not entirely hostile, she is fully aware of her power and gazes down at the viewer rather disdainfully. Her bodice is embellished with gold brocade while her neckline and sleeves are finished with a trim of delicate lace that may have been acquired in Mechelen or Binche. The sovereign's ensemble is completed with an opulent bodice brooch set entirely with diamonds. She wears matching diamond pendant earrings, while a precious stone hangs over her forehead suspended from a small tiara, one of her favourite pieces, which she wore for many portraits.

The imperial crown can be seen at her side (see p. 156). Draped across her shoulders is a mantle lined with ermine – a privilege of the upper class. If this portrait was in fact painted in 1765, it was certainly before August, since her husband, Emperor Francis I, died on the seventeenth of that month.

Maria Theresa (1717–1780) was a woman of character. Her accession to the throne in 1740 triggered the War of the Austrian Succession. This conflict lasted until 1748 since, at the instigation of the Prussians, other countries contested her right to accede to the throne, especially as she was a woman. But she handled the situation skilfully and proved to be a sovereign who safeguarded the wellbeing of her subjects with authority and compassion. In 1776, for example, she abolished the use of torture during interrogations. She also tried to strengthen her power in Europe by arranging political marriages for her numerous children – sixteen in all, although three died very young – but without great success. Maria Amelia married Ferdinand, Duke of Parma, an insignificant grandson of Louis XV. Maria Christina married Prince Albert of Saxony, Duke of Teschen, and, together with her husband, became governor of the Austrian Netherlands, although this did not entail an extension of her influence. Finally, another of her daughters, Marie Antoinette, married King Louis XVI of France and shared his fate at the guillotine during the Revolution. **JW**

BIBLIOGRAPHY : Vienna 1980, pp. 106–9, 187–8, 263–4, 291 ;
Hamann 1988, pp. 340–4.

Chatelaine decorated with putti

Julien le Roy (1686–1759), Paris, 18th century
Gold, diamonds, jasper and enamel, chatelaine : 192 mm ;
watch : 45 mm
Brussels, Musées Royaux d'Art et d'Histoire (inv. 2845)

This chatelaine holds a fob watch, a key and a seal with an ancient head in relief. Items have been lost from two of the hooks. The chatelaine is decorated with four small, hexagonal pictures in pink and white. At the top a putto is waving a veil above his head while another is handing him a basket of flowers. They symbolize the play of attraction and rejection between two lovers. Below this another putto is holding a flower stem above two turtledoves as a sign of fertility, while further down a small Cupid has put down his bow and arrow, signifying that the hunt is over now that the marriage has been celebrated. The back of the watch shows a more animated scene in which two putti, apparently at loggerheads, represent the tribulations of marriage. One brandishes a bow and arrow, while the other protects himself with a shield. The watch, the attachments for key and seal, and the frames to the enamelled panels all glitter with small rose-cut diamonds. The chatelaine was a typical gift for a high-ranking bride. The allusions to love and marriage are playfully overt. JW

BIBLIOGRAPHY : Ripa 1603, p. 297 ; Deurne 1968, no. 268 ;
Antwerp 1995, no. 34 ; Tokyo 2003b, no. III–37.

Chatelaine with watch

Watch : Abraham Colomby, Geneva, c. 1745
Gold, diamonds, silver, pearls and enamel, chatelaine : 200 mm ;
watch : 37 mm
Brussels, Musées Royaux d'Art et d'Histoire (inv. 2842)

The chatelaine is topped with a pearl and enamel crown beneath which hang two little half-moon plates decorated with a floral motif in the shape of a bow. Each is crowned with a row of pearls and linked by seven small chains. Below these are five chains holding a watch, the back of which shows the diamond-encircled portrait of a young woman in a dark hat with red feathers. Small rose-cut diamonds are set around the hat ; the young woman is wearing earrings and a diamond brooch. Like the watch face, the portrait is surrounded by two rows of diamonds. Hanging at either side are a watch key, an unstamped seal, two small urn-shaped plates and a trefoil cross.

The commonly used term 'chatelaine' is short for 'chaîne châtelaine'. In Ancient Rome a young bride would receive the gift of a key, symbol of her responsibilities in running the home. The chatelaine is derived from this, and would be hung with all

kinds of accessories in addition to the house keys : a watch – a mark of high social status at the time – a seal, a sewing kit and sometimes even a small pair of scissors. The eighteenth century saw the creation of some exquisite examples of chatelaines. JW
BIBLIOGRAPHY : Antwerp 1968, no. 263 ; Tokyo 2003b, no. III–36.

Necklace with three pendant bows

c. 1710
Silver, diamonds and velvet, necklace : 320 mm ;
central pendant : 27 mm
Private collection

This necklace is made up of eleven elements with smaller connecting links. The most striking pieces are the three bows with pendants, the largest placed in the centre, which are joined together by small bushes laid sideways. The final links at either end are roses through which ribbons can be threaded to fasten the necklace. The diamonds used are high, flat rose- and table-cut stones and smaller stones with facets. Wherever they are set in a line, roses usually alternate with tables. The piece has one notable particularity : at one end the final link contains two rows of three very long table-cut diamonds ; at the other end the corresponding diamonds are rose cut. The back is undecorated. The stylistic variation between the various elements and the manner in which the stones are set suggests that this piece incorporated several older stones. Be that as it may, its quality is beyond question and its overall harmony is immediately apparent. '*Colliers de chien*' chokers of this kind were very fashionable throughout the eighteenth century. JW
BIBLIOGRAPHY : Antwerp 1993, no. 87 ; Tokyo 2003b, no. II–23.

Small girandole parure

Spain (?), second half of the 18th century
Silver and diamonds, brooch : 60 x 70 mm ;
girandoles : 44 x 39 mm
Private collection

The brooch and girandole earrings – which can be used as brooches – are decorated with ribbons, vines and, in the centre of each, a large rose-cut diamond. Each piece has three teardrop pendants and all are entirely set with flat rose-cut diamonds. This girandole parure, whose name refers to chandeliers with several branches, is a form of ceremonial jewellery indicating the social status of its owner. Queens and princesses of the time often wore such pieces in official portraits. JW
BIBLIOGRAPHY : Evans 1989, pl. 138 ; Antwerp 1995, no. 35 ;
Tokyo 2003b, no. II–22.

Aigrette

England (?), c. 1780
Silver, diamonds, 112 x 70 mm
Antwerp, Diamond Museum of the Province of Antwerp
(inv. CMD02/2)

The silver aigrette comprises five feathers or '*paillons*' joined at the bottom by a ribbon. The diamonds on each *paillon* are all rose-cut with closed settings. The piece takes its name from the egret or heron, whose feathers were particularly favoured by the high society of the day. In the eighteenth century the finest feathers would be gathered on a comb and worn in the hair or as a corsage ornament. However, because they were so fragile, connoisseurs favoured alternative versions made from precious materials. The English were less inclined towards the frivolity of French rococo, explaining the relatively sober appearance of this piece. It was later mounted with a pin at the level of the second feather allowing it to be worn as a brooch. Men of high rank would also sometimes wear an ornament of this kind on the front of their hats.

This aigrette is from the collection of Jerome and Bernice Zwanger, patrons of the Metropolitan Museum of Art, New York. WL

BIBLIOGRAPHY : Antwerp 2002, pp. 61, 68–70 ; Tokyo 2003b, pp. 93, 253 ; Antwerp 2004, pp. 8–9 ; Antwerp 2004b, pp. 24, 52 ; London 2006, p. 34 ; Antwerp 2006b, pp. 60-2, 91-2.

Feather

Mid-18th century
Gold, silver, diamonds and rubies, 92 x 43 mm
Private collection

This peacock feather ornament is outlined in rubies, with a further row of rubies running down the centre and enclosing a yellow diamond 'eye'. The feather is slightly curved, as if blown by the wind. It would have been worn in the hair, perhaps together with real feathers, as depicted in the portrait of Princess Cunigonde of Saxony from 1755 by Pietro Antonio Rotari (1707–1762) (see p. 149). DSC

Three-feathered aigrette brooch

Netherlands, late 18th century

Gold, silver and diamonds, 140 x 90 x 30 mm

Private collection

A rosette enhanced with a central diamond encircled by fourteen smaller diamonds supports a collection of leaves and gently curved feathers mounted on a trembler spring. The piece is set throughout with small rose-cut diamonds. The back is silver. Jewellery featuring feathers first became very popular in the seventeenth century and was generally worn in the hair. During the eighteenth century feathers were also worn as brooches, notably due to the changing fashions in hats and hairstyles. JW

BIBLIOGRAPHY : Antwerp 2002, no. 27 ; Tokyo 2003b, no. III–25.

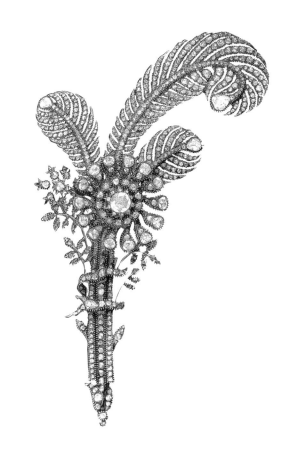

Aigrette

Portugal, c. 1800–10

Gold, silver and diamonds, 130 x 85 mm

Lisbon, Museu Nacional de Arte Antiga (inv. 1197 Joa)

'Aigrette' is the French name for the little egret (*Egretta garzetta*), a small white heron whose very decorative crosier-shaped plumes were once quite popular as hair ornaments. From the seventeenth century, real egret feathers, which were very expensive and fragile, were progressively replaced with jewelled imitations also called aigrettes. In the following century, aigrettes began to be worn as brooches as well. This particular piece is composed of three large feathers set *en tremblant* and decorated entirely with brilliant-cut diamonds. The largest feather is placed at the centre, while the two others extend out toward the sides, giving an attractive effect of volume. The three feathers are gathered together at the bottom under a large yellow rose-cut diamond, which was probably added later. Two arrows and a small bow – an obvious allusion to Cupid, the god of love – also appear at the base of the piece. Symbolic jewellery such as this was often commissioned to seal a romantic relationship. This aigrette was, in fact, created at the request of the Count and Countess of Mesquitella for the 13 September 1807 wedding of their eldest son to the granddaughter of the famous Marquis of Pombal, prime minister to Joseph I (1714–1777). With its dimensions, the quality of the mount and the refinement and lightness of the design, this aigrette is an exceptionally fine example of Portuguese jewellery. LO

Portrait of the young Louis xv in royal ceremonial dress

Jean Ranc (1674–1735), 1718–19

Oil on canvas, 226 x 168 cm

Versailles, Châteaux de Versailles et de Trianon (inv. MV4386)

In 1716, the year after the death of Louis xiv, Hyacinthe Rigaud painted the first official portrait of Louis xv. Two years later a portrait of the young king, then aged eight, was commissioned from Rigaud's pupil Jean Ranc. Although, as in Rigaud's composition, Louis xv is represented with certain items used during the coronation of every French monarch – the sceptre, hand of justice and crown – he would not be crowned in Reims until 25 October 1722. So this is a ceremonial portrait, rather than a portrait of the king dressed for his coronation. The sceptre, hand of justice and crown, all associated with the throne and coronation robes, are used here as emblems of royal power.

Ranc depicts the royal insignia with great precision. A *lettre de cachet* dated 11 June 1719 enabled him to borrow the precious items held in the basilica of Saint-Denis and to copy them from life (Archives nationales, Paris, K136, no. 19, cited by Engerand). In his right hand the king holds the silver-gilt sceptre, surmounted by a five-petalled fleur-de-lis. Unlike other hands of justice, the example shown here, next to the crown, has a hand of silver rather than ivory. Both insignia were made in 1594 for the coronation of Henry iv in Chartres. The gold crown was made in 1610 by the goldsmith Aubin du Carnoy and used at the coronation of Louis xiii.

Louis xiii in Philippe de Champaigne's *Vow of Louis xiii* (1638, Musée des Beaux-Arts, Caen), and Louis xiv in his portrait by Rigaud (1701, Musée du Louvre) had already appeared with the sceptre and hand of justice of Henry iv, their father and grandfather respectively. By portraying himself with the same insignia, Louis xv signifies his own place within the Bourbon dynasty. JT

BIBLIOGRAPHY : Engerand 1900, pp. 20–1 ; São Paulo 2007, pp. 84–6.

Personal sword of King Louis xv

Paris, c. 1750

Gold, steel and chrysoprase, 970 mm

Paris, Musée du Louvre, Département des Objets d'Art
(inv. MR 433)

The hilt of this richly decorated sword in an elegant rocaille style has a pommel, guard and grip in gold inlaid with pale green shards of chrysoprase. The steel blade, triangular in section with a pattern of gold lines and engraved fleurs-de-lis, bears the king's initials. Louis xv is thought to have worn this sword frequently as an element of ceremonial dress. Indeed, it was a mark of rank to wear a sword and monarchs and members of the high aristocracy seldom appeared in public without one. JW

Bracelet clasp with portrait of King Louis XV, belonging to the Marquise de Pompadour

Jacques Guay (1711–1793), France, c. 1750 ;
setting : anonymous, c. 1750
Gold, silver, emeralds, diamonds and sardonyx cameo, 45 x 35 mm
Paris, Bibliothèque Nationale de France, Département des
Monnaies, Médailles et Antiques (inv. BAB 927)

This sardonyx cameo portrait of Louis XV – crowned with laurel and facing in profile towards the left – is part of a bracelet clasp signed GUAY F[ECIT], for Jacques Guay. The frame is an emerald crown of laurels tied with ribbons made from rose diamonds. Madame de Pompadour (1721–1764) wore the cameo as the clasp to a pearl bracelet, which she proudly displayed as

proof of her high standing with the king during the years 1745–64. The pair to it was set with a contemporary sardonyx cameo bust of Henry IV of France, founder of the Bourbon dynasty. DSC
BIBLIOGRAPHY : Babelon 1897, no. 927, p. 354 ; Paris 2002, no. 113.

Ring with portrait of King Louis XV

Jacques Guay (1711–1793), France ; cameo signed by
Madame de Pompadour, c. 1750
Gold and sardonyx cameo with two layers, 19 x 15 mm
Paris, Bibliothèque Nationale de France, Département
des Monnaies, Médailles et Antiques (inv. BAB 931)

The oval bezel of this gold ring is set with a sardonyx cameo head of Louis XV facing in profile towards the right and signed POMPADOUR F[ECIT]. As patroness of the arts, Madame de Pompadour not only learnt how to use the burin and make prints, but she also mastered the art of gem engraving, tutored by Jacques Guay whom she installed in a studio in her apartment at Versailles. Recreating the features of the king in this cameo and wearing it on her finger must have been a source of great pride, and would have helped reinforce her position as queen of the arts and royal favourite. DSC
BIBLIOGRAPHY : Babelon 1897, no. 931, pp. 346-7 ; Paris 2002, no. 109.

François Boucher, *Madame de Pompadour*, 1758.

Hermaphrodite cameo of Madame du Barry

Cameo : Italy, 16th century ; setting : France, c. 1770
Gold, enamel and chalcedony cameo with two layers, 37 x 48 mm
Paris, Bibliothèque Nationale de France, Département des
Monnaies, Médailles et Antiques (inv. CHAB 493)

The oblong gold plaque with dark blue enamel border is set with a cameo of Hermaphrodite, partially draped and reclining on a couch beneath a tree, serenaded by two Cupids and fanned by a third with an ivy leaf. As mistress of Louis xv in the final years of his life, Madame du Barry acquired magnificent diamond jewellery, but this plaque, which she wore in the centre of a necklace, demonstrates her taste for themes in line with the contemporary classical revival in the arts. DSC

BIBLIOGRAPHY : Babelon 1897, no. 493, p. 257.

Bracelet clasp with cameo representing the birth of the Duke of Burgundy

Jacques Guay (1711–1793), France, 1751

Sardonyx with two layers and copper setting, 36 x 28 mm

Paris, Bibliothèque Nationale de France, Département des

Monnaies, Médailles et Antiques (inv. BAB 659)

The oval cameo represents an armed Minerva, brandishing her shield to protect the infant lying on a cushion at her feet. The personification of France, wearing a crown of laurel and a shield charged with fleurs-de-lis, holds out her arms in welcome. The cameo has a reserved border. Signed GUAY F[ECIT] for Jacques Guay and dated M.DCC.L.I., this jewel was exhibited in the Salon of 1757. Engraved after a drawing by François Boucher (1703–1770), the cameo is a declaration of the joy of the French nation on the birth of its future king, the eldest son of the Dauphin Louis (1729–1765) and his wife. Their hopes were dashed when the Duke of Burgundy died prematurely in 1761 at the age of ten. Madame de Pompadour wore this cameo with its pair set in bracelets. DSC

BIBLIOGRAPHY : Babelon 1897, no. 659 p. 306–7 ; Paris 2002, no. 116.

Bracelet clasp with cameo representing the alliance of France and Austria

Jacques Guay (1711–1793), France, 1756

Sardonyx cameo with two layers and gold setting, 34 x 28 mm

Paris, Bibliothèque Nationale de France, Département des

Monnaies, Médailles et Antiques (inv. BAB 660)

Signed GUAY, for Jacques Guay and dated 1756, this oval cameo depicts two standing women, dressed in classical drapery, joining their hands in friendship over an altar on which burns a sacred fire. A snake biting its tail, the symbol of eternity, encircles the altar. The shields beside each woman are ornamented with the national emblems of France and Austria, and a mask and broken torch lie between them. The border is reserved. Madame de Pompadour mounted this cameo as a bracelet clasp, demonstrating her pride in her immense political influence, since she had planned the Austrian alliance, which was followed by the Seven Years War. More than the king's favourite, the queen of fashion and of the arts, Madame de Pompadour was in effect the prime minister of France in petticoats. DSC

BIBLIOGRAPHY : Babelon 1897, no. 660, p. 307 ; Paris 2002, no. 110.

Cameo of Emperor Francis I, Empress Maria Theresa and their children

Louis Siriès, Florence, 1755

Onyx cameo, gold setting, pearls and emerald, 90 x 125 mm

Vienna, Kunsthistorisches Museum, Kunstkammer

(inv. ANSA XII 74)

During the Renaissance, gemstones, cameos and other intaglio work skilfully executed in semi-precious stones such as chalcedony, carnelian, agate and onyx were particularly prized and were often used to decorate rings, chains, clasps and hat medallions. With the arrival of the baroque period, however, these materials fell out of fashion. But in Florence, Francis III Stephen of Lorraine, who reigned as Grand Duke of Tuscany from 1736, revived the tradition, which had previously thrived in the region. In 1748, he called to his service Louis Siriès, a French jeweller considered by his contemporaries to be one of the most accomplished artisans in his field. It was Siriès who crafted this exceptionally large onyx cameo. On the front is a portrait of Francis III, elected as Emperor of the Holy German Empire under the name Francis I, together with his wife Maria Theresa and twelve of their children.

The young Marie Antoinette, future queen of France, is shown seated on her mother's lap. On the back of the piece, encircled by a laurel wreath, is an inscription paying tribute to the imperial couple's fertility. It is clear from the design of the decoration and the size of the stone that this piece, set into a narrow gold band, was not meant to be worn as an ornament but rather to be used as a ceremonial object in the imperial treasury. FK

BIBLIOGRAPHY : Schallaburg 2000, pp. 254ff., no. 11.14 ; Florence 2006, pp. 98ff., no. 34.

Ring with trophy surmounted by a crown

France, second half of the 18th century
Translucent blue enamel and rose-cut diamonds
Paris, Département des Objets d'Art, Musée du Louvre, on permanent loan from the Musée National de la Renaissance, Ecouen (inv. ECL 15595)

This ring shows a trophy of arms on the enamel of a vertical oval chaton. Suspended from the royal crown is a coat of arms, behind which can be seen a bow, a quiver and a sword arranged on a bed of laurel leaves. The trophy and border are set with small rose-cut diamonds.

The ring was worn either by a courtier, or by a person recognized for their merit. However, the quality of cut is rather mediocre for a piece belonging to the king, either Louis XV or Louis XVI. The ring was part of the Rothschild legacy of 1906. JW

Ring with portraits of King Louis XVI and Queen Marie Antoinette

France, c. 1774
Gold, silver, diamonds and sardonyx cameo, 23 mm
Tokyo, Albion Art Collection

The hoop divides at shoulders mounted with diamonds to support the oval bezel with beaded border enclosing a sardonyx double portrait cameo of Louis XVI and Queen Marie Antoinette. Both are facing in profile towards the right, surmounted by the diamond-set royal crown of France. On the back there is a silver wire monogram of the letters LM. The ring is housed in a stamped leather ring box.

From the time of their marriage in 1770 the royal couple were frequently portrayed in miniatures, ceramics and hardstone cameos such as this, for presentation to their friends, political and diplomatic allies and courtiers. Most represented the king or queen individually, and double portraits are rare. Although majestic looking, these profiles are youthful, suggesting that the cameo marks the beginning of their reign. Following the execution of the royal couple in 1792, the possession of rings like these would have been considered evidence of treason by the revolutionary authorities, and subsequently few have survived. DSC

Engraving of Queen Marie Antoinette's necklace

After Charles-Auguste Boehmer and Paul Bassenge, c. 1785

Etching on paper, 50.7 x 39.6 cm

Versailles Châteaux de Versailles and Trianon (inv. Gravures 1455)

As the printed inscription indicates, this engraving is an exact depiction of the extraordinary necklace made by Paris jewellers Charles-Auguste Boehmer and Paul Bassenge at the very end of the reign of Louis XV (1710–1774). Boehmer and Bassenge were specialist traders in jewels and precious stones, whose clients included the Versailles court and the greatest foreign monarchs. To make this necklace, intended as their masterpiece, they spent several years amassing pearls and five hundred and forty pear- or brilliant-cut diamonds of peerless quality.

This double piece was tied with a ribbon at the back of the neck. The upper part consists of a choker enhanced with several pendants, including a larger central element comprising a pear-cut diamond edged with pearls and crowned by three brilliants. This is counterbalanced by the second necklace, consisting of two rows of diamonds separated by a row of pearls, worn on the breast and shoulders. The rows are joined in the centre with a large brilliant and end in four stylized tassels in pearls and diamonds, based on lace patterns.

The jewellers were hoping that Louis XV would buy the piece as a last gift for his mistress Madame du Barry, but at 1,600,000 pounds, the king considered it too expensive, a view that seems subsequently to have been shared by other great lords and sovereigns. When Marie Antoinette, wife of the future Louis XVI, was invited to buy, she also declined to make such a costly acquisition, despite her immoderate love of jewellery. Besides, she preferred not to appear with a necklace originally intended for the king's mistress. But in 1785, Madame de la Motte, a dangerous mistress of intrigue, informed the jewellers that the queen now 'wished' to buy it through an intermediary. Playing on the difficult relations between Marie Antoinette and the cardinal bishop of Strasbourg, Louis-René de Rohan, who was hoping to regain his sovereign's favours, Madame de la Motte involved him without his knowledge in her wicked plan to acquire the piece for herself. This led to one of the greatest scandals in history, the famous 'affair of the diamond necklace'. The monarchy was permanently weakened by the trial, during which the queen was brought into disrepute.

This engraving of the necklace, gives an idea of the brilliance of its jewels, and provided a model for the creation of various replicas. VB

199

Empire and romanticism: Napoleon and George IV

DIANA SCARISBRICK

The catastrophic effect of the French Revolution of 1789 led to the collapse of the *ancien régime* in Europe and brought the demand for expensive jewellery from France almost to a standstill. The fortunes of most jewellers did not revive until Napoleon Bonaparte succeeded in imposing law and order following his appointment as Consul in 1799, and after his declaration as Emperor in 1804, when he determined to restore Paris to her former position as the creative centre for luxury and fashion. There was a political motive too, for he believed, like Louis XIV before him, that dazzling displays of jewellery would assert his authority To make his court the most brilliant in Europe, he encouraged the trade by buying wonderful jewellery for his first wife, Josephine, her successor, Marie Louise, and for his mother and sisters, which they displayed at grandiose ceremonies – his coronation, marriages, state balls – evoking the splendour of Versailles during the reign of Louis XIV. The crown jewels, which had been dispersed during the Revolution, were reinstated and magnificent additions were made to them. Exhibitions held in the Louvre promoted good craftsmanship and a new style was devised to express the character of the Napoleonic regime.

This Empire style, which shows the influence of the painter, Jacques-Louis David and the imperial architects, Charles Percier and Pierre Fontaine, complemented the rather theatrical courtly robes designed by Jean-Baptiste Isabey. The principal element is classical in its symmetrical and uncomplicated shapes, but the motifs – palmettes, honeysuckle, Greek fret – derive from antiquity. Cameos and intaglios, both ancient and modern, also play an important role. As an alternative to the rare, hardstone engraved gems, cameos of malachite, shell and coral were imported from Italy.

The best jewellers of the Empire style were Marie-Etienne Nitot and his son François-Regnault Nitot, to whom Napoleon gave the most commissions, followed by Marguerite, Sensier, Gibert, Piteux, and Friese and Devillers. All excelled at creating parures – matching sets of comb, tiara, earrings, necklace, belt buckle and pairs of bracelets displaying quantities of diamonds, pearls and coloured stones – which were sumptuous but never heavy. Since their purpose was to demonstrate rank, the tiara and comb crowning the head were made in imposing designs conferring extra height, dignity and authority on the wearer. Earrings, which were usually long pendants either of the three-drop girandole design or the simpler top and drop style, lit up the face. Most necklaces were composed of clusters linked by chains of diamonds, and were worn with matching bracelets at the wrists and belts emphasizing the fashion for high waists.[1] The importance of diamonds in creating the desired effect was explained by John Mawe in his *Treatise on Diamonds and Precious Stones* (1813): 'the various colours combined with high lustre that distinguish the ruby, the emerald, the sapphire and the topaz, beautiful as they are, upon a near inspection are entirely lost to the distant beholder, whereas the diamond without any essential colour of its own imbibes the pure solar ray and then reflects it with undiminished intensity … proclaiming to the surrounding crowd the person of the monarch.'

Some Empire jewellery had a more specifically political function. Most important were the cameo portraits of Napoleon engraved by the best artists in Rome – Nicola Morelli and Giuseppe Girometti – emphasizing his role in history as the heir to the emperors of ancient Rome. These were further embellished, or 'habillé', by rose-diamond and laurel crowns and drapery. These cameo portraits and miniatures of the emperor, the empress and their son the king of Rome, were enclosed in medallions and rings and, like other jewels, bore the imperial ciphers, N[apoleon], J[osephine], M[arie] L[ouise], and the symbols of the star, the bee and the thunderbolt.

Once again, France asserted its supremacy in the creation of jewellery, for such was the impact of the Empire style that it was copied throughout Europe. Parisian jewellers remodelled the Bavarian crown jewels, and their designs were diffused abroad by lavish gifts from the emperor and the empress and by the fashion magazines that reported the new fashions.

< Jean Auguste Dominique Ingres, *Napoleon I on his imperial throne*, 1806.

202

Nowhere was this influence greater than in England, in spite of the war between the two countries, which went on almost without interruption from 1793–1815. Court receptions in London were the scene of splendid displays of jewellery, and even away from the capital the aristocracy asserted their position by wearing fine clothes and rich ornaments when dining at home in their country estates. They had their own political jewellery, expressing loyalty by wearing portraits of the leaders of the struggle against Napoleon: the monarch, George III and his son the future George IV, the statesman, William Pitt, and the heroic Admiral Nelson and Duke of Wellington. Jewels embellished with the symbols of the kingdoms of England, Scotland and Ireland – the rose, the thistle and the shamrock – marked the act of Union of 1801. Oak leaves alluded to the fortitude of the British people, the Maltese cross to the conquest of that island and palm branches to the victory over Napoleon.[2] By buying at advantageous prices from the desperate French émigrés, the crown jeweller, Rundell, Bridge and Rundell, had acquired a magnificent stock of pearls and precious stones, and its reputation was such that Napoleon promised to award the firm to the marshal who could capture London in the planned invasion.[3] In Germany the products of the foundries of Berlin also assumed a patriotic character when, to finance the war against Napoleon, women sacrificed their gold jewels, replacing them with iron ornaments of distinctly classical style

The period following the end of the Napoleonic regime in 1815 was also a time of social and political transformation, which saw the restoration of the old monarchical system in France. The crown jewels were now worn by the Duchess of Angoulême and her sister-in-law, the Duchess of Berry, but remodelled so as to remove their Napoleonic character. After the July Revolution of 1830, when Louis Philippe came to the throne, he attempted to promote an image of bourgeois simplicity and subsequently left the crown jewels untouched. However, this soon changed and women were expected to appear at official functions 'in full court dress' led by his wife, Queen Marie Amelia and her daughters and daughters-in-law, all wearing important jewels. The eldest daughter, Louise Marie, on her marriage to Leopold I was given a handsome corbeille of jewels appropriate for her role as Queen of the Belgians.[4]

France continued to take the lead and most women visitors to Paris replenished their wardrobes and bought new jewels there. The celebrated makers Jean-Baptiste Fossin, Jacques-Eberhard Bapst, Paul-Nicolas Menière, François Mellerio, Charles Christofle, Léon Rouvenat, François Desire Froment-Meurice and Madame Janisset, competed for foreign and domestic customers by creating something new and beautiful every season. The fashion for full-skirted dresses, caught in at the waist and balanced by puffed sleeves and wide necklines,

Antoine-Jean Gros, *Maria Theresa Charlotte of France, Duchess of Angoulême*, 1819.

< Robert Lefèvre, *Empress of the French, Marie Louise, depicted as Regent of the Empire*, 1814.

the hair elaborately drawn up high at the back or crowned with turbans, gave plenty of scope for jewels which appear in profusion on the head, arms, hands,[5] throats and waist.

For the very rich there were versions of the grandiose empire-style parures mounted with diamonds, pearls and precious coloured stones, but the classicism of the past was now transformed into richer, more substantial designs influenced by nature rather than by the art of Greece and Rome. Enamel was introduced for extra colour and gold mixed with alloys for use in different shades of pink and green.

The themes of jewellery from this period are extraordinarily diverse. As before, the classical world provided certain motifs – ears of corn, Greek fret, vine leaves and honeysuckle – but the chief inspiration came from the less remote past of the Middle Ages and the Renaissance evoked by the novels of Sir Walter Scott and Victor Hugo. Motifs from medieval architecture, trefoils, quatrefoils and pointed arches from Renaissance sculpture and painting were eagerly adopted by women who liked to think of themselves as the new Catherine de' Medici. Heraldic symbols, demonstrating pride in one's rank and ancestry, decorated bracelets, watchcases, chatelaines and rings, and were often ordered as wedding presents. From the court of Louis XIV derived the Sévigné brooch worn at the breast, the three-drop girandole earring and the motif of the winged angel head. Most popular of all was the revival of the naturalistic jewellery of the eighteenth century, produced in great variety: leaves of ivy, olive, chestnut and waterlily, flowers of eglantine, hawthorn, lily and jasmine, and even fruits such as redcurrants and cherries. Other revivals from that period include the ribbon and bowknot jewel, and rings with pointed oval bezels called 'marquise' after the famous favourite of Louis XV, Madame de Pompadour. Jewels with a patriotic character commemorated the success of the French military campaign in Algeria, especially the victory over Abd al-Kadir in 1847, which inspired bracelets and brooches decorated with the tassels, crescents and arabesques of Islamic jewellery.[6]

French influence could be felt in Vienna, where the leading talent was the French émigré Emmanuel Piote (1781–1865), who founded the imperial court jewellery business of Köchert. In London, in addition to Rundell, Bridge and Rundell, the most prominent jewellers were Storr and Mortimer, Thomas Hamlet, Robert Garrard and Joseph Kitching.

All European monarchs in the period after 1815 attached importance to jewels as an expression of power and authority but none cared for them with the passion of George IV. As early as 1792 he had justified his expenditure in a memorandum which stated: 'The importance of the monarchy to the civil order of this country is inestimable, the necessity of attaching splendour to the person and family indispensable.'[7] He invariably cut a magnificent figure, whether presiding over a ball, or resplendent in Field Marshal's uniform with his Garter Star on his breast and diamonds in his hat. Ever generous, at Christmas and New Year's Day he gave expensive jewels to his sisters, sisters-in-law and daughter, Princess Charlotte, which they could enjoy showing off at court functions. Aware of new trends, he introduced romanticism into English jewellery with commissions for Gothic-style crosses, a pair of bracelets copied from the ninth-century Iron Crown of Monza and a ring inspired by one owned by the fourteenth-century Bishop of Winchester, William of Wykeham. However, his greatest enthusiasm was for jewels expressing patriotic themes, and these have an unmistakably English character. His purchase of a suite illustrating Jacques's 'Seven Ages of Man' speech from *As You Like It* reflects his admiration for the genius of William Shakespeare.[8] His coronation in 1821, the first in England for sixty years, was the pretext for expenditure on expensive souvenirs such as rings, lockets and medallions with his portrait and cipher, emphasizing his royal rank. Since the emblems of his three kingdoms meant so much to him, he had them incorporated into the diamond regal circlet which he wore over his velvet cap in the procession from Saint James's Palace to Westminster Abbey.[9] They appear again in the suite with the rose, thistle and shamrock alternating between tasselled knots, combined with crosses and the orb of sovereignty which he gave Lady Gwydyr, wife of his Lord Great Chamberlain, and which epitomizes the taste of this 'roi grand seigneur' for elegant jewels expressing a sense of history and a patriotic spirit.

1. Morel 1988, pp. 245–93.
2. Scarisbrick 1994, pp. 324–9.
3. Cloake 1988, p. 240.
4. Vachaudez 2004, pp. 11–23.
5. Vever 1975.
6. Paris 2000.
7. Aspinall 1963–71, vol. IV, pp. 223–4.
8. William Shakespeare, *As You Like It*, II, 7, ll.139–166.
9. Twining 1960, pl. 60a.

< Thomas Lawrence, *George IV*, c. 1821.

Portrait of Empress Josephine in her coronation gown

Studio of François Gérard (1770–1837), 1808

Oil on canvas, 85 × 67 cm

Rueil-Malmaison, Musée National des Châteaux de Malmaison
et de Bois-Préau (inv. MM 40.47.8085)

The empress wears the costume designed by Jean-Baptiste Isabey for her coronation in 1804. The parure of pearls, emeralds and diamonds is typical of the sumptuous but elegant style devised for her by the court jeweller, Marie-Etienne Nitot et Fils. Napoleon encouraged Josephine's passion for jewellery and she was a loyal customer of Nitot et Fils from the Consulate until her death in 1814. DSC

Napoleon I in his coronation robes

Anne-Louis Girodet-Trioson (1767–1824), 1811–12,
probably after a sketch of 1804

Oil on canvas, 93 × 74 cm

Brussels, Musée Royal de l'Armée et d'Histoire Militaire
(inv. 2000 82)

The emperor, who has just been crowned, is depicted wearing his coronation robes, a red coat lined with ermine and decorated with bee motifs. In his left hand he holds a sceptre as tall as a man and surmounted by a seated eagle, while his right hand hovers protectively above the orb, the hand of justice and an open book, almost certainly the Constitution of Year XII of the Republic (1804), or possibly the Civil Code of 21 March of the same year.

The emperor's choice of attributes at his coronation was fairly eclectic: the laurel crown of the Roman emperors, the orb and hand of justice of the Capetians and the robe of the Bourbons. The bee motif so favoured by the emperor was not new either, as it had been frequently used in the high Middle Ages. Legend describes men attacked by a swarm of bees who suddenly discover their religious vocation and even declare themselves to be divine; subsequently a cloud of bees is the symbol of a superior person. Some claim that the bee motif is the origin of the French fleur-de-lis: turn the bee upside-down and you have a stylized lily. However, Napoleon's bees are in fact a reference to the gold bees found under Louis XIV in the tomb of Childeric, father of Clovis, the founder of the first royal dynasty, further legitimizing his power.

The emperor placed his brothers on the thrones of several of the states he conquered: Joseph became first King of Naples, and then King of Spain; Louis became King of the Netherlands and Jerome King of Westphalia. Napoleon's sister Caroline was Queen of Naples alongside her husband, Marshall Joachim Murat. Napoleon took as his second wife Marie Louise, the daughter of Emperor Francis II of Austria. In this way he combined the politics of family alliances with military conquest in his bid to unify Europe.

In 1811 Girodet-Trioson was commissioned to paint thirty-six ceremonial portraits to be distributed throughout France. Only twenty-four were finished by the time of Napoleon's fall. JW

BIBLIOGRAPHY: Estevenin-Davenne 1987, pp. 34–8; Jourdan 1998, p. 166; Antwerp 1999, no. 6.

Cloak clasp of Emperor Napoleon I

Before 1815
Silver gilt, 190 x 110 x 40 mm
United Kingdom, Levens Hall Collection, Cumbria

This pair of silver-gilt bees formed the clasp to Napoleon's travelling cloak, which was found in the carriage abandoned on the field at Waterloo. The carriage and its contents were awarded to the Duke of Wellington who distributed these historic items to George IV, friends and relations. The bees were given to the duke's niece, Mary Wellesley, who married Sir Charles Bagot in 1807. Napoleon adopted the bee, symbol of thrift and industry, as a political emblem to replace the fleur-de-lis of the *ancient régime*. DSC

Golden eagle

Paris, First Empire, early 19th century
Gold and lapis lazuli, 71 x 40 mm
Private collection

On 18 May 1804, Napoleon was proclaimed Emperor of the French and hastily sought a new symbol of sovereignty in order to make a clean break with the monarchy of the *ancien régime*. On 12 June, despite various proposals from his advisors – elephant, lion, bees – the Council of State settled on the cockerel. The emperor was not much impressed by farmyard fowl and seemed to prefer the idea of the lion but, at the last minute and almost certainly under the influence of Dominique Vivant Denon, chose the eagle instead. Less than two months later the imperial eagle was adopted by the decree that established the seal and arms of the emperor.

The eagle, a heraldic figure derived from the Roman eagle, was re-established by Charlemagne, used in the crusades and became the emblem of the Germanic Holy Roman Empire. The form chosen by Napoleon was 'in the ancient style', based on the expressive Roman eagles rather than their heraldic successors.

The eagle became the main component of the new imperial arms. The day after his coronation Napoleon had it set on all the standards carried by his troops, as shown in the painting by Jacques-Louis David, *The Distribution of the Eagle Standards*, 5 December 1804 (Musée National du Château de Versailles).

The eagle with half-open wings seen here was one of the drafts for the imperial eagle submitted to the emperor. Napoleon ultimately preferred a fiercer image, so this suggestion was rejected. FC

BIBLIOGRAPHY : Fierro/Palluel-Guillard/Tulard 1995.

Portrait cameo of Emperor Napoleon I

Cameo : Nicola Morelli (1771–1838), 1804–15 ; setting : France

Gold, silver, diamonds, onyx cameo and lapis lazuli, 52 x 42 mm

Tokyo, Albion Art Collection

The front of the oval frame is set with an onyx cameo portrait of Napoleon I facing in profile towards the right, crowned with diamond laurel leaves tied with ribbons. The drapery at his neck is also set with diamonds and fastened with a clasp bearing the cipher N and pinned with symbolic bees. A chased golden eagle holding a thunderbolt in its claws is attached to the lapis-lazuli plaque at the back. The frame is plain gold with a suspension loop. The political character of the portrait is emphasized by the imperial pose, laurel crown and warrior's cloak, the symbols of bee, eagle, thunderbolt and the cipher N. This is one of several portraits commissioned from Morelli in Rome by the emperor, destined for setting in the lids of jewellery or snuffboxes. Napoleon I gave this cameo to William Fraser of Delhi as a gift in return for books, falcons and food sent to alleviate the boredom of exile in St Helena. DSC

Presentation snuffbox of Emperor Napoleon I

Victoire Boizot, France, 1808–13

Gold, diamonds and enamel, 20 x 77 x 56 mm

Paris, Fondation Napoléon, Donation Lapeyre (inv. 1097)

The lid of this gold, oblong snuffbox bears the diamond crowned cipher N, within a royal-blue enamel border of trails of leaves and flowers, which continues round the sides. The practice of giving snuffboxes as presents to diplomats or those who had rendered important services to the ruler evolved during the eighteenth century, and was continued by Napoleon as soon as he was appointed Consul in 1800. Traditionally made by the best goldsmiths, the decoration of these boxes varied, as did their intrinsic value. This example, with the imperial initial embellished with diamonds, is one of the most expensive types. DSC

Coronation ring of Empress Josephine in its box

1804

Ring : gold, rubies, brilliants and cut glass on foil, 20 mm ;
box : wood carved with scales and set with diamond points
Inscription engraved on the silver-gilt plate on the box lid
'Coronation ring of the emperor Napoleon and the empress
Josephine blessed by pope Pius VII 2 xber 1804'
Rueil-Malmaison, Musée National des Châteaux de Malmaison et
de Bois-Préau (inv. N. 107)

Napoleon's coronation ceremony in Notre-Dame on 2 December 1804 included the blessing of two gold rings mounted with stones from the crown collections by the goldsmith Marguerite. Napoleon's ring was set with an emerald, symbol of divine revelation, and Josephine's with a ruby, emblem of joy. Whereas Napoleon's ring has disappeared, Josephine's remained in Napoleon's family and was given by King Jerome to his daughter-in-law Princess Marie-Clothilde of Savoy. However, after 1815 the fallen emperor's sisters and brothers were forced to sell many of their stones at a loss, so it is no surprise to find that the ruby has been replaced by cut glass and its red sparkle is now replicated using foil. The ring was given to the Musée de Malmaison by Prince Louis Napoleon and his sister Clothilde, Countess of Witt. CJ

BIBLIOGRAPHY : Morel 1988, p. 254 ; Malmaison 2004, p. 106.

Presentation ring with portrait of Pope Pius VII

Rome, 1804
Gold, silver, rose-cut diamonds and sardonyx cameo,
25 x 22 x 29 mm
Private collection, courtesy Albion Art Jewellery Institute, Tokyo

The upper side of this oval ring with swivel bezel is bordered with diamonds enclosing a sardonyx cameo bust of Pope Pius VII (Barnaba Chiaramonti 1740–1823). He wears a zuchetto (skull cap) and stole inscribed with his name in gold letters, and faces in profile towards the right. The paved diamond ground on the reverse side is overlaid with gold representing the arms of the Chiaramonti family : a mountain crowned by a triple processional cross above the word PAX (Peace), three stars, and three blindfold onyx blackamoors. Although unsigned, the quality of this excellent portrait suggests that it must have been executed by one of the leading artists of the day in Rome, possibly Morelli, Berini or Girometti, all of whom were supported by the pope, a great patron of the arts. The embellishment with the rose-cut diamonds suggests that the pope intended it for

presentation to a person of high rank. Persecuted by Napoleon in the years following the coronation, the pope bore the humiliation of exile with a dignity and courage that won him many admirers. The ring came into the possession of the Grand Marshal of the court of Alexander I of Russia, Prince Nicolas Borissovitch Youssoupoff (1751–1831) who was in Paris for the coronation of Napoleon in 1804 to which the pope had been invited. He brought many gifts representing contemporary Roman art chosen for the purpose by Antonio Canova. DSC

The Coronation of Napoleon, now in the Louvre. Where she led others followed, not only in France but also across Europe. The twelve young noblewomen who carried Queen Victoria's train at her coronation in Westminster Abbey in 1837 also wore silver ears of corn tiaras, expressing the hopes of the nation that the new reign would be prosperous. DSC

Tiara with ears of corn

Early 19th century

Gold, silver and diamonds, 60 x 145 x 135 mm

Private collection, courtesy Albion Art Jewellery Institute, Tokyo

The tiara incorporates twelve ears of corn, fixed obliquely and slightly bent, as if blown by the wind. The six ears on each side meet above the centre of the forehead, supported by a plain gold frame. Golden ears of corn, sacred to the goddess Ceres and therefore symbolic of prosperity and abundance, were worn on the head in antiquity. They were revived in the reign of Napoleon for tiaras, but reinterpreted, as here, in diamonds. Princess Pauline Borghese is depicted wearing a tiara of this design at her brother Napoleon's coronation of 1804 at Notre-Dame, in Jacques-Louis David's great record of that event,

League of Princes ring

Germany, 1813
Gold and enamel
London, D.S. Lavender Antiques

The gold ring is mounted with an octagonal bezel enamelled with a winged genius lamenting the dissolution by Napoleon of the Holy Roman Empire in 1806. The figure is surrounded by the coats of arms of the various powers that joined the coalition to overthrow Napoleon and it bears the inscription FURSTENBUND (League of Princes). DSC

> ## Parure of Countess Vilain XIIII

c. 1810
Silver, gold, amethysts and diamonds (cut in brilliants)
Bazel church council, on loan to the Provinciaal Diamantmuseum, Antwerp

The necklace from the parure of Countess Vilain XIIII comprises twenty-four links, alternately large and small, each set with an oval amethyst on foil in a closed mount. Brilliant-cut diamonds surround the amethysts in the large links. The matching pair of earrings comprises pear-shaped amethysts in a closed mount, surrounded by eighteen old-cut brilliants in an open mount. These are suspended beneath a rosette comprising a round amethyst on foil in a closed mount, crowned by fourteen old-cut brilliants in an open mount. Countess Vilain XIIII, born Sophie Louise Zoe de Feltz (1780–1853), was the first owner of this parure made around 1810. In 1802, aged twenty-one, the baroness and daughter of an Austrian diplomat married Count Philippe Vilain XIIII, a descendant of one of the oldest families of the Flemish nobility. As the years went by, members of the Vilain family came to occupy important civil functions and played a major role in the history of Belgium. From 1780 they greatly contributed to the development of the village of Bazel in eastern Flanders. In 1800 Philippe Vilain XIIII, one of the family's most important figures, became closely associated with

Napoleon's entourage. As lady-in-waiting to Empress Marie Louise, Napoleon's second wife and daughter of Emperor Francis I of Austria, Zoe de Feltz had sustained relationships with the emperor and his wife and for this reason had a special role at the christening of the King of Rome in 1811. While Princess Aldobrandini held the christening bonnet, Countess Vilain XIIII and the Countess of Beauvau held the pitcher and saltcellar. Zoe de Feltz received a necklace and earrings of amethysts and brilliants as a souvenir of the occasion. In the same year the emperor ennobled her husband Philippe Vilain XIIII, who became a Count of the Empire, a title confirmed in 1816 by King William I. On 15 May 1852, a year before her death, Zoe gave the parure to Bazel church where it was worn by a statue during annual processions until the 1970s. However, the loss of an earring during one of these ceremonies put an end to this tradition. The earring was eventually found, somewhat damaged, along the route of the procession. Since then a diamond has been missing from the rosette. The parure was subsequently placed in the safe of Bazel church council. WL / LG

BIBLIOGRAPHY : Bennett/Mascetti 1989 ; De Wilde 1996 ; De Cerval 1998 ; Bury 2000 ; Phillips 2000 ; Samet 2000 ; Denissen/De Ren 2001 ; Denissen 2002 ; Tokyo 2003b ; Phillips 2004.

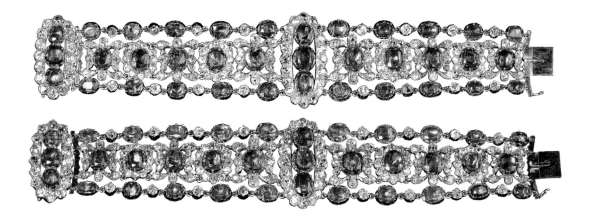

Bracelets of the Duchess of Angoulême

Contemporary copy, first half of the 19th century

Gold, silver, diamonds and rubies, 180 x 76 mm

Private collection

These bracelets were made as exact contemporary copies of the pair from the ruby and diamond parure of the Empress Marie Louise (1791–1847) in 1811. Paul-Nicolas Menière and Jacques-Eberhard Bapst subsequently modified them for the Duchess of Angoulême and the originals are now in the Louvre. These replicas convey something of François-Regnault Nitot's extraordinary talent for combining richly coloured stones with quantities of small diamonds. DSC

> ## Jewellery box

Jean-Baptiste Claude Odiot (1763–1850), Paris, 1809–19

Silver gilt and silk, 225 x 295 x 213 mm

Lisbon, Palácio Nacional da Ajuda (inv. 4859)

This highly valuable box in the Empire style, resting on the open wings of four doves, was made in the workshops of Jean-Baptiste Claude Odiot, official supplier to Napoleon and his family. Odiot also had the great honour of making the cradle of the King of Rome, preserved in the Schatzkammer, Vienna. This box is richly decorated. The longer sides are ornamented with two Cupids holding a circular garland of laurel leaves emphasizing the lock. Decorative floral scrolls attached to their bodies drop down and then climb up flowering tripods on either side. The scene is framed by pilasters at each corner, which also flank the scenes shown on the shorter sides. These are skilfully decorated with scrolls, trophies and garlands, which also appear on the lid surmounted by two small winged putti spinning thread in high relief. A slightly projecting frieze of leaves runs round the edge of the lid and the base of the box. Napoleon's second wife Empress Marie Louise (1791–1847) owned a similar box, also made by Odiot after a design by Garneray around 1810. Tsar Alexander I commissioned an identical box to give as a gift. CV

BIBLIOGRAPHY : Rosas Junior 1954 ; Lisbon 1992, pp. 276–7.

< Portrait of Pauline Bonaparte,
Princess Borghese

Robert Lefèvre (1755–1830), 1809

Oil on canvas, 63 x 51.5 cm

Rueil-Malmaison, Musée National des Châteaux de Malmaison

et de Bois-Préau (inv. MM. 74.6.1)

The artist Robert Lefèvre painted a number of portraits of the imperial family, including several of Napoleon 1's sister, Pauline Bonaparte (1780–1825), who married Prince Camillo Borghese in 1803. In 1806 a full-length portrait was commissioned for the Galerie de Diane at the Tuileries. Exhibited in 1808, it was hung in the Salon de Famille in the Palace of Saint-Cloud in 1809. This head and shoulders portrait reprises the full-length painting, with a few changes to the clothing, jewellery and background. Here the princess wears a parure of cameos set with diamonds, comprising a tiara-comb, bandeau, earrings and a brooch. The cameos depict the profiles of heroes or emperors from classical antiquity. Antonio Canova based the tiara's central cameo, representing Perseus, on the marble statue in the Vatican.

Napoleon was keen to restrict imports and wanted to set up a school for the engraving of fine stones in Paris to rival that of Rome. The fashion for cameos, which lasted until around 1880, became a real passion under the empire, as reflected in the *Journal des Dames et des Modes* of 16 March 1805: 'A fashionable woman wears cameos on her belt and cameos on her necklace, cameos on each of her bracelets and a cameo on her tiara.' CJ / DSC

Cameo parure of Grand Duchess Wilhelmine de Hesse-Darmstadt

Cameos : Rome ; setting : anonymous, 1804

Gold, enamel, onyx cameos and pearls, 380 x 408 x 170 mm

Eichenzell, Hessische Hausstiftung, Kronberg i.T.

Grand Duchess Wilhelmine of Hesse-Darmstadt (1788–1836) gave this parure to her daughter Marie (1824–1880) who married Alexander II of Russia in 1841. The jewels have been listed in the inventory of the Hesse family since 1883. The set comprises a bandeau, comb, pair of earrings, necklace, pair of bracelets and a slide. The gold setting is designed as pairs of openwork ivy leaves with dark blue quatrefoils each centred on a pearl between. The cameos, all contemporary work, are described below.

BANDEAU

Comprising a band of ivy leaves graduated towards each end, it is set with the following onyx cameos from left to right :

- Head of Neptune, facing right in profile, signed DORELLI.
- Head of a king, facing right in profile, signed DORELLI.
- Head of Medusa, after the celebrated intaglio from the Strozzi

ing his club, after the celebrated intaglio by Gnaios, facing right in profile, signed MASTINI.

EARRINGS

These are of the top and drop style.
• Tops: bearded mask facing front.
• Drops: Hadrianic heads facing left on one earring and right on the other.

SLIDE

This piece is mounted with a chalcedony bearded head with draped neckline, seen from behind, facing left.

NECKLACE

The oblong clasp at the back is set with three pearls within a raised border, enamelled dark blue. The necklace is graduated towards the ends and set with the following onyx cameos from left to right:
• Hadrianic head, facing right in profile, signed DORELLI.
• Head of Apollo, facing right in profile.
• Head of a young woman with her curly hair kept in place by a bandelette above the nape of the neck, facing left in profile. Signed KAP (for Giuseppe Capparoni). As this is the centre cameo it is slightly larger than those to each side.
• Head of a young woman with hair in a chignon, facing left in profile.
• Hadrianic head, facing left in profile, signed DORELLI.

BRACELETS

Each of the clasps is set with a cameo in an oval frame outlined in dark blue enamel with an inner border, from left to right:
• Sardonyx head of a young woman, hair in bandelettes, facing right in profile.
• Sardonyx head of a young woman, wreathed, facing left in profile. DSC

collection, facing left in profile. This is larger than the others, marking the centre of the bandeau.
• Bust of a young woman, hair kept in place by a bandelette and swept into a chignon at the back. She has a draped neckline, her shoulder emphasized by a touch of pink, facing left in profile.
• Head of a man of Hadrianic period, facing left in profile.

COMB

This mounted with a torsade of pearls below the gallery and

centred on a sardonyx head of the young Hercules, shoulder-

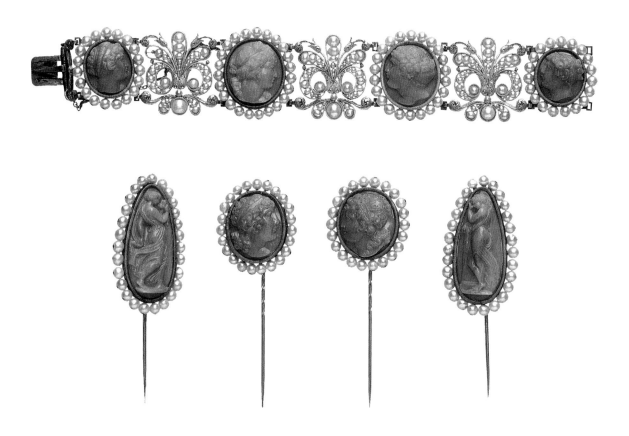

Demi-parure of Queen Hortense of Holland

Mounts : French, early 19th century

Gold, coral cameos and natural pearls ; bracelet : 25 x 170 mm

Rueil-Malmaison, Musée National des Châteaux de Malmaison et
de Bois-Préau (inv. MM. 40.47.6926)

This jointed bracelet is composed of four coral cameos engraved
with figures in the antique style and bordered with pearls, alternating with three gold filigree palmettes set with natural
pearls. The four large pins are surmounted with coral cameos
– two round and two oval – also surrounded by pearls. The set
is displayed against a background of wine-coloured velvet in a
dark red leather case.

This demi-parure belonged to Hortense de Beauharnais
(1783–1837), Queen of Holland. She was the daughter of Empress
Josephine and married Louis Bonaparte, one of Napoleon's brothers. Showered with favours by the emperor, her adoptive father,
Hortense received countless pieces of jewellery, most of which
she was forced to sell after the fall of the empire in 1815. This
modest set nevertheless remained in the possession of the
queen, who gave it to the wife of Count Marchand, one of the two
executors of Napoleon's will in St Helena. It was passed on to
Marchand's daughter, Malvina Mathilda, who married Edward
Desmazières, heir to the title of count. Count Alberic Desmazières-
Marchand donated it to the Musée de Malmaison in 1924.

With its delicate mount and coral cameos surrounded by
pearls, this set is a perfect example of the art of empire-period
jewellery design. CJ

BIBLIOGRAPHY : Malmaison 2004, p. 108.

Parure of Queen Sophia of Sweden

Simon Petiteau, Paris, 1820–30

Mark SP with a French stamp 1819–139

Gold and malachite ; tiara : 190 mm ; necklace : 445 mm

Stockholm, Nordiska Museet (inv. 990.047)

This parure composed of a tiara, large necklace, two bracelets, earrings and a large corsage brooch was created using four different types of gold. Malachite is a stone occasionally seen in parures – a gold, pearl and malachite parure from the same period is conserved in the collections of the Fondation Napoléon. The stones in this parure are carved with classical scenes deriving from the work of the Danish sculptor Bertel Thorvaldsen (1770–1844). A scene depicting 'Night' in the large malachite of the brooch picks up the theme of 'Day' in the tiara's central stone. An 1815 Roman relief by Thorvaldsen inspired both scenes. The necklace also features cameos depicting Hercules, Hebe and Hygieia, all derived from pieces sculpted by Thorvaldsen in Rome in 1808. The sculptor had a strong influence on glyptic work during this period.

The tiara bears the mark of the jeweller Simon Petiteau, who was born in Châteauroux in 1782 and worked in Paris until 1860. We can therefore assume that the parure was made in Paris, where gold cannetille had reached new heights. It represented a convenient cost-effective alternative to diamonds and created a unique effect. The tiara's scrolls and palmettes are reminiscent of the First Empire and combine harmoniously with realistically rendered Lilliputian flowers and grape clusters. It is thought that the suite belonged to the collection of Queen Desirée of Sweden (1777–1860), who owned several parures of this type. Queen Sophia, born Princess of Nassau (1836–1913), probably inherited the suite, and her descendants donated it to the Nordiska Museet. cv

BIBLIOGRAPHY : Stockholm 1949, no. 689 ; Nordiska 1952, p. 89 ; Isacsson 1999 ; Stockholm 2000, p. 99, no. 118.

Portrait of Queen Hortense of Holland

Jean-Baptiste Regnault, (1754–1829), c. 1810

Oil on canvas, 73 x 59.5 cm

Rueil-Malmaison, Musée National des Châteaux de Malmaison
et de Bois-Préau (inv. MM. 40.47.7232)

This portrait is a reprise of one that appears in the large Jean-Baptiste Regnault painting *The Wedding of Jerome Bonaparte and Princess Catherine of Württemberg*, completed in 1810 and now exhibited at Versailles.

Hortense de Beauharnais (1783–1827), daughter of Josephine, became Queen of Holland when she married Napoleon's brother Louis Bonaparte. She always remained very close to the court and to the emperor, who showered gifts and jewellery on her. She owned a number of very valuable parures, including a diamond suite that she later sold piece by piece. She returned some of it to Napoleon in 1815 when he left France for exile in St Helena.

Hortense is depicted wearing a parure composed of a comb, tiara, necklace, pendant earrings, two bracelets and a belt. The stones are most likely emeralds set with diamonds. No trace remains of this parure or the gemstones and mounted jewellery she inherited after the death of Empress Josephine in 1814. This is hardly surprising, since after the Bourbon Restoration, Hortense, who held the title of Duchess of Saint-Leu, was forced – like most of the princesses – to sell off her gemstones and necklaces in an attempt to maintain a certain lifestyle. Helen Fahnestock-Hubbard donated this portrait to the Musée de Malmaison in 1927. CJ

Parure of Princess Catherine Bagration

Tiara, earrings and comb : attributed to Fossin and Fils,
Paris, 1880

Gold, silver, diamonds and pink spinels,
tiara : 70 x 385 mm ; comb 30 x 140 mm

Private collection

The tiara is formed from a series of arcades enclosing spinel drops swinging within diamond frames. These are interspersed with spinel and diamond clusters and surmounted by scrolls supporting the arcading. The whole ensemble rests on a rope-twist diamond base. The gallery of the comb is made up of spinel and diamond clusters with scrolls. The pendant earrings incorporate briolette spinels with diamond caps hanging within diamond loops. The necklace consists of graduated spinel and diamond clusters, separated by pairs of diamond calyxes to each side of a collet diamond from which hang diamond and spinel drops meeting at an oblong spinel centrepiece within a diamond border. It is hung with a large oval cluster between two small drops.

This spectacular parure is a rare surviving example of the grand jewellery devised for the First Empire and adopted for court wear in the following period. The Russian born Princess Catherine Bagration (1783–1857), heiress to her great uncle, Prince Potemkin, was extremely beautiful and was renowned for her many love affairs. As a young woman she settled permanently in Paris, living in great state at 45 rue du Faubourg St-Honoré. Her transactions with Fossin and Fils fill many pages of the ledgers in the Archives of Chaumet, Paris. DSC

Emeralds of Empress Catherine II mounted in a necklace

England, c. 1830
Gold, silver, diamonds and emeralds,
375 mm ; centrepiece : 50 x 36 mm
Tokyo, Albion Art Collection

The emeralds are incorporated into a suite comprising a diamond and emerald necklace with matching earrings. The necklace is composed of a graduated row of twelve step-cut emeralds, each in pierced gold collets, alternating with fourteen cushion-shaped diamonds in silver collets. The necklace is fringed with fourteen pear-shaped emeralds, meeting at a detachable central octagonal domed emerald within a border of twelve cushion shaped emeralds hung with an emerald drop and fastened by an emerald clasp. Each earring is composed of an emerald briolette within an openwork diamond border. This important set would have been worn with a tiara and plumes on the head with the low-cut dresses that were de rigueur for court receptions. Because of their association with the Empress Catherine the emeralds would be noticed and remarked on.

According to family tradition, the emeralds were given by Catherine II to the 2nd Earl of Buckinghamshire (1723–1793) during his embassy to St Petersburg in 1762–5, and were worn by his wife Caroline, (d. 1817). Their daughter, Amelia, Viscountess Castlereagh, later marchioness of Londonderry (1762–1829), bequeathed them on to her nephew, 7th Marquess of Lothian (1794–1844), and they remained in the family until a recent sale. DSC

Amethyst parure

Mellerio dits Meller, Paris, c. 1825
Gold in several colours and amethysts,
necklace : 480 mm ; brooch : 60 x 30 mm ; comb : 170 x 110 mm ;
earrings : 50 x 20 mm
Collection Mellerio dits Meller

This parure consists of a tiara, top and drop earrings, necklace and brooch, with open-set amethysts in oval gold settings outlined in cannetille borders. The nine amethysts in the tiara surmount chased gold roses, leaves, palmettes, stars and scrolls, repeated in the necklace as pendants to the smaller medallions between the larger ones. The rich combination of deep purple amethysts and chased gold in this parure would have been highly admired at formal social events. It could have been one of several, each set with different coloured stones, so that the owner could choose the most suitable to match a particular outfit. DSC

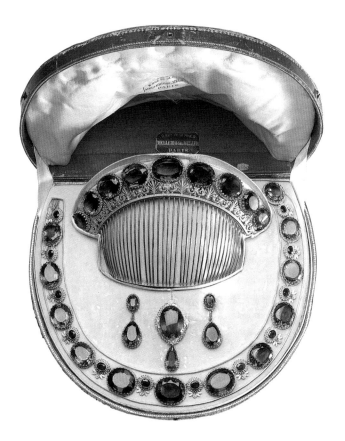

Ball parure

Stamp of Louis-Eugène Révillon, 1819–38

Gold, woven chains and citrines,

comb : 48 x 150 mm ; necklace : 68 x 445 mm ; bracelets :

50 x 150 mm ; pendant earrings : 40 mm ; belt buckle : 50 x 40 mm

Rueil-Malmaison, Musée National des Châteaux de Malmaison et

de Bois-Préau, Villeneuve-Esclapon bequest, 1952

(inv. MM 51.2.146 to 151)

Semi-precious gemstone parures were very fashionable during the Restoration. They differ from those of the Empire period and are characterized by large amounts of worked gold, in particular cannetille and crenellation, rediscovered techniques that came back into fashion with the new interest in antique jewellery. CJ

BIBLIOGRAPHY : Paris 2000, p. 94 ; Malmaison 2004, p. 108.

Mourning tiara of Queen Hortense of Holland

First third of the 19th century

Bronze gilt and jet, 70 x 200 mm

Rueil-Malmaison, Musée National des Châteaux de Malmaison
et de Bois-Préau, on loan to Château de Compiègne

(inv. MM 40.47.7169)

This tiara was probably part of a mourning parure also comprising a necklace, bracelets, earrings and possibly a bandeau. Hortense de Beauharnais, Queen of Holland (1783–1837), had to face the deaths of several family members, two of which were particularly painful for her: she lost her five-year-old son Napoleon Charles in 1807 and another son, Napoleon Louis, died in 1831.

Madame Donzel, the great-niece of Valérie Mazuyer, Queen Hortense's goddaughter and last lady-in-waiting, donated this piece to the Musée de Malmaison in 1939. CJ

BIBLIOGRAPHY : Malmaison 1993, p. 108 and 2004, p. 107; Boston 2000.

>> Portrait of Queen Marie Amelia

After François Dubois (1777–1860), 1835

Oil on canvas, 288 x 144 cm

Brussels, Royal Collections of Belgium

This painting, conserved in the Belgian royal collections, is a copy of a portrait commissioned from the painter Louis Hersent in 1836 by King Louis Philippe for his daughter Queen Louise. The original was intended for the apartments of the Queen of the Belgians in the French royal residences. It represents Queen Marie Amelia (1782–1866) at full length, dressed in a silk, satin and lace court dress. The sovereign wears the pearl, sapphire and diamond comb-crown that appears in her 1839 inventory of personal jewellery. This piece, together with a large stomacher also worn by the queen in the Hersent painting, and two secondary brooches created by the jeweller Bapst constituted one of the sapphire parures of the House of Orleans. It was passed on to the Count of Paris through direct inheritance, and he had it sold at Sotheby's despite much protest from the family.

The necklace, earrings and skirt ornaments, all set with identical stones, are part of the second sapphire and diamond parure that Louis Philippe bought back from Queen Hortense,

daughter of Empress Josephine. Through a marriage in the family this second suite, refurbished by the jeweller Bapst, also ended up in the hands of the Count of Paris, who, following covert negotiations, decided to sell it to the Louvre, where it is still on display today. The two parures are set with diamonds, pearls and Ceylon sapphires of exceptional quality. Their splendour seems to provide ample evidence that although the July Monarchy can be characterized by simplicity, it was not without flair. For reasons of conscience, Queen Marie Amelia refused to wear the crown jewels, yet she owned seven complete parures of the most flawless stones. The restraint is perhaps relative. Granddaughter of the great Maria Theresa and niece of the hapless Marie Antoinette, Marie Amelia, daughter of King Ferdinand I of the Two Sicilies, married Louis Philippe of Orleans in 1809. She had eight children, including Louise, who, through marriage to Leopold I, became the first Queen of the Belgians. CV

BIBLIOGRAPHY : De Brem 1993, p. 85.

Three bracelets with miniatures of King Louis Philippe, Queen Marie Amelia and their daughter, Princess Clementine

Mellerio dits Meller, Paris

Miniatures : François Meuret (1800–1887), after Franz Xaver Winterhalter (1805–1873), c. 1845

Gold and miniatures, 50 x 160 mm each

Bernard De Leye Collection

These three bracelets of chased gold links bear the stamp of the jeweller Mellerio dits Meller. This company, which still exists on Rue de la Paix, was founded in 1613 by a family of Lombard origins who decided to settle in Paris. Very soon Mellerio became supplier to the court. Under Louis Philippe they had very close relationships with all the members of the house of Orleans. These miniatures are all signed by François Meuret, an artist attached to the July Monarchy who obtained a first class medal at the Salon of 1843. They show King Louis Philippe after a portrait by Franz Xaver Winterhalter dated 1839 (Musée du Château, Versailles MV5219), Queen Marie Amelia, née Princess of the Two Sicilies, after a painting dated 1842 (Musée du Château, Versailles MV5111) and their third daughter Princess Clementine of Orleans, later Princess Augustus of Saxe-Coburg-Gotha, after a painting dated 1838 (formerly Forbes Collection).

These bracelets illustrate the popularity of sentimental jewellery during the reign of Louis Philippe, fulfilling the desire to immortalize the significant events of everyday life, such as births, anniversaries and marriages. Typically, these ornaments did so by use of elaborate symbolism, and also through minia-

tures, painted on ivory, enamel or porcelain, often surrounded with pearls or diamonds. Miniatures were worn as pendants, rings or around the wrist as bracelets. Like the Saxe-Coburg-Gothas, the Orleans family were very fond of miniatures and the eight children of Louis Philippe and Marie Amelia liked to exchange pieces of this kind as gifts. For her wedding to Archduke Maximilian in 1857, Princess Charlotte of Belgium, future Empress of Mexico, received a remarkable bracelet signed by the London jeweller Hancock from her Orleans uncles and aunts. At its centre was a miniature of the late Queen Louise of Belgium, immortalized by Queen Victoria's official watercolourist William-Charles Ross (1794–1860). Moreover, on the day of their wedding at Compiègne in 1832, Leopold I had given his bride, the future Queen Louise, a pendant miniature of himself, which she wore during the ceremony. cv

BIBLIOGRAPHY : London 1987 ; Paris 2000, p. 103 ; Tokyo 2003, pp. 135, 291 ; Vachaudez 2004.

< **Collar of the Order of the Holy Spirit of the Duke of Nemours**

Attributed to Jean-Charles Cahier (1772–1849), Paris, 1829

Gold and enamel, 1590 mm

Bernard De Leye Collection

This collar comprises a succession of twenty-nine panels in which solid gold fleurs-de-lis surrounded by tongues of fire alternate with military trophies and the initial H, recalling the founder of the order, flanked by royal crowns, horns of plenty and tongues of fire in red enamel. The eight-pointed cross, interspersed with fleurs-de-lis in gold, has the dove of the Holy Spirit at its centre. On the reverse Saint Michael can be seen killing the dragon. The Order of the Holy Spirit was instituted by Henry III in Paris in 1578, in the midst of the wars of religion, and was regarded as the most illustrious of the French chivalric orders. Henry decided to dedicate it to the 'blessed Holy Spirit' because he had acceded first to the throne of Poland and then to the throne of France (one year later) on Pentecost Day.

The order had its headquarters at the Convent of the Grand Augustins in Paris. It was abolished during the Revolution, but later reinstated under Louis XVIII (1755–1824) and continued under the reign of Charles X (1757–1836). At this time the order's ceremonies were held in the chapel of the Tuileries. On taking the throne in 1830, Louis Philippe (1773–1850), who was made Knight of the Order of the Holy Spirit by King Louis XVI in 1789, abolished all the chivalric orders apart from the Legion of Honour. This collar of the Order of the Holy Spirit was thus one of the last pieces to be made in Paris. It was given to Prince Louis of Orleans (1814–1896), Duke of Nemours, when he was awarded the order in 1829 by his father King Louis Philippe. Comparison with the collar preserved in the Louvre (inv. OA 11859) suggests that this piece can be attributed to the Parisian gold and silversmith Jean-Charles Cahier. The collar was bequeathed to the Duke of Alençon (1844–1910), second son of the Duke of Nemours, and then to Duke Emmanuel of Vendôme (1872–1931), husband of Princess Henrietta of Belgium. The family has recently parted with the collar. cv

Georgiana Koberwein, 1883

Oil on canvas, 69 x 56 cm

Harold Brown Esq.

When Princess Charlotte, only daughter and heir to her father George IV, died in childbirth in 1817, the country was faced with a serious problem of succession. At the age of fifty-five the king did not intend to remarry and was counting on his six brothers to perpetuate the line. However, Frederick, Duke of York, died before him and Ernest Augustus, Duke of Cumberland, was not eligible as he was King of Hanover. Augustus, Duke of Sussex, was at that time more interested in amorous affairs and did not marry a woman of his own rank until much later. George IV was succeeded by William IV, but he too died without any heirs. And so the race for the throne began. Barely a year after Charlotte's death Adolphus, Duke of Cambridge, and Edward, Duke of Kent, had both married, the former at the age of forty-four, the latter fifty-one. The Duke of Kent proved victorious in this singular competition with the birth of a plump, well-formed girl, named Victoria after her mother, a sister of poor Charlotte's inconsolable widower Prince Leopold. The girl lived in relative anonymity at Kensington Palace. Gradually, however, her destiny began to take shape. She acceded to the throne in 1837 and remained there until 1901, a long reign that was to become the Victorian 'era'. In 1840 she found her ideal husband in the person of her first cousin Prince Albert of Saxe-Coburg-Gotha. Their union produced nine children before coming to a sudden end with the prince's death in 1861. The queen never got over her loss and wore mourning dress for the rest of her life. For many years she refused to appear in public. It took the tenacity of her Prime Minister to persuade her to return to her official life. However, she had never neglected her duties. Her reign coincided with a period of unprecedented prosperity, at a time when the British Empire was more powerful and prosperous than ever before. This was fully reflected in the world of jewellery, where there was a constant stream of commissions. There was even a real coronation, when Victoria was proclaimed Empress of India in 1876.

Often known as the grandmother of European royalty, since her descendants have occupied most of the thrones in Europe, Victoria was immortalized in 1883 by Georgiana Koberwein. In this portrait, the queen wears a magnificent diamond necklace with matching pendant earrings, made in 1858 using twenty-eight stones from a ceremonial sword and a badge of the Order of the Garter. Only the pear-cut diamond hanging from the necklace and the two drop diamonds of the earrings come from another piece of jewellery formerly set with the Timur ruby, a priceless gem from the treasury of the maharajahs of Lahore, presented to the queen in 1851 by the Honourable East India Company. The necklace weighs a total of 161 carats and Queen Elizabeth II wore it with the earrings on her coronation day. Queen Victoria also wears a small crown, made in at her own request in 1870. The queen was exasperated by the weight of the Imperial State Crown and by the interminable process that had to be respected to take it out of the Tower of London. Nonetheless the small crown comprises 1162 brilliants and 138 rose-cut diamonds from a fringe collar dismantled for the purpose. Over the black of the queen's dress, lightened by a veil of Honiton lace, can be seen the ribbon of the Order of the Garter, held in place by a bar brooch comprising two rows of collets, which had previously been worn singly. Victoria also wears the diamond-studded Order of the Garter, the Order of the Crown of India and the Order of Albert and Victoria. Whereas the queen's profile always pre-empts that of the Prince Consort, it can be observed that, in the case of the decoration worn by the Queen, the prince pre-empts his royal wife, an exception chosen by Victoria herself. The bar brooch, small crown, necklace and earrings remain part of the inalienable treasure of the crown jewels. The painting was formerly in the collections of the Princes of Hohenzollern and hung in Sigmaringen Palace. cv

Coronation parure of King George IV of England

Rundell, Bridge & Rundell, London, 1824
Gold, diamonds, rubies, amethysts, emeralds and pearls,
pendant : 52 mm ; brooch : 45 mm ; earrings : 35 mm
Private collection

The parure consists of a necklace with a pendant globe hanging from the Maltese cross in the centre, a pair of globe earrings and a brooch, both also attached to Maltese crosses. The necklace is composed of tasselled gold knots inspired by those in the collar of the Knights of the Order of the Garter alternating with the emblems of England, Scotland and Ireland – the rose, thistle and shamrock – set with diamonds and coloured stones. In addition to their Christian symbolism, the Maltese crosses allude to the occupation of that island by the British navy, and the globes echo the orb of sovereignty, which the king holds in his hand during the coronation ceremony. The design demonstrates George IV's patriotic pride in British history. The bill of £147 for this set of 'elegant coronation ornaments' is in the Royal Archives in Windsor Castle. George IV gave the parure to the wife of his Lord Chamberlain,

Clementina Drummond, Lady Gwydyr, as a memento of the coronation ceremony. DSC

BIBLIOGRAPHY : Hartop 2005, no. 73, fig. 68, p. 78.

Tudor rose bracelet clasps (?)

England, c. 1830
Gold, silver, enamel and diamonds, 40 x 35 mm each
Private collection, courtesy Albion Art Jewellery Institute, Tokyo

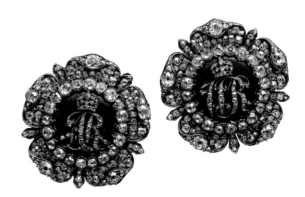

The diamond Tudor roses frame the crowned diamond initials w[ILLIAM] R[EX] and A[DELAIDE] R[EGINA] applied to a royal-blue enamel ground. Symbolizing the kingdom of England, Tudor roses were frequently adopted as patriotic mementoes by British royalty in the nineteenth century. These examples would have been worn as brooches or as bracelet centrepieces by one of the children of William IV (1765–1837). He and his queen, Adelaide, who had no surviving children together, ruled from 1830–37. The roses belonged to the FitzClarence family, by descent from one of William IV's sons by his mistress, Mrs Jordan. DSC

Pendant with miniature of Queen Marie of Hanover

Germany, mid-19th century

Gold, silver, diamonds and miniature, 41 x 26 mm

Private collection, courtesy Albion Art Jewellery Institute, Tokyo

The pendant encloses a miniature portrait bust of Queen Marie of Hanover (1818–1907) surrounded by a diamond border edged with diamond points and surmounted by a royal crown. In 1843 Queen Marie married George V, Duke of Brunswick and Luneburg, and future King of Hanover (1819–1878). DSC

Marshal's baton presented by King George IV to his son King of Hanover

John Northam, England, 1821

Gold and velvet, 520 mm

London, S.J. Phillips

This long baton is covered with crimson velvet with applied crowned lions. Each end is decorated with bands of foliage in gold of various colours, surmounted by a figure of Saint George on horseback transfixing the dragon with his spear, and at the base by a plaque inscribed F[R]OM HIS MAJESTY GEORGE IV KING OF THE UNITED KINGDOM OF GREAT BRI[T]AIN AND IRELAND TO FIELD MARSHAL HIS ROYAL HIGHNESS ERNEST DUKE OF CUMBER-LAND KG 1821. The initials KG stand for Knight of the Order of the Garter. Symbolizing the authority of the commander of an army, the baton was given by George IV to his brother Ernest, Duke of Cumberland (1771–1851) who succeeded to the throne of Hanover in 1837 which had been united with England since 1714. Queen Victoria was barred from ruling Hanover on account of the Salic Law, so the two kingdoms separated and the throne passed to her uncle, the Duke of Cumberland, the fifth son of George III. An able soldier and efficient king, when he lay in state his coffin was surmounted by the crown and sceptre of Hanover, his busby and sabre, the collars of the Orders of the Garter and Saint George, and the Field Marshal's baton. DSC

>> Insignia of the Order of the Garter presented by King George IV to the Kings of Hanover

Star : Rundell, Bridge & Rundell, London, 1835 ;

Garter, Great George and Lesser George : Robert Garrard, 1878

Gold, silver, enamel, diamonds and rubies

Tokyo, Albion Art Collection

The star was made for the future George V of Hanover (1819–1878) on his appointment to the Order of the Garter, 15 August 1835, by his uncle, William IV. The other items were made for his son, Prince Ernest Augustus, Duke of Cumberland (1845–1923), son of George V of Hanover, on his appointment to the Order of the Garter by Queen Victoria on 22 June 1878. The group consists of the following four items :

STAR

The star is centred on a cross set with five rubies on a paved diamond ground. This is encircled by a buckled garter enamelled in blue and inscribed in diamonds with the motto HONI SOIT QUI MAL Y PENSE within diamond rays set in four larger and four smaller points. On the reverse is inscribed RUNDELL BRIDGE & CO, JEWELLERS TO THEIR MAJESTIES AND ROYAL FAMILY 32 LUDGATE HILL LONDON and there is a number on the pin. The star was worn pinned to the coat or cloak.

GREAT GEORGE

The enamelled gold Great George depicts the freestanding figure of Saint George, wearing Roman armour and a helmet and mounted on horseback. He holds his lance ready to attack the dragon who has a green body and red wings. The grassy green base is strewn with leaves and flowers and encircled by a guilloche border of blue ribbons with a suspension loop for hanging the figure from the collar of the order.

GARTER

The garter bears the motto HONI SOIT QUI MAL Y PENSE inscribed in pierced diamond letters between diamond collet borders. There are diamond quatrefoils between the words and two more quatrefoils to each side of the flower on the tab, which terminates in a line of small diamonds. The buckle is also executed in diamonds.

LESSER GEORGE

The sash garter badge, or Lesser George, has at its centre an onyx cameo of Saint George on horseback, his lance raised to slaughter the dragon at his feet. This is set within a diamond border surrounded by a buckled garter enamelled blue and bearing the motto HONI SOIT QUI MAL Y PENSE inscribed in pierced diamond letters with diamonds dotted between the words and two quatrefoils on the tab. Around the edge is a foliate diamond border surmounted by a collet diamond between two tulip-shaped flowers. The setting is transparent throughout with a suspension loop for attaching the badge from a blue ribbon sash at formal, but not the grandest, ceremonial events.

These items remained in the collection of the Royal House of Hanover after the degradation of Prince Ernest in 1915, when England and Germany were at war and as an enemy national he, with the other German relations, was stripped of his British honours and titles by George V. Whereas it is customary to return insignia on the death of the knight, since Prince Ernest Augustus had been degraded, his heirs must have considered that this was not necessary, and hence it was kept in the family.

Appointment to the 'most noble' Order of the Garter is the highest honour the English monarch can bestow. Founded by Edward III in 1348, the ceremonies associated with the order take place at Windsor Castle. The motto, which translates 'Shame on him who thinks evil of it', is in the spirit of fourteenth-century courtly chivalry. The number of knights is limited to twenty-four. This insignia was made by the crown jewellers Rundell, Bridge and Rundell in 1835 and by Robert Garrard in 1878, and represents the best craftsmanship of mid-nineteenth-century England for the Royal House of Hanover. DSC

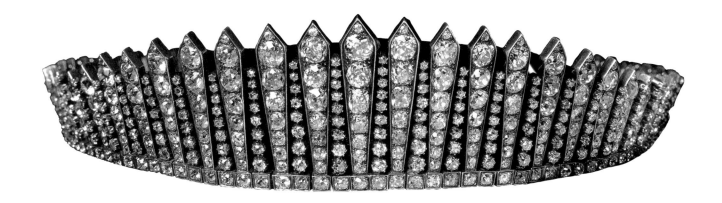

Diamond fringe tiara

England (?), late 19th century

Gold, silver and diamonds, 50 x 180 x 170 mm

Private collection, courtesy Albion Art Jewellery Institute, Tokyo

Lines of diamonds alternate with diamond-set points to create a kind of halo evoking the kokoshnik ('cockscomb'), the traditional headdress of Russian peasant women. This fashion originated in the Romanov court before spreading to most of Europe's royal houses and aristocratic families. The French crown jewels included a similar tiara, as did the collection of the grand duchesses of Saxe-Weimar-Eisenach. Today, tiaras of this kind can be found in the collections of Queen Sylvia of Sweden, Princess Elisabeth of Denmark, Princess Marie-Aglae of Liechtenstein, the Duchess of Westminster and Princess Michael of Kent. Franz Xaver Winterhalter's painting *The First of May 1851* shows Queen Victoria holding Prince Arthur, the future Duke of Connaught, and wearing a similar tiara dating from 1830. The piece had originally been a necklace made using brilliants from the collection of King George III. The young Queen Victoria (1819–1901) first wore it as a tiara at a gala opera performance in 1839. The piece then passed to Queen Mary, to Elizabeth the Queen Mother and finally to Queen Elizabeth II, who still wears it from time to time, thereby perpetuating a fashion born in the early nineteenth century. CV

BIBLIOGRAPHY : Twining 1960, pp. 191–2, pl. 72a ; Field 1987, pp. 41–3 ; Munn 2001, pp. 160–1 ; Tokyo 2007, pp. 56–7.

Tiara of Princess Alice, Grand Duchess of Hesse

England (?), c. 1860

Gold, silver and diamonds, 220 x 220 x 70 mm

Germany, Hessische Hausstiftung, Kronberg i.T.

The tiara consists of a wide bandeau surmounted by foliage and tall pinnacles. When Princess Alice of Great Britain (1843–1878) married Prince Louis IV of Hesse-Darmstadt (1837–1892) in 1862, her widowed mother, Queen Victoria, gave her a diamond tiara, probably based on a design by the art-loving Prince Consort Albert. For Princess Alice, his involvement must have had a special significance, as she had nursed Albert devotedly when he was dying of typhoid fever. She wore the tiara often, notably at the wedding of her brother, the Prince of Wales, to Princess Alexandra of Denmark in 1863. On this occasion Queen Victoria described Alice as 'looking extremely well in a violet dress, covered with her wedding lace, and a violet velvet train, from the shoulders trimmed with the mini veil beloved Mama had worn at Vicky's wedding. Louis in the Garter robes leading her'. After Princess Alice's death at the age of thirty-five, the tiara was not seen again for about twenty years. The next to wear it was Grand Duchess Victoria Melita (1876–1936), first wife of Princess Alice's only son Grand Duke Ernst Ludwig (1868–1937). She was herself a granddaughter of Queen Victoria, through her father Prince Alfred, Duke of Edinburgh. The Grand Duke divorced her in 1901 and remarried in 1905. The tiara was then passed on to his second wife, born Princess Eleonore of Solms-Hohensolms-Lich (1871–1937) who wore it in a spectacular photograph dated 1908, a few months before the birth of her second son, Prince Ludwig. In 1937, the jewel escaped destruction when the aeroplane taking Grand Duchess Eleonore, her son, Grand Duke Georg Donatus, his wife and two of his children, crashed, killing them all. The tiara survived intact, protected by its strong metal travelling case which was recovered from the wreckage. The family was travelling to England to attend the wedding of Prince Ludwig to The Honourable Margaret Geddes who, until now, is the last princess of the House of Hesse to have worn Princess Alice's tiara. CV

238

Bracelet with miniature of Queen Victoria

Miniature : John Simpson, England, mid-19th century

Gold, silver, diamonds, rubies, emeralds and miniature,

bracelet : 180 mm ; miniature : 55 x 48 mm

Private collection, courtesy Albion Art Jewellery Institute, Tokyo

This gold bracelet has a flexible band and the centrepiece encloses a miniature of Queen Victoria (1819–1901) wearing a tiara, earrings and a pearl necklace, by John Simpson after a portrait by Franz Xaver Winterhalter. The reverse is inscribed MEINE THEUREN NICHTE STEPHANIE VON VICTORIA RAM (9TEN MAI 1858) indicating that the bracelet was a gift from Queen Victoria to her relation, Stephanie of Hohenzollern (1837–1859), during her brief stay in England on her journey from her native Germany to Lisbon. There she married Pedro V, the young King of Portugal, but sadly she died the following year. An expensive bracelet such as this emphasized the bond between two queens, both to each other and to diplomatic relations between their two countries. DSC

Presentation snuffbox from Queen Victoria

Mark of Robert Garrard, London, 1855–6

Gold, diamonds and enamel, 45 x 100 x 70 mm

Paris, Musée du Louvre (inv. OA 11978)

This snuffbox, in the neo-baroque style, bears a rocaille motif on the lid. Queen Victoria's monogram, VR for Victoria Regina, can be seen on a blue enamel ground, surrounded by five large, old diamonds, of which the nearest to the front of the lid appears to be hanging from a chain, with a grid pattern of diamonds set on either side. The inside of the box bears the inscription in French : A GIFT FROM HER MAJESTY QUEEN VICTORIA TO HIS EXCELLENCY MR A. FOULD. Achille Fould (1800–1867) was a French banker who, under the Second Empire, oversaw a trade agreement between France and the United Kingdom. Queen Victoria gave him this snuffbox to thank him for his services. JW

BIBLIOGRAPHY : Tokyo 2003b, no. V–3.

Prince Albert locket

c. 1840

Gold, silver, diamonds and enamel, 76 x 45 mm

Private collection, courtesy Albion Art Jewellery Institute, Tokyo

This oval gold locket is enamelled in royal blue and decorated with a diamond Gothic-style letter A[LBERT] surmounted by a crown. Inside there is the inscription 'Captain John Hamilton on his wedding July 6 1840'. Prince Albert of Saxe-Coburg-Gotha, who married Queen Victoria in February 1840, gave this locket to Captain Hamilton, presumably a member of the royal household. It illustrates the huge significance of these gifts with which royalty acknowledged services and loyalty, in addition to oiling the wheels of diplomacy. DSC

Portrait of Empress Eugenie

Franz Xaver Winterhalter (1805–1873) (workshop copy), 1853

Oil on canvas, 237 x 155 cm

Beloeil, Château de Beloeil collection

A frequent visitor to the Tuileries Palace during the reign of King Louis Philippe, Franz Xaver Winterhalter had already won over many European courts. The quality of his portraits was indeed wonderfully suited to the spirit of the times. So it was no surprise when a newspaper in Karlsruhe, his adoptive home, announced that he had been called to Paris by the new emperor and his wife to paint their portraits. Winterhalter at once travelled to the French capital, where he was the first to be admitted to the informal gatherings held by the empress and known as the Compiègne series. He immortalized Empress Eugenie, then twenty-seven years old, in this official portrait in which her hand seems lightly to be touching a crown, symbol of her status. In the purest tradition of royal portraits, the décor includes a perspective view of attractive gardens and a column skilfully draped in rich velvet. The empress is wearing the great pearl and diamond tiara from the crown jewels, which was sold in 1887 and passed into the collections of the princes of Thurn and Taxis before returning to France, where it is now on display in the Galerie d'Apollon in the Louvre. Around her neck Eugenie wears many strings of pearls, also from the royal treasury, and necklaces casually wound round her wrist as was customary at the time. Instead of a stomacher she has a profusion of lace to decorate the crinoline patiently sewn in Charles Frederick Worth's Paris workshops.

Winterhalter sets the tone. He enables the imperial couple to make it generally known – as countless copies of this portrait were made and sent throughout France – that the Second Empire marked a return to the magnificence that had characterized the First Empire. Indeed, the great jewellers had never worked at such a fevered pitch. Born Eugenia de Montijo (1826–1920), the young Spanish aristocrat married Napoleon III in 1853. cv

BIBLIOGRAPHY : London 1987, p. 47 : Tokyo 2003b, pp. 154-5, 265-6.

> Brooch from the currant-leaf parure of the crown jewels

Alfred Bapst, Paris, 1855

Silver and diamonds, 88 x 55 mm

Private collection

This brooch features paved diamond leaves centred on a large cushion-cut diamond and suspended diamond 'berries'. It was

240

originally one of sixteen elements that linked together to make the currant-leaf garland worn by the Empress Eugenie as a necklace. It formed part of a set with the famed *tour de corsage* and stomacher. According to Morel this was 'one of the royal House of Hanover's most splendid parures of the nineteenth century'. This author also discusses the background to the disastrous dispersal of the French crown jewels by the Third Republic in 1887, an act motivated entirely by political spite. Aware of the significance of this incomparable collection, symbolizing the power and authority of the monarchy, the Republican majority in the Chambre des Deputés voted for its dispersal, thereby destroying symbolicaly any possibility of restoring the Bourbons to the throne of France. This brooch was part of lot 11, bought by various jewellers including Garrard, Bapst and Tiffany. DSC

BIBLIOGRAPHY : Morel 1988, p. 341, pp. 365–81.

Copy of the 'Regent' made for Empress Eugenie

Second half of the 19th century
Cubic zirconia, 20 x 30 x 30 mm
Paris, Musée du Louvre (inv. SN844)

The 140.64-carat Regent diamond is so called because it was acquired in 1717 from the British merchant, Thomas Pitt, by Philip II, Duke of Orleans, when acting as Regent of France. On account of its size and quality it was the most important of the French crown jewels, dispersed in 1887, and it has been in the Louvre ever since.

Recognizing its significance, Napoleon I had it set into the hilt of his sword which he wore not only as Consul but also at his coronation in 1804, and later in 1812 in the pommel of the imperial glaive (sword), symbolizing the military victories which had won him absolute power. In the Second Empire the Empress Eugenie wore it in her hair and it was for her that this copy was made. DSC

BIBLIOGRAPHY : Morel 1988, pp. 185–90.

Empress Eugenie's bracelet

1850
Diamonds and emerald, 190 mm
Private collection

This bracelet comprises two joined bands, whose openwork is intended to show off fourteen circular diamonds set as solitaires. These are arranged in two rows of seven on either side of a central decoration in diamonds, itself set with a remarkable rectangular emerald of 7.25 carats. Formerly owned by Empress Eugenie, wife of Napoleon III, the bracelet was bought by Russell Sturgis, who gave it to his daughter Lady Portsea. When the Second Empire fell, Eugenie found refuge in Great Britain. Although the crown jewels remained in France, she was able to take her own personal jewellery with her, hastily wrapped in old newspaper, including her renowned collection of emeralds. She gave an entire box of these to her goddaughter, Queen Victoria Eugenia of Spain, and sold a fine set at Christie's in 1872. During her years in exile the empress was obliged to part with certain pieces of jewellery to cover her household expenses. This magnificent bracelet was almost certainly one of those sold during her lifetime to a member of the British establishment. CV

Bracelet-bandeau with medallions of the imperial family

Miniatures : Philippe Prochietto dit Porcher (1825–1890),
Geneva, illegible markings on the back of the clasp, after 1854
Gold, miniatures on enamel, 35 x 220 mm
Rueil-Malmaison, Musée National des Châteaux de Malmaison
et de Bois-Préau, held at the Château de Compiègne
(inv. MM PO 2097)

Napoleon III presented this bracelet to a princess of the court on the occasion of her wedding. It is composed of five portrait medallions of the imperial family : King Jerome, brother of Napoleon I and former king of Westphalia ; Empress Eugenie, after an 1854 portrait by Franz Xaver Winterhalter ; Napoleon III ; Princess Matilda, daughter of King Jerome and cousin of Napoleon III, after an 1850 pastel by Eugène Giraud ; and

Prince Jerome Napoleon, brother of Princess Matilda. There are several similar bracelets mounted by the Parisian jeweller Mellerio and depicting members of the Orleans family around 1840. This one joined the national collections in the 1920s along with a large number of objects donated by Baroness d'Alexandry d'Orengiani (1850-1927). Although of English origin, she was very attached to the Second Empire and was close to Empress Eugenie at the end of her life. CJ

Empress Eugenie's locket

France, second half of the 19th century
Gold, silver, diamonds, pearls and sapphire cameo,
chain : 380 mm ; locket : 70 x 34 mm
Tokyo, Albion Art Collection

The cover of the oval gold locket is set with a sapphire cameo of Queen Hortense (1788–1836) playing the lyre in the character of a Muse. The portrait is framed in a diamond border within a pearl and diamond laurel crown. The daughter of the Empress Josephine, Hortense married the brother of Napoleon, King Louis of Holland, and was the mother of Napoleon III, Emperor of France, who must have inherited the cameo. Inside the locket there is a photograph of his wife, Empress Eugenie (1826–1920), whose imperial crown and cipher surmount the locket, which hangs from a gold chain interspersed with globes. This historic locket was given as a gift from the empress to Lady Burgoyne who brought her across the Channel to England after the collapse of the Second Empire in 1870. It was the only jewel the empress took with her on such a dangerous journey and was much valued on account of the significance of the cameo and also because it would have contained photographs of the emperor and their son, the Prince Imperial. However, she was so grateful to Lady Burgoyne and her husband for transporting her to safety in their yacht that, despite losing her throne, she continued to act like an empress by presenting her with this remarkable memento. DSC

Chatelaine watch with cipher
of Empress Eugenie

Jules Fossin (1808–1869), 1853

Gold, enamel, diamonds and baroque pearl, 104 x 31 mm

Rueil-Malmaison, Musée National des Châteaux de Malmaison
et de Bois-Préau (inv. MM 40.47.6922)

This round pocket watch, designed to be worn at the waist suspended from a belt, has a blue-enamelled back bearing the letter E surmounted by a crown of brilliant-cut diamonds. The
bow-shaped hook embellished with a single pearl at its centre
is linked to the watch with a ring and a jointed gold hook.

It was common at court to give gifts of jewellery and other
valuable objects to people in one's entourage and to guests of high
standing. Rings, bracelets and medallions bearing sovereigns'
monograms were commissioned from jewellers and widely distributed. The gift of a personal piece of jewellery was rarer. This
watch, commissioned from official court jeweller Jules Fossin,
is said to have been a gift from Emperor Napoleon to his wife
Eugenie (1826–1920) on the occasion of their January 1853 wedding. The empress later gave this watch as a token of friendship to Countess de la Bédoyère, one of her thirteen ladies-in-
waiting at the palace. She was the wife of the only son of
General de la Bédoyère; the museum also owns the jewellery
he was wearing when he was shot in 1815 for his association
with Napoleon. The countess's granddaughter, Madame Jean
Reimbert, born Nina de la Bédoyère, donated this watch to the
Musée de Malmaison in 1934. CJ

BIBLIOGRAPHY : Malmaison 1991, p. 58 and 2004, p. 110 ;
Paris 1998, p. 80.

Gift box with a miniature of
Emperor Napoleon III

Maurice Mayer, jeweller to the Emperor

Miniature : Gabriel Aristide Passot (1797–1875),

mid-19th century

Gold, enamel, precious stones ; miniature : oil on ivory,

28 x 95 x 60 mm

Paris, Fondation Napoléon, Donation Lapeyre (inv. 1060)

On 2 December 1852 the President-Prince Louis Napoleon,
nephew of Napoleon I, was crowned emperor with the name of
Napoleon III. The lid of this gold gift box is decorated with a
miniature by Gabriel Aristide Passot showing a portrait bust of
the emperor in the uniform of a brigadier, wearing the cross
and broad sash of the Legion of Honour. This miniature is
based on the large full-length portrait painted by Franz Xaver
Winterhalter of around 1852 (Museo Napoleonico, Rome), in

nier a silver medal at the Exposition Universelle. Only the empress's crown survives in the collections of the Musée du Louvre; that of the emperor disappeared when a portion of the crown jewels were sold off in May 1887.

This flask for smelling salts, whose crystal body is engraved with a double E – Eugenie's monogram – is distinguished by its cap, which is modelled on the royal crown. Eight gold eagles, their wings outstretched, surround a red jasper stopper. Above each eagle is an arch set with eleven diamonds, culminating in a central pearl. Between each eagle is a fleuron set with two diamonds. Beneath, a band is set with eight round rubies, eight rectangular emeralds and eight round rose-cut diamonds. A rose-cut diamond is used for the thumb-rest. KH

> ### Diamond corsage bouquet
Mellerio dits Meller, Paris, c. 1870
Silver, gold and diamonds, 120 x 120 x 30 mm
Mellerio dits Meller

The corsage bouquet, which had come into fashion in the eighteenth century and was copied directly from nature, made its reappearance in the romantic period, particularly under the Second Empire. The magnificent diamond bouquet in the French crown jewels and a similar one at the Victoria & Albert Museum, London, are fine examples. This delightful leafy branch with paved diamonds is mounted with a set of small bells on tiny spiral springs. The jeweller Mellerio patented this technique, which enabled pieces to tremble at the slightest movement and so to reflect the greatest possible amount of light, in 1854. CV

BIBLIOGRAPHY : Tokyo 2003, pp. 166, 301.

which the emperor wears the imperial mantle and large collar of the Legion of Honour. The present image is bordered by twenty-four white stones set on a blue enamel ground. KH

Flask for smelling salts with the monogram of Empress Eugenie
Mid-19th century
Crystal, pearl, diamonds, rubies, emeralds, gold and jasper, 102 mm
Paris, Fondation Napoléon, Donation Lapeyre (inv. 1138)

On 30 January 1853, in Notre-Dame in Paris, Napoleon III married Eugenia Maria de Montijo de Guzmán, who had been born in Granada, Spain in 1826. She thus became empress of the French under the name Eugenie. The jeweller Alexandre-Gabriel Lemonnier (c. 1808–1884) was commissioned to create crowns for the rulers. He created an initial model with precious stones from the crown of Charles X. This can be seen in Franz Xaver Winterhalter's well-known official portrait of the emperor and empress. In 1855, it was replaced by a simpler version. Although smaller and lighter, Eugenie's crown was designed along the same lines as that of Napoleon III. It was composed of arches formed by the wings of eight eagles in chased gold, alternating with eight palmettes extended by a large palm leaf. To this were added 102 brilliants taken from the French crown jewels, as well as 1,252 brilliants and 56 emeralds purchased with imperial funds. The crowns were delivered in August 1855, and they earned Lemon-

> ### Brooch in the shape of a bow
Mellerio dits Meller, Paris, c. 1880
Silver, gold and diamonds, 110 x 120 mm
Mellerio dits Meller

Made popular by masters such as Gilles Legaré in the seventeenth century, then by others including Augustin Duflos, Jean-Henri Pouget and Jean Bourget in the eighteenth, the bow was a favourite ornament of elegant ladies, who appreciated the novelty of these precious beribboned baubles. The lines were initially fairly rigid, but a greater originality soon came in, following the principles of the rococo style. Although this bow dates from the 1880s, it is similar to Pouget's designs as shown on pages 47 and 48 of his *Traité des pierres précieuses* published in 1762. Bows came into vogue again under the Second Empire and remained popular throughout the eighteenth century.

244

Notable examples include the large diamond corsage bow in the French crown jewels and the magnificent bow given by the residents of Kensington to the future Queen Mary on the occasion of her marriage to the Duke of York, son of Edward VII, in 1893. This fine and particularly decorative example shows a highly sinuous ribbon in diamonds forming four loops. The original box has been preserved and bears the stamp MELLERIO DITS MELLER with the crowned initials E.C.C. CV

BIBLIOGRAPHY : Tokyo 2003, pp. 166, 301.

< Peacock feather aigrette

Probably Mellerio dits Meller, Paris, c. 1880

Gold, silver, diamonds, emeralds and sapphires, 110 x 85 mm

London, Sandra Cronan Limited

To each side of the central shaft, set with a continuous line of diamonds, are diamond barbs graduated in size towards the base. The large 'eye' is set with a cabochon sapphire surrounded by a row of diamonds within an outer border of calibre-cut emeralds. Symbolic of glory and majesty, the peacock offered a challenge to the leading French jeweller, Mellerio, who from the 1860s decided to imitate nature and produced the tail feathers in metal and precious stones. Each of the great jewellery houses, notably Gautrait, Boucheron and Mellerio, created a series of jewels on the peacock theme.

This example is a striking ornament, and would have been worn to the side of the head as an aigrette, mounted on a frame as a tiara, or pinned to the bodice as a brooch. DSC

Demi-parure with stomacher

France (?), 1850–70

Gold, silver and diamonds

Corsage in three parts : 100 x 100 mm ; 90 x 70 mm ; 85 x 40 mm ;

bracelet : 240 x 60 mm

Private collection

These pieces in the naturalist style, so typical of the mid-nineteenth century, are set with rose-cut diamonds. The components of the corsage can be worn as separate brooches, since the drops are detachable. The bracelet can also be worn as a diadem and, given its length, seems better suited to this function. The original case had a space for pendant earrings. The church of Saint Martin in Aalst has a similar corsage in three parts, but with glass instead of diamonds.

Jewellers were always keen to flatter the egos of their clients, who wore jewellery primarily in order to glitter when they were out in society. The technique of mounting jewellery on springs so that it would tremble with the wearer's every movement dates from the seventeenth century. In the nineteenth century jewellers took inspiration from nature, creating fluid, mobile shapes that would move with the slightest breath of air. Pendant pieces were often made to imitate the laburnum, which, in Victorian symbolism, evoked the 'beautiful dreamer'. JW

BIBLIOGRAPHY : Antwerp 1968, no. 281 ; Robijns 1980, 606–7 ; Antwerp 2002, no. 39 ; Tokyo 2003b, no. V–1.

Jakob Speltz, Frankfurt, 1859

Gold, silver and diamonds, 92 x 66 x 35 mm

Luxembourg, Collection Grand-Ducale

This piece is one of a set of three old-cut diamond brooches dating from the mid-nineteenth century. Each brooch was designed as a cascade of wild roses, the fully opened flowers, buds and leaves decorated with paved diamonds on a mount of silver on gold. The brooch presented here is the largest of the three. According to the inventory of 1859, the bouquet originally contained 595 brilliants. The back of all three bouquets have square, partially numbered tenons, which seemed to have allowed them to be mounted onto a structure, almost certainly a tiara. The lower part has hooks that must originally have held ivy-leaf pendants. The inventory of 1859 does not detail the different possible combinations. It mentions only the association of rose bouquet no. 3 with a garland of two sprays of flowers and ivy leaves mounted *en tremblant*. These bouquets could probably be combined into one or several larger pieces. The two sprays, without the roses, are now combined in a fixed tiara.

Today the brooches are worn only for important official events, such as the state visit to the Netherlands made by the grand duke and duchess on 24–26 April 2006.

The three brooches were made in 1859 by the jeweller Jacob Speltz of Frankfurt, reusing diamonds belonging to the House of Nassau-Weilburg, and make their first appearance in the inventory of 1859, which also includes a design for larger bouquets with buds on either side of the open flower. This bouquet is shown with ivy-leaf pendants and described in position v. The 'Sechs Gehänge' comprises 18 solitaires, 233 small brilliants in a double ivy leaf and 18 single ivy leaves, and 78 small brilliants in the six upper eyelets and at the lower six ends. Today these elements no longer exist. The bouquets were altered in 1896, at the instigation of Grand Duchess Adelaide Marie (1833–1916), born Princess of Anhalt-Dessau, second wife of Grand Duke Adolf I. The jeweller Koch of Frankfurt took out 12 large diamonds to include them in a new rivière with stones from the pendants. He replaced them in the bouquets with yokes comprising a total of 97 small diamonds, probably taken from the ivy leaves of the pendants. There is a distinct difference of technique between the piece as a whole and the centre of the buds, replaced in 1896. While the original piece has an open mount, the centres are set in boxes closed at the back. The boxes were then soldered into the cavities left when the large diamonds were removed. These brooches are splendid examples of the fashion for the naturalistic style and also recall the large corsage rose of Princess Mathilde, which was made in the same period. The brooches are kept in their original cases of dark blue velvet, with the monogram c surmounted by a crown. The same monogram can be seen on the cases of the large tiara and of the two bracelets, which date from 1812. The cover of the inventory of 1859 has the same design. As the inventories of the 'Hausschmuck' (family jewels) were kept in the 'Chatoulle' (safe), it is highly likely that the monogram c stands for 'Chatoulle', signifying that these pieces belong to House of Nassau-Weilburg trust. The 'Hausschmuck', or jewellery of the Nassau-Weilburg family, was established in 1766 at the instigation of Prince Karl-Christian (1735–1788) and his wife Carolina of Orange-Nassau-Dietz (1743–1787). They used part of their jewellery to establish a collection to be held in trust and bequeathed from one head of the family to the next, as stipulated in the family 'Erbvertrag' or contract. The trust jewellery can be transformed to suit the tastes of the day but, unlike personal jewellery, can never be sold or given away. All the women's jewellery belonging to the house of Nassau was thus taken apart in 1812 to create new pieces, almost certainly in preparation for the wedding of Crown Prince Wilhelm of Nassau (1792–1839)

248

and Princess Louise of Saxe-Hildburghausen (1794–1825). The older pieces that have been preserved date from this transformation enshrined in the inventory of May 1813. Pieces were later modified in 1829 for Wilhelm's second marriage to Pauline of Wurttemberg (1810–1856) and again in 1859, during the reign of Duke Adolf (1817–1905), who was Grand Duke of Luxembourg from 1890 to his death. The twentieth century has seen the collection enhanced with pieces set with coloured stones, acquired either by legacy, purchase or transformation. The last great phase of transformations and new creations occurred in the 1970s. MP

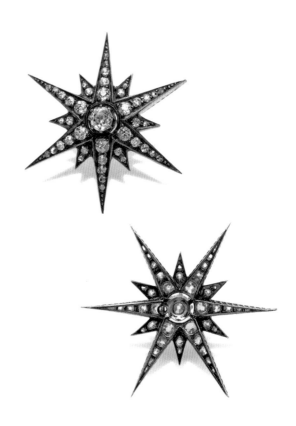

> ### Portrait of Empress Elisabeth of Austria
Recent copy by Anton Mag. Sever after Franz Xaver Winterhalter,
1865 (original painting)
Oil on canvas, 269.5 x 163 cm
Vienna, Museen des Mobiliendepots (inv. MD 068306)

Famous throughout Europe for his graceful brushwork, Franz Xaver Winterhalter was called to the Viennese court by Emperor Francis Joseph to paint the portrait of his wife Empress Elisabeth (1837–1898). Born a duchess in Bavaria, Elisabeth had married Francis Joseph, her first cousin, in 1854. In addition to two more intimate portraits showing Elisabeth with her hair loose and falling to her waist, the artist also painted the celebrated full-length portrait that is still on display at the Hofburg Imperial Palace in Vienna. The slender, bare-shouldered empress – set off by the stormy landscape in the background – is dressed in a spectacular crinoline of sequinned tulle embroidered with silver stars by the Paris designer Charles Frederick Worth. Elisabeth's lady-in-waiting, Fanny Angerer, formerly hairdresser at the Burgtheater, designed the spectacular crown hairstyle that we see here, which the empress studded with stars made by Viennese jeweller Alexander Emanuel Köchert. In 1862 he supplied her with twenty-seven such pieces.

The star was one of the most popular motifs of nineteenth-century jewellery and attracted many sovereigns, who commissioned complete sets to wear as hair ornaments, brooches, corsages and tiaras. Queen Alexandra, wife of Edward VII, owned a set of diamonds similar to those of the French crown jewels. Princess Victoria of Hesse, one of Queen Victoria's grandchildren, wore stars set with a central pearl, while Isabella II's daughter, the Infanta Eulalia, had rubies at the centre of her stars. The Spanish Queen also acquired a complete star parure from the Paris jeweller Mellerio, indicating that stars were popular as early as 1850. CV

BIBLIOGRAPHY : London 1987, pp. 153, 217 ; Stockholm 2000, p. 117 ; Tokyo 2003b, pp. 153, 265.

Star brooches
France (?), c. 1860
Gold, silver and diamonds, 50 mm each
Edmond Rochtus Collection

Each star comprises a central diamond from which radiate twelve points, alternately long and short, set with small eight-facet diamonds. Stars such as these were worn as brooches but could equally well be fixed to a tiara. Initially five-pointed, they became a popular element in women's jewellery in the mid-nineteenth century and soon acquired up to sixteen points. Among the best-known star parures is that of Queen Maria Pia of Portugal (1847–1911) created by the jeweller Estevão de Sousa between 1862 and 1866. This particularly impressive set included a tiara of twenty-five, five-point stars, a necklace of eighteen stars, a stomacher with nineteen stars, two stars at the shoulders, a large star brooch, sixteen star clips, a long bracelet of twenty stars, earrings and a comb decorated with five stars. Thus adorned for the ball, the Queen could outshine even the starriest night. Indeed, when she opened the ball at the Ajuda Palace in honour of the visit of the Prince of Wales in 1876, journalists observed, 'the queen was dressed in the national colours of white and blue. The edge of her train was entirely embroidered with stars and stars made of diamonds were sewn on the *bouillonnés* of her dress. Her hair was also dressed with stars

and her chignon with a star tiara.' Other famous examples of star jewellery include the impressive tiara with two rows of stars belonging to the grand duchesses of Oldenburg, which was only worn on ceremonial occasions, the stars worn by Empress Elisabeth in her portrait of 1865 by Franz Xaver Winterhalter and the star jewellery of Amelia of Portugal and the Empress Eugenie. We do not know whether these sovereigns were aware that in the Revelation of Saint John the head of the woman who appears in the heavens is crowned with twelve stars symbolizing the signs of the zodiac. CV

BIBLIOGRAPHY : Lisbon 1992, pp. 64–7 ; Morel 1998, pp. 344, 366 ; Stockholm 2000, p. 117 ; Tokyo 2003b, VI–10, VI–19.

Nine stars from a tiara

Garrard, London, c. 1870

Gold, silver and diamonds, 63 x 190 x 145 mm

Private collection, courtesy Albion Art Jewellery Institute, Tokyo

Worn on a tiara, the nine diamond stars would be set on the frame, arranged in two groups of four on either side of the larger central star. The twelve pointed rays of each star are set in two layers, alternately short and long. All-white diamond stars were versatile as they could be worn with dresses of every colour as well as white and black. Besides being worn as a set on the tiara, they could be detached and worn separately as brooches or fixed on hairpins for less formal occasions. Worn as a tiara, the diamonds blazing out from the stars, the wearer would appreciate the additional height and brilliance and feel like the queen of the night. DSC

> ## Star tiara

Mid-19th century

Gold, silver, rubies and diamonds, 58 x 146 x 105 mm

Private collection, courtesy Albion Art Jewellery Institute, Tokyo

Decorated with rubies and diamonds, this tiara comprises an openwork bandeau filled with leaves and flowers buds centred on a twelve-point star. The bandeau is set between diamond borders and surmounted by nine more stars, four to each side of the largest in the centre, with rubies and diamonds between them. Each star has a ruby in its centre and the inner group of six rays is set with diamonds, those outside with rubies, considered to flatter blonde hair. The star, so well suited to the display of diamonds, was one of the most popular motifs in jewellery during the second half of the nineteenth century. Flowers were also popular, and both are combined in this attractive design. The fashion for stars was due principally to Empress Elisabeth of Austria who was painted by Franz Xaver Winterhalter in 1865 at the height of her youthful beauty and with diamond stars set off by her chestnut hair. DSC

Bracelet of Empress Elisabeth of Austria

Germany, bearing the mark WAZ, with an Austrian importation mark for the year 1867–8 and a French importation mark of 1893 for the gold and silver, c. 1845–55

Gold, silver, diamonds, enamel and rubies, 200 mm

Private collection

This remarkable heraldic bracelet was a wedding gift to Empress Elisabeth (1837–1898) on her marriage to Emperor Francis Joseph in 1854. The large imperial crest at the centre of the composition is flanked by sixteen escutcheons representing provinces of the empire. They are arranged in double rows of four and surrounded by laurel garlands. The presence of the arms of Lombardy-Veneto, a province lost by the emperor in 1859 during his war with France and Sardinia, confirms the period when the bracelet was made. The jeweller chose to use only paved rose-cut diamonds. The foil backing to the stones is coloured with pink, pale green and blue powder, and with gold and silver. The laurel garlands by the clasp end in a cabochon ruby. The detailed work of the piece makes it easy to identify the provinces represented. To the left of the large imperial arms, from right to left and top to bottom, are the arms of the provinces of Carniola, Transylvania, Slavonia, Hungary, Tyrol, Illyria, Croatia and Dalmatia. To the right, in the same order, are the arms of the provinces of Lombardy-Veneto, Salzburg, Galicia, Silesia, Bohemia, Lower Austria, Carinthia-Styria and Moravia. In the centre is the double-headed eagle sable on a gold ground, emblem of the empire, crested by the tripartite arms of the Habsburgs surrounded by the great collar of the Order of the Golden Fleece: in 1, for the County of Habsburg: or, a lion rampant gules armed langued and crowned azure; in 2, for Austria: gules a fess argent; in 3, for Lorraine: or on a bend gules three allerions argent.

This highly symbolic bracelet asserts Habsburg supremacy over all the selected provinces. The empress rejoiced in an impressive set of titles, notably Queen of Hungary, Bohemia, Dalmatia, Croatia, Esclavonia, Galicia, Lodomeria, Illyria and Jerusalem; Grand Duchess of Tuscany and Cracovia; Duchess of Lorraine, Salzburg, Styria, Carinthia, Carniola and Bucovina; Grand Duchess of Transylvania; Margravine of Moravia; Duchess of Upper and Lower Silesia, Parma, Piacenza, Modena, Guastalla, Auschwitz, Zator, Friuli, Ragusa and Zara; Princely Countess of Habsburg, Tyrol, Kyburg, Göritz and Gradisca; Princess of Trient and Brixen; Margravine of Istria and of Upper and Lower Lusatia; Countess of Hohenhems, Feldkirch, Bregenz and Sonnenberg; Lady of Trieste, Cattaro and the Wendish Mark; Grand Voyvode of Serbia… and so on. CV

Historic replica of the Habsburg regalia

Emperor Rudolph's crown: 1835, metal and glass, 310 x 300 mm

Saint Stephen's crown: E. Krahl, 1792, wood and metal, 210 x 200 mm

Sceptre: gilded turned wood, 490 x 40 mm

Orb: brass and glass, 175 x 110 mm

Vienna, Bundesmobilienverwaltung-Hofmobiliendepot Möbel Museum

Over the past few centuries many countries adopted the tradition of the public lying-in-state for a deceased monarch. The regalia served as the symbol of royal dignity. Some monarchies, however, used replicas. The monetary value of these funerary crowns obviously bears no relation to the worth of the real thing. The Austrians had faithful copies made of two crowns. The Habsburgs were the emperors of the Holy Roman Empire and of Austria, and were also kings of Hungary and Bohemia. The crowns of these two kingdoms, Saint Stephen's crown and King Wenceslaus's crown, were not kept in the treasury in Vienna and so they were not readily available for the funeral of a Habsburg monarch.

In 1792 it was decided to have an accurate copy of the Hungarian royal crown made for the funeral of Emperor Leopold II. For the funeral of Emperor Francis I in 1835, a replica was produced of Emperor Rudolph II's crown (1604), which had meanwhile become the symbol of the Austrian empire. In 1916 these replicas graced the coffin of Emperor Francis Joseph. PD

Bracelet with swan motifs

Germany (?), third quarter of the 19th century

Gold, silver, diamonds, rubies and sapphires, 45 x 65 x 63 mm

Edmond Rochtus Collection

An open rococo cartouche with the heads of two winged angels forms the central element of a triple bracelet in gold. The cartouche is decorated with several diamonds and three rows of high-set sapphires. On either side a swan with curved neck and a ruby for its eye stands on a flower stem in silver. As well as elegance, nobility and courage, the swan also symbolizes the power of poetry and serenity in the face of death, hence the term 'swansong'. In this particular case the swan is a reference to the romantic King Ludwig II of Bavaria (1845–1886), whose favourite motif it was. He gave this bracelet as a gift to the court actress Hermine Bland-Steiner. JW

BIBLIOGRAPHY : Antwerp 1968, no. 287 ; Westkunst 1989 ; Antwerp 1995, no. 135 ; Tokyo 2003b, no. VII–12.

Fob watch with portraits of the Emperor and Empress of Austria

Watch : James Moore French, London, c. 1854

Gold and enamel, 49 x 16 mm

On permanent loan to the Sparkassenstiftung Pforzheim au Schmuckmuseum Pforzheim, coll. Ph. Weber (inv. 30776)

The front and back of the case show head and shoulder portrait miniatures of the Emperor Francis Joseph and Empress Elisabeth in their wedding clothes. They were married in 1854 and regarded as an ideal couple. A great many depictions of the young lovers were distributed throughout the world on objects of all kinds, including watches, vases and dishes. In reality the young emperor, born in 1830 and crowned in 1848, very much needed to improve his image as the early years of his reign had been troubled and marked by many unfortunate decisions on his part. The empress, the celebrated Sissi, soon distanced herself from life at court and spent her time travelling and practising sports. Her rebellious nature earned her the sympathy of the people and later tragedies raised her to iconic status. Her only son, Crown Prince Rudolf, killed himself in 1889 over an impossible love affair, while she herself was murdered in Geneva in 1898. Today Sissi plays an important posthumous role in tourism in Austria. JW

BIBLIOGRAPHY : Thomas/Leiter 1999, pp. 186–7 ; Antwerp 1999, no. 215.

The European monarchies in splendour

CHRISTOPHE VACHAUDEZ

In the mid-nineteenth century Europe enjoyed a period of peace and prosperity, which further heightened the prestige of its kingdoms and former principalities. In the same period the Industrial Revolution saw the emergence of new social classes and indirectly favoured the aristocracy, who were able to perpetuate their own art of living with panache.

In Britain this period of opulence, marked by progress and creativity, coincided with the Victorian era. Queen Victoria succeeded Georges IV in 1837. She was only eighteen years old and had spent little time at the magnificent court of her uncle, a knowledgeable aesthete who did not care how much he spent, to the dismay of his horrified Chancellor of the Exchequer. His commissions from London jewellers filled entire pages of their great bound ledgers. On acceding to the throne, the young Victoria inherited a collection that was certainly large, but not terribly spectacular, since it was suspected that the jewellery cases of the duchesses of Buccleuch, Bedford and Sutherland contained far finer pieces.[1] Moreover, a significant proportion of these jewels, bequeathed to the House of Hanover by Queen Charlotte, wife of George III, had been claimed by Victoria's uncle Ernest, King of Hanover. The matter was not resolved until nearly twenty years later when, in 1858, the Count of Kielmansegge was given the task of repatriating some pieces to Germany. Although the intrinsic value of Queen Charlotte's nuptial crown, stomacher, rivière and diamond cross was far from negligible, the disputed pieces also had a symbolic value that rendered resolution of the conflict still more difficult.

Queen Victoria was not much interested in her dress ; however, she was always ready to wear jewellery when her duties as monarch required it. In 1840 she married one of her cousins, Albert of Saxe-Coburg-Gotha, and the situation changed somewhat. In addition to making architectural sketches the prince, who was interested in sciences and many artistic disciplines, also designed the jewellery that he was in the habit of giving to his wife. So these pieces gained an additional dimension in the Queen's eyes and she wore them with new enthusiasm. Victoria's reign also marks the height of sentimental jewellery which, in this case, was designed by the beloved, but which, more generally speaking, recalls a dear one through an inscription, miniature or some symbolic element. As the mother of nine children, the Queen had no trouble perpetuating this practice with gifts of bracelets, rings and pendants decorated with portraits or locks of hair to her many relations. The Saxe-Coburgs, who colonized many European thrones, passed on the fashion, already well established in the Orleans family, where Louis Philippe and Marie Amelia were constantly commissioning items of commemorative jewellery.

However, it should be noted that Prince Albert also designed magnificent gala parures, set with opals, rubies, turquoises, sapphires and diamonds, which enhanced the royal treasure. There is no lack of references to the creations of 'Dearest Albert' in the Queen's abundant correspondence. Jewellers such as Hancock, Garrard, Hennell, Hunt and Roskell, and Howell James were certainly not complaining. Moreover, the grand style remained in favour with the kingdom's rich and powerful, who bought quantities of new jewellery or had older pieces adapted to the tastes of the day. Meanwhile the Prince Consort was making innovatory use of oriental motifs, combining fleurs-de-lis and fans in a tiara designed for his eldest daughter, and based his design of a coronet of sapphires and diamonds for his wife on a chignon ornament worn by Queen Henrietta Maria, wife of Charles I, in a painting by Anthony van Dyck. In the early 1840s he also designed an orange branch in porcelain, which the queen wore with earrings.

In this he was in step with the naturalist style, whose success was at its peak at the time that Hunt and Roskell presented their celebrated bouquet of diamonds at the Great Exhibition of 1851. While the neo-gothic style can be seen in the design of some pieces, such as the diamond tiara given by Queen Victoria to her daughter Alice in 1862 for her wedding to the Grand Duke of Hesse, the jeweller Hancock brought enamel back into prominence, using it in his design for pieces in the neo-Renaissance style, worthy of those painted by Hans Holbein. The

257

< George Hayter, *The Coronation of Queen Victoria*, 1838 (detail).

The Mellerio stand at the Exposition Universelle of 1867 including the laurel-leaf tiara of Queen Margherita of Italy (see p. 272).

< Queen Alexandra, wife of King Edward VII, wearing a tiara made for her wedding and a dress decorated with stars.

parure he created in 1856 for Lady Granville, niece of the sixth Duke of Devonshire who, with her husband, was to represent Queen Victoria at the coronation of Tsar Alexander II, is spectacular. In its originality it was specifically designed to eclipse the torrents of diamonds worn by the Russian grand duchesses. Hancock used pieces from the family's collection of antique cameos and intaglios and set them in an ensemble comprising seven pieces in gold enhanced with diamonds and motifs in red, green and blue enamel, which echo the colours of the engraved stones. The whole offers a marvellous illustration of the stylistic eclecticism reigning in the second half of the nineteenth century.

Queen Victoria was terribly affected by her husband's death in 1861 and took the court with her into an endless period of mourning, during which the royal jewels were piously placed back in their boxes. For a time the diamond fringe tiara of 1830 based on the traditional headdress of Russian peasant women, Prince Albert's sapphire brooch, the large necklace given to the queen by the Sultan of Turkey and the gifts from the Maharajas all disappeared.

Across the Channel the July Monarchy was over and King Louis Philippe and Queen Marie Amelia were suffering the torments of exile. They had just sought refuge in Britain, at the Claremont Estate, which their son-in-law, King Leopold I, had placed at their disposal. In 1848 the nephew of Napoleon Bonaparte and grandson of Josephine de Beauharnais was elected President of the Republic and, on 2 December 1852, reinstated the Empire, reigning as Napoleon III. Like his uncle, he understood that a resplendent court would earn him a degree of prestige in the eyes of the other powers and that for this he needed to marry as quickly as possible. On 30 January 1853, in Notre-Dame, Paris, he exchanged vows with a twenty-seven-year-old Spanish aristocrat by the name of Eugenia de Montijo de Guzmán. The fortunate lady was a mere countess, but the emperor gave a simple justification for his marriage – strongly criticized by his family : 'Royal marriages create a false sense of security. One does not become accepted by ageing one's crest and seeking at all costs to enter a family of kings.'[2] The empress was to prove his trump card when it came to seducing the monarchs of Europe and fully re-establishing Paris in its role as capital of the arts and good taste. Describing Eugenie in a letter of 1 May 1855 to her uncle King Leopold, Queen Victoria wrote, 'it is not such a great beauty, but such grace, elegance, sweetness, and nature. Her manners are charming ; the profile and figure beautiful and particularly *distingués*.'[3]

Fortunately, Eugenie had a real interest in jewellery, to the delight of the French designers. The crown jewels that Queen Marie Amelia had always refused to wear were exhumed from their cases and presented to the Empress. For Napoleon III, wearing jewellery laden with history helped legitimize his position. Eugenie loved the perfection of the parures of rubies, sapphires, turquoises and diamonds made by Menière, Evrard and Frédéric Bapst for the Duchess of Angoulême, and decided to preserve them intact, as she did the tiara of the emerald parure ; but she chose to have the pearl and diamond parures remodelled. She entrusted this delicate task to a series of tried and tested jewellers, who worked on the above-mentioned pieces as well as a large collection of precious stones from the

Wedding of the future Emperor Charles I and Princess Zita Bourbon-Parma at Schwarzau, 21 October 1911.

crown of Charles x, royal ornaments and jewellery formerly placed at the disposal of the king and dauphin. Viette were asked to incorporate the magnificent Regent diamond into the design for a tiara. Jewellers Marret and Baugrand created a diamond comb to be worn behind the chignon, while Kramer produced a large belt of precious stones and a corsage bow to which two pendant stones were attached. Meanwhile Théodore Fester designed the great corsage bouquet in 1855 and Gabriel Lemonnier was commissioned to create the pearl tiara. However, the Bapst jewellers distinguished themselves with the great currant-leaf parure, the shoulder bows, the tiara in the Greek style, the diamond needle tiara, the coiffure balls, the briar roses and the stars that the empress wanted as part of her coiffure.[4] Fontenay, Mellerio, Rouvenat, Froment-Meurice and Oscar Massin complete the long list of jewellers who supplied the court and participated with great success in the Expositions Universelles mounted in Paris (1855, 1867) and Vienna (1873).

During this time there was a constant stream of parties at the Tuileries, Saint-Cloud, Fontainebleau and Compiègne, where Eugenie established her famous 'series'. As the portraits by Franz Xaver Winterhalter amply show, the crinoline held sway and pearls were worn in long sautoirs, either around the neck or casually draped into a bracelet at the wrist. They were now more highly prized than the diamonds that had flooded the market

since 1867 as a result of intensive mining in South Africa. The Second Empire shows an extraordinary patchwork of styles. The empress, who admired Marie Antoinette, favoured the ornamental motifs that had been in vogue during the reign of Louis xvi, and doves, ribbons, flowers and seashells reappeared. But at the same time the neo-gothic style, well served by the talents of Viollet-le-Duc, also found favour with Eugenie, who was overseeing the renovation of the Château de Pierrefonds and was similarly interested in the trends for a return to the virtues of antiquity. Napoleon iii's acquisition of the Campana collection in 1861 almost certainly influenced the enthusiasm that gripped Paris and found concrete expression in a return to prominence of palmettes, Greek frets and laurel leaves.

However, all these trends were royally supplanted by naturalism. Flowers were mounted so that they trembled, a process patented by Mellerio in 1854, further increasing the realism of compositions in perfect imitation of the humblest plant or bloom. The passion for corsages led jewellers to create striking leafy garlands that so covered bodices as to create something akin to naturalist breastplates; or else they would simply highlight the décolleté, dotted with pendant stones, insects and rosebuds. The empress set the fashion for this style, exemplified by the magnificent diamond currant-leaf parure, the large bouquet of crown jewels and an elegant lilac flower from the workshops of Léon Rouvenat for her corsage. Meanwhile the emperor's first cousin, Princess Mathilde, liked to wear a gigantic rose in Brazilian diamonds pinned to her bodice and a diamond-studded imperial eagle in her hair. For jewellery had lost nothing of its symbolic nature and those close to the emperor were quick to display their political obedience. Similarly, the choice of plants used was not always insignificant. It might evoke a heraldic feature, an important event or, like the emerald trefoil given to Eugenie by Napoleon III, express a feeling. Feathers, too, seduced queens and elegant aristocrats to such an extent that, for her silver wedding anniversary the Belgian Queen Marie Henrietta, wife of Leopold II, received from the ladies of Belgium a tiara of jointed ostrich feathers entirely studded with diamonds.

Not content with having the crown jewels at her disposal, the empress also built up an impressive personal collection, which she took with her into exile, hastily packed into cases with newspaper. Princess Mathilde also owned some remarkable pieces, including a unique set of black and grey pearls. As Frédéric Masson of the Académie Française observes, 'Her jewellery chest seemed inexhaustible; she might take out, for example, her seven-string pearl necklace, her black pearl necklace, the three-string pearl necklace that the Emperor Napoleon had given to the Queen of Westphalia on her wedding day, the diamond rivière with huge stones, the diamond necklace with uncommonly fine settings, or the imperial diadem that sat so well on her head. Always the piece was priceless and of such powerful beauty as to defy all competition.'5 The truth of these words could be verified by the connoisseurs jostling for a place at the auction of the princess's jewels held in Paris in 1904.

In Italy, Queen Margherita had a passion for the accumulation of pearls. Some of the strings she bought were long enough to reach her knees. The sovereign performed her role to the full, since the House of Savoy, which had ruled a large part of the Italian peninsula only since 1861, had to assert its supremacy. Designed by the jewellers Musy of Turin, Mellerio and Boucheron of Paris and Hancock of London, the magnificent pieces worn by the wife of King Umberto I had the desired effect.

In Vienna, the Habsburg Empire was still at the height of its brilliance. The city was the centre of a vast empire ruled with an iron hand by Francis Joseph I, who ascended to the throne in 1848. In 1854 he married his first cousin Elisabeth, Duchess of Bavaria. The empress was radiantly beautiful and admired by all, however her unstable character often took her away from the capital, where she was liked by few. When she was there, she sometimes went to balls and the other official ceremonies held at court, which provided her with an opportunity to wear the great parures of the ancestral treasury. Certain major houses supplied a cohort of archdukes and archduchesses, as well as the many famous families who gravitated around the imperial house. Biedermann, Hübner and most of all Köchert, to name but a few, gave Viennese jewellery its glory. For the empress Köchert notably redesigned the emerald and ruby parures, the latter having come directly from Marie Antoinette through her daughter the Duchess of Angoulême. He also made a series of diamond stars for Elisabeth who, by wearing them in her portrait by Winterhalter, made them popular throughout Europe.

While Britain and Austria were enjoying a degree of stability, the same could not be said of Spain, where Isabella II was deposed in 1868, a victim of her own goodness and inexperience. She fled to Paris and saw her meagre resources melt away like snow in sunlight. Her only remaining option was to sell her jewellery collection, known to be one of the finest in Europe. It took several days to exhaust the royal coffers filled with emeralds, topazes, sapphires, aquamarines and diamonds. Her mother, Queen Maria Christina, followed suit a few months later. Jewellery was easy to transport and bore witness to the magnificent days of a reign, so could prove very useful to monarchs who had lost their money. It became a providential currency, as it had been in more distant days when it was exchanged for hostages or sold to finance a war, a crusade or an expedition.

Many Russian grand dukes, driven out by the Bolshevik revolution, would also have to part from their precious pieces. But for the time being a different wind was blowing through the newspaper columns, whose writers found it hard to grasp the aims of a newly fledged government. Meanwhile, the crown jewels of France, having been evacuated to Brest during the Commune and put on public display from 1878 to 1884, were auctioned in May 1887, following the passing of the Law of Alienation. This dispersal did not reflect a real need to generate cash, but was a political manoeuvre intended to counteract any idea that the monarchy could be restored. The Third Republic was still taking its first steps and wanted to reinforce its position. The sale dealt a fatal blow to the supporters of royalty, of whom there were still many. Nevertheless, despite the fall of the Second Empire and this disastrous sale, which continued to distress the upper echelons of the jewellery world, Paris retained its creative supremacy.

In the absence of a royal court, habits were maintained to varying degrees, but necklaces, bracelets and tiaras were still worn in profusion. Boucheron, Mellerio, Cartier and Chaumet shared a cosmopolitan, international clientele. The American industrialists and millionaires who eagerly crossed the Atlantic to soak up the culture of the Old Continent also favoured the arts of luxury, buying mainly from Boucheron and Cartier. The opulence of the parures they commissioned gave them an ostentatious means to proclaim their success. They were able to penetrate the very closed world of the aristocracy, who were prepared to accept marriages of convenience for a bit of ready cash. So the Duke of Marlborough married Consuelo Vanderbilt and May Goelet married the Duke of Roxburghe. In Britain the

Ghetta Carell
Roma

262

colourful Prince of Wales, who had been waiting for years to accede to the throne, wiled away his time with lively parties. Meanwhile his very beautiful wife, born Princess Alexandra of Denmark, cultivated an extreme elegance. Slender, svelte and glittering with jewels, she made a striking contrast with Queen Victoria, who was small, dumpy and dressed all in black. The Princess of Wales, who set a fashion for chokers in order to hide a scar on her neck, wore jewellery in abundance. She took an active part in the social life of the country, long abandoned by her mother-in-law. Fancy-dress balls were a great success and duchesses were forever having their parures taken to pieces so that they could be adapted to the most original costumes, as Empress Maria Theresa rubbed shoulders with Cleopatra and Elizabeth I.

This festive world wanted to glitter and did not count the number of pieces it bought. The tiara was the most important element in the parure. It was more successful than ever and regarded as the epitome of elegance, whether in the form of a waterfall, a seashell, a bouquet of fuchsias or outstretched wings. Imbued with powerful symbolism, tiaras were associated with the prestigious ceremonies and great events of royal life, and continued to entice a world in the throes of transformation, as the perpetuation of a tradition to which the European monarchies were frantically clinging. If the First World War was to be the swan song of monarchical Europe, for the moment there was no hint of the upheavals to come. On the contrary, the ceremonies had never been more splendid. The year 1893 saw the weddings of both Maria of Saxe-Coburg-Gotha and the future King Ferdinand of Romania and the future George V and Princess Mary of Teck. In 1894 it was the turn of the Tsarevich Nicholas, who married Princess Alix of Hesse, and Princess Victoria-Eugenia of Battenberg, who married King Alfonso XIII of Spain, while Prince George of Greece married Princess Marie Bonaparte in 1907. The wedding presents were put on display and brought great delight to the populace, who spent hours filing past closely monitored glass cases to admire the riot of pieces set with the rarest precious stones.

The grand style was compulsory among the monarchies. They had little taste for Art Nouveau, which produced jewellery that was far too simple either to satisfy their taste for luxury and ostentation, or to represent royal dignity in the proper manner. Cartier was dubbed 'jeweller of kings and king of jewellers' by King Edward VII and acquired a solid reputation. He spread the use of platinum and established the garland style, a return of the decorative motif from the Louis XVI period, now applied

to jewellery. Soon Cartier was supplying the courts of Spain, Belgium, Britain, Yugoslavia, Romania and Monaco. However King William III of the Netherlands preferred Mellerio, who created a complete parure that is still worn today by Queen Beatrix. The great receptions of the aristocracy continued apace, with celebrations in which princesses, archduchesses and queens competed in their choice of parures, from the coronation of King George V to the wedding of Princess Zita of Bourbon-Parma and the Archduke Charles, future emperor of Austria in 1911, or that of the Kaiser's daughter Princess Victoria-Louise to the Duke of Brunswick in 1913. Their jewellery proclaimed loud and clear the power, wealth and dignity of those who wore it. When the Austro-Hungarian Empire fell in 1918, the crown jewels mysteriously disappeared, as though their fate were tied to that of the fallen sovereigns.

Some great families suffered radical change after the First World War and sold a proportion of their jewels. However the European courts soon returned to their former splendour, as proved by the magnificence of the wedding of Princess Astrid of Sweden to Leopold, Duke of Brabant and future king of the Belgians, doubly celebrated in Stockholm and Brussels in 1926. As in the other Nordic monarchies, which were very attached to tradition, the wedding ceremonies were lengthy and full of pomp. Every lady invited had to wear a tiara. The wedding of Princess Marie-José of Belgium to Prince Umberto of Piedmont, future king of Italy, in 1930, was conducted in accordance with the same requirements and brought its share of trouble. One of those invited, Leopold II's daughter Princess Clementine, was greatly amazed to find that guests were expected to bring sixteen different outfits, all of which required jewellery to match. The princess was obliged to make a hasty appeal to her sister to help her assemble the necessary pieces.[6] Times have changed, but the wearing of jewellery, so crucial to the monarchical system, continues in style in the courts of the Old Continent, triumphantly proving its importance in the public imagination and its essential role in the expression of power and hierarchy.

1. Field 1987, p. 9.
2. Dufresne 1986, p. 46.
3. Letters 1908, vol. III, p. 122.
4. Morel 1988, pp. 334–50.
5. Morel 1988, p. 357.
6. Vachaudez 2004, p. 72.

< Queen Marie-José of Italy, born Princess of Belgium,
wearing the jewels of the House of Savoy.

Portrait of Queen Theresa of Bavaria

Julie Gräfin von Egloffstein (1792–1869), 1836
Oil on canvas, 135 x 103.5 cm
Munich, Wittelsbacher Ausgleichfonds, (inv. WAF B I a242)

Queen Theresa (1792–1854), wife of Ludwig I of Bavaria, born Princess of Saxe-Hildburghausen, is wearing a pearl necklace with matching earrings and a pearl and diamond tiara which is now in the Treasury of the Residenz, Munich. The queen wears her hair in the fashionable Parisian style and is dressed in a red velvet gown with ermine edges to the sleeves. Bird of paradise feathers and a cashmere shawl complete her magnificent gala attire. The tiara seems to have been placed at the disposal of Amalia, wife of King Otto I of Greece, who was the son of Ludwig I and Queen Theresa. She wears it in several portraits, including a full-length painting by Carl Rahl, now on display at the Residenz, Bamberg. **CV**

Tiara of Queen Theresa of Bavaria

Attributed to Caspar Rieländer, Munich, c. 1825
Gold, silver, pearls and brilliants, 65 x 180 x 100 mm
Munich, Bayerische Verwaltung der staatlichen Schlösser,
Gärten und Seen, Residenz München, Schatzkammer
(inv. Res. Mü. Schk 252 WAF)

This tiara, now preserved in the treasury of the Munich Residenz, comes from the collection of Queen Theresa of Bavaria (1792–1854), wife of King Ludwig I. It was probably created in the workshops of Munich jeweller Caspar Rieländer. The piece is generally believed to have been completed in 1825, a date which would coincide with the Bavarian sovereigns' accession to the throne. The tiara is composed of sixteen diamond arches, each of which houses a drop pearl mounted *en tremblant* on an elegant 'love knot' in turn topped by a drop pearl in a fleuron mounting. The queen presented the tiara to her daughter-in-law, Princess Amalia (1818–1875), wife of Prince Otto of Bavaria, who was also briefly King of Greece. The tiara was then passed on to Prince Rupert, who gave it to his wife, Princess Antonia of Luxembourg. She was the last member of the family to wear it before it joined the permanent collections of the Residenz.

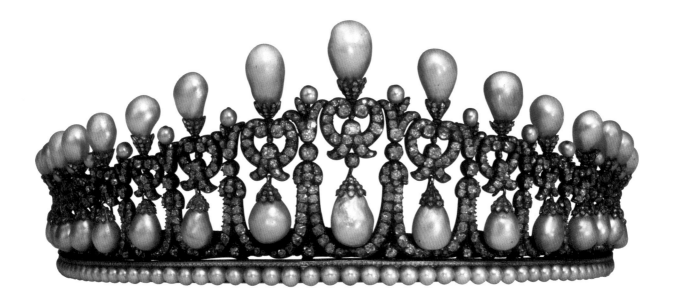

The design as we know it was particularly popular and many copies of it are listed in the *Almanach de Gotha*. A similar tiara was part of the trousseau of Princess Augusta of Hesse-Cassel (1797–1889) who in 1818 married the Duke of Cambridge, an uncle of Queen Victoria. The new duchess wore this tiara to her niece's coronation in Westminster Abbey. The piece was later passed on to her daughter Augusta Caroline (1822–1916), who had become Grand Duchess of Mecklenburg-Strelitz through marriage. It remained in the family until 1981, at which time it was put up for auction. It seems that it was purchased by the Princess of Waldburg-Zeil, born Princess Gabrielle (1931) of Bavaria, a direct descendant of Queen Theresa. Queen Mary of Great Britain (1867–1918), who greatly admired her Aunt Augusta Caroline's tiara, had a copy made in London by the jeweller Garrard in 1914. Still conserved in the royal collections of Great Britain, the piece regained its former fame after Queen Elizabeth loaned it to the Princess of Wales, who wore it quite often, though without its upper row of drop pearls. Other tiaras identical to the one at the Residenz have been counted among collections belonging to the princes of Yussupov and Württemberg, and the maharajahs of Patiala. **cv**

BIBLIOGRAPHY : Twining 1960, p. 37, pl. 28a ; Munich 1970 ;
Marquardt 1983 ; von Roda 1983, pp. 68–74 ; Seelig 1987, pp. 46–57 ;
Field 1987, pp. 113–15 ; Fuchs 1996, pp. 1853–7 ; Munich 1999 ;
Stockholm 2000, pp. 100–1 ; Munn 2001, pp. 134–5.

< **Portrait of Queen Amalia of Greece**
Joseph Stieler (1781–1858), 1836/7
Oil on canvas, 74 x 60 cm
Munich, Wittelsbacher Ausgleichfonds, (inv. WAF B I a286)

Painted around the time of her marriage by Joseph Stieler – painter of the so-called 'Gallery of Beauties' at the court of Bavaria – Princess Amalia of Oldenburg (1818–1875), eldest daughter of Grand Duke Augustus, is wearing a large floral tiara, a chaton rivière and very large, long pendant earrings whose shape recalls those of the Queen Theresa's ruby parure in the Treasury of the Residenz, Munich. The tiara, sold at Christie's in 1931, formerly rested on a lattice structure decorated with briolettes, which still exists and is now part of the jewels of the house of Bavaria. The set was created in Paris in 1817 by the jeweller Borgeois and later adapted, at the request of King Ludwig I, by court jeweller Kaspar Rieländer. Princess Amalia married Otton of Bavaria in 1836, thereby becoming Queen of Greece. The prince had acceded to the Greek throne in 1832 and was maintained there, not without some difficulty, until 1862. The exiled monarchs went to Bavaria, where they took up residence in the Bamberg Palace. The tiara remained in the house of the Wittelsbachs and was notably worn in this form by the sister of Queen Elisabeth of Belgium, Duchess Marie Gabrielle in Bavaria, on her wedding day. **cv**

Tiara of Archduchess Isabella of Austria

Köchert, Vienna, 1825–30

Gold, silver, diamonds and peridots, 85 x 200 x 160 mm

Tokyo, Albion Art Collection

This tiara is composed of a succession of seven scrolls with a leaf design, each encircling a cushion-cut peridot held in place by claw settings. It was part of a complete parure, which, according to custom, was designed by imperial jeweller Köchert in Vienna for Princess Henrietta of Nassau-Weilburg, wife of Duke Charles of Teschen (1771–1847). The suite was passed on to their son, Archduke Charles-Ferdinand (1818–1874), who married a sister of Marie Henrietta, Queen of the Belgians, and then to

his son, Archduke Frederick, Duke of Teschen (1856–1936), who gave it to his wife Isabella (1856–1931), born Princess of Croÿ. The archduchess, who had eight children, wore the parure to the coronation of Emperor Charles I as King of Hungary in 1916. She had a strong character and one of the most beautiful jewellery collections in the imperial family. In April 1937, one year after the death of Archduke Frederick, the tiara, necklace, brooch, earrings and two stomachers from the parure were put up for sale at the Dorotheum in Vienna. Count John of Coudenhove-Kalergi bought them and left the jewellery to his daughter, Countess Maria, who settled in California. After her death, the pieces were found wrapped up in newspapers and bath towels. They were sold at Sotheby's in 2001. CV

Tiara of Princess Mary Immaculate of Saxony

Germany, c. 1830

Gold, silver, diamonds and pearls, 90 x 150 x 105 mm

Tokyo, Albion Art Collection

The frame of this tiara features half-pearl and diamond motifs arranged in an alternating pattern, while seven pear-shaped pearls mounted on fleurons surmount back-to-back festoons. This type of tiara-crown could be worn at the back of the head as a chignon ornament. This style (see Scarisbrick 2000, p. 64), initiated in the seventeenth century by Marie de' Medici and continued by her daughter Henrietta Maria in London, remained popular for centuries, captivating Queen Hortense, daughter of Josephine de Beauharnais and Princess Mathilda, a cousin of Napoleon III, as well as Queen Victoria. The tiara was the prop-

erty of Princess Mary Immaculate of Saxony (1874–1947). She wore it to the 1911 wedding of her nephew, Archduke Charles, future emperor of Austria and Princess Zita of Bourbon-Parma in Schwarzau. The Archduke's mother, Marie Josepha, was a sister of Prince John George of Saxony. cv

BIBLIOGRAPHY : Boston 2000, p. 64.

> Tiara of the Countess of Flanders

c. 1830

Gold, silver, diamonds and pearls, 35 x 140 x 135 mm

Private collection, courtesy Albion Art Jewellery Institute, Tokyo

This tiara, which can be closed to form a full circlet, comprises a continuous band of diamonds mounted with upward-curving

rows of diamonds. Where the ends of these meet they are surmounted by festoons comprising three leaves set with diamonds and a central pearl, while a pearl fleuron appears in the space between them. Although the design is quite simple, the tiara, which can be worn equally well on the brow or high on the head, is striking for the quality and the size of its diamonds and pearls and for the fleurons – a motif associated with royalty – reminiscent of ripe strawberries, which bring a majestic aspect to the whole. The tiara is thought to have been made for Grand Duchess Stephanie of Baden (1789–1860) who was an adopted daughter of Napoleon. Her second child, Princess Josephine (1813–1900), probably received it as a wedding present when she married Prince Charles of Hohenzollern-Sigmaringen in 1834. An oil painting at Sigmaringen Castle depicts her wearing the tiara. She seems to have bequeathed it to her daughter, Princess Stephanie (1837–1859), who was briefly queen of Portugal and whose sculpted bust in Hohenzollern Castle shows her wearing the tiara. On Stephanie's death the tiara passed to her sister Marie (1845–1912) who, through her marriage to Count Philip of Flanders, became sister-in-law to King Leopold II of Belgium and mother to the heir to the throne, later Albert I. Her daughter, Princess Henrietta (1870–1948), inherited the tiara and wore it quite frequently. In 1896 Henrietta married a grandson of King Louis Philippe of France and became Duchess of Vendome. This historic diamond and pearl tiara was sold, with other jewellery, by Henrietta's only granddaughter. However a similar version remains in the possession of the descendants of Grand Duchess Stephanie's daughter, Princess Marie of Baden, whose first husband was the Duke of Hamilton and Brandon. It would seem that the Grand Duchess had a similar tiara made for each of her children. CV

Tiara of Queen Margherita of Italy

Mellerio dits Meller, Paris, 1867

Gold, silver and diamonds, 55 x 185 x 180 mm

Private collection, courtesy Albion Art Jewellery Institute, Tokyo

The tiara consists of fourteen sections, each with three paved-diamond laurel leaves and two berries graduated towards the large five-petalled flower at the front, the stamens framing the square stone at its centre. The different elements of the tiara can be separated to form smaller ornaments. This tiara was exhibited by the Parisian firm of Mellerio at the Exposition Universelle held in Paris in 1867, where it was bought by Victor Emmanuel II of Italy for his future daughter-in-law. Margherita of Genoa Savoy (1851–1926). Victor Emmanuel had recently been proclaimed monarch of the newly united Italy, and the capital city was now to be Rome and not Turin, so this fine tiara had a political significance. As the wife of the future Umberto I resided in Rome, a laurel-leaf tiara – symbol of the victory and authority of the Ancient Roman emperors –was an extremely appropriate gift. Jewellers to Empress Eugenie and Queen Isabella II of Spain, Mellerio mastered the court style of the Second Empire, one of the most outstanding periods in the history of Parisian jewellery. When it was exhibited at the Exposition Universelle, where Mellerio was awarded a gold medal, the art critic Jules Mesnard admired the tiara for its pure classicism and for so successfully combining a rich effect with such good taste. In Queen Margherita, who wore her wonderful collection of jewels to perfection, Italy had a sovereign who was born for her royal role : beautiful, dignified and unfailingly gracious. DSC

Engagement ring of the queens of Italy

Italy, second half of the 19th century

Gold, rubies and diamonds, 25 x 22 x 23 mm

Tokyo, Albion Art Collection

> Tiara of Queen Marie of Serbia

Bolin (?), St Petersburg, c. 1880

Gold, silver, diamonds and paste replacement for emeralds

Van Cleef & Arpels Collection

This gold ring features shoulders with ribbon and scroll motifs supporting an oval bezel set with an 8.71-carat step-cut ruby and surrounded by a border of sixteen cushion-cut diamonds in a claw setting.

The piece is historically significant as it was the engagement ring used by several sovereigns of Italy. In 1868 King Umberto I presented it to his future wife Princess Margherita of Savoy-Genoa, who received splendid parures from her own family and that of her husband. Subsequently, wanting to ensure that the court of the unified Kingdom of Italy was the most brilliant in Europe, she acquired other pieces of jewellery that she wore with great distinction. Certain pieces belonged to the State while others were her personal property. After the 1900 assassination of Umberto I in Monza, she returned all of the jewellery that belonged to the State, entrusting it to Helen, the new queen. But she was free to do as she liked with those belonging to her personally, such as this ring, which was passed on to her grandson Umberto II. He in turn gave it to his fiancée Marie-José, whom he married in 1930. When they left Italy in 1946 after a very brief reign, the royal couple deposited the jewellery belonging to the State at the Bank of Italy but they kept this ring in their private collection.

This intensely red ruby originated in Burma, present-day Myanmar. According to Marco Polo, ruby mines in this region and in the Mogok area in particular have been in operation since the twelfth century. Rubies symbolize love, vitality and power, which is why they are frequently used in engagement rings and consistently found in royal crowns. The twelfth-century visionary, Hildegard of Bingen, claimed that rubies eliminate melancholy and gloominess, bringing greater happiness to its wearer. They are also the carbuncle of tales and legends and believed to shine at night like a live coal, or *carbunculus* in Latin. **CV / DSC**

The tiara is in the shape of a halo with a border of brilliant-cut diamonds at the base and top. The space in between is filled in with seven large cabochon emeralds in diamond frames, divided by diamond latticework. The emeralds belonged to Marie of Hesse (1824–1880), wife of Tsar Alexander II (1818–1881), and then to her daughter-in-law, Princess Elisabeth of Hesse (1864–1918), wife of Grand Duke Serge (1857–1905) and sister of Empress Alexandra (1872–1918), consort of Tsar Nicolas II

Queen Marie of Serbia wearing her tiara.

274

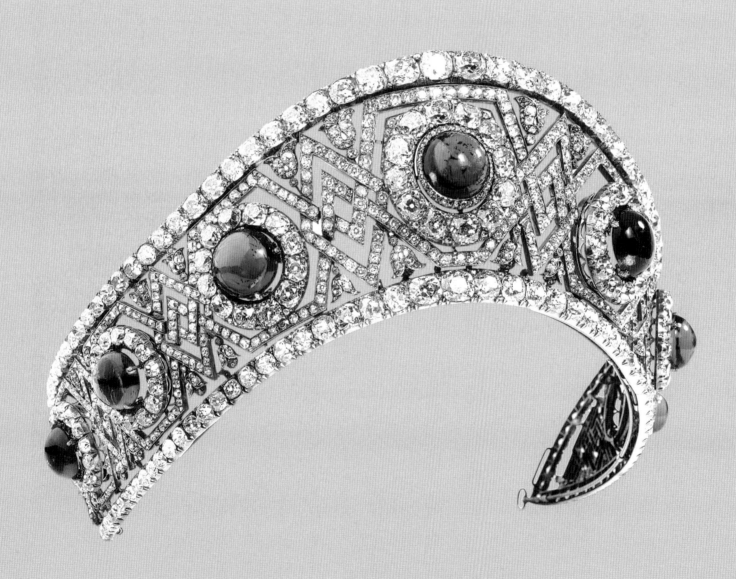

(1868–1918). Although the date of the tiara itself is uncertain, we can assume that it probably was a wedding present. The Grand Duchess chose to wear it in 1894 on the occasion of her brother's wedding in Coburg. Following the assassination of her husband, Grand Duke Serge, in 1905, Ella, as she was known in the family circle, retired from public life and founded the religious order of Martha and Mary on the proceeds of the sale of some of her jewels. The rest were entrusted to her brother-in-law, the Grand Duke Paul (1860–1919). When the Tsar because of a morganatic second marriage exiled him, the Grand Duchess Serge, childless, brought up his daughter, the Grand Duchess Marie (1890–1958). In 1908, she married Prince Wilhelm of Sweden (1884–1965), a son of King Gustav v (1858–1950), and received the tiara and matching necklace as a gift from her aunt. While in exile in Romania with her second husband Prince Serge Putiatin (1893–1966), she sold them in 1922 to King Alexander of Serbia (1888–1934) for his bride-to-be, Princess Marie of Romania (1900–1961). The bride's mother, Queen Marie (1875–1938), described the emeralds as 'imperial stones the like of which I hadn't seen since Russia'. Whereas Cartier remodelled the necklace, the tiara has remained intact. The Queen of Serbia wore it for most of her official portraits and took it into exile with her, allowing her daughter-in-law, Alexandra of Greece, wife of King Peter ii (1923–1970), to borrow it only once for a reception in Buckingham Palace in honour of the marriage of the future Queen Elizabeth ii. Queen Alexandra recalled in *For Love of a King* (1956): 'my head ached and hurt unbearably under the weight of the heavy tiara of emeralds which I wore… my tiara bit viciously into my head.' In 1949 the tiara was sold to Van Cleef & Arpels, who removed the emeralds but left the rest untouched. **CV**

Princess Olga of Yugoslavia wearing her tiara, by Cecil Beaton, 1939.

< **Tiara of Princess Moina Abamelek Lazarev**
Boucheron, Paris, 1907
Gold, silver and diamonds, 82 x 210 x 190 mm
Tokyo, Albion Art Collection

The tiara rests on a narrow line of diamonds above a base of collet-set diamonds. It comprises a series of foliate vine scrolls interspersed with large diamonds within diamond borders on stems centred on a large yellow diamond similarly surrounded. The collet diamond base was added to give extra height. The classical design derived from the ironwork that decorated Parisian architecture in the Louis xvi period and is enhanced by the golden blaze of the yellow diamonds. Princess Moina Abamelek Lazarev (1878–1955) was heiress to the vast Demidoff estates in Russia. She bequeathed the tiara to her nephew, Prince Paul of Yugoslavia who gave it to his wife, Olga, formerly Princess of Greece. **DSC**

278

Tiara of Grand Duchess Hilda of Baden

Herman Schmidt-Staub (Pforzheim-Karlsruhe), 1907

Platinum, gold and diamonds, 600 x 400 x 400 mm

Karlsruhe, Badisches Landesmuseum (inv. 83/81)

The tiara of the Grand Duchess Hilda rests on a wreath of stylized laurel leaves between a line of running scrolls and an upper row of square and rectangular cut stones. It is surmounted by a curved line of channel-set diamonds interspersed with stones set lozenge-wise rising to a point at the centre. The space between is filled with intersecting Louis xvi-style festoons and swags, which hang with freely swinging open-set diamonds. Although the front of the tiara is platinum, the back is executed in yellow gold. The garland style of the tiara suggests that it was probably made on the occasion of the enthronement of Grand Duke Frederick II in 1907. Thereafter, Grand Duchess Hilda (1864–1952), born a Princess of Nassau, wore this tiara on great occasions such as the wedding of her niece Sophie of Luxembourg to Prince Ernst-Henry of Saxony in 1921 and the eightieth birthday of her brother-in-law King Gustave v of Sweden in 1938. She never missed a single christening engagement or wedding. With her sweet face and silver hair, finished off with a hat or adorned by a tiara, she was a constant fixture in photographs of family gatherings at that time. Since she had no children, she left her jewels to the six daughters of her brother, Grand Duke William iv of Luxembourg. Antonia, wife of Prince Rupert of Bavaria, inherited the tiara, which was later acquired by the Badisches Landesmuseum, in 1984. It has thus returned to the palace where Grand Duchess Hilda had spent a part of her life. cv

< Grand Duchess Hilda of Baden wearing her tiara, c. 1910.

Tiara of Princess Marie of Greece

Cartier, Paris, 1907

Millegrain platinum and diamonds, 60 x 190 x 180 mm

Private collection, courtesy Albion Art Jewellery Institute, Tokyo

The tiara consists of twin paved-diamond olive branches meeting at a pear-shaped diamond suspended over the brow at the centre. The classical olive-branch tiara was not only fashionable in the final years of the *belle époque*, it was also particularly appropriate for Marie Bonaparte (1882–1962) as it evoked the tiaras worn by the women in her family during the First Empire of Napoleon I, from whose brother Lucien she was descended. As if to emphasize this connection, Princess Marie wore the tiara low on the brow, just as the Empress Josephine had done. Since the tiara was one of the jewels ordered at the time of her marriage to Prince George of Greece the olive branch had a special significance for Marie who was to live with him in Athens. Symbolic of peace and prosperity the olive was the attribute of the goddess Athena, who protected the city and whose shrine was the Parthenon on the Acropolis. As a result of this marriage Princess Marie was related to all the royal families of Europe and therefore would have attended many important events requiring formal dress and tiara. Cartier was so proud of the jewels commissioned for the marriage that they were displayed to the public and photographed in the press. DSC

Princess Marie Bonaparte, 1907.

Tiara of Archduchess Marie Anne
of Austria, Duchess of Parma

Moritz Hübner, Vienna, 1903

Silver, gold and diamonds

Tokyo, Albion Art Collection

This diamond tiara composed of two jointed arches with a succession of rings radiating from a festooned central ornament was designed by Viennese jeweller Hübner and presented as a wedding gift to Archduchess Marie Anne of Austria (1892–1940). One of the daughters of Archduke Frederick, Duke of Teschen, and Princess Isabella of Croÿ, she was also the goddaughter of Empress Marie Anne, widow of Ferdinand I of Austria. She married Duke Elias of Bourbon-Parma in 1903, thereby becoming sister-in-law to Zita, future empress of Austria, who had been born princess of Bourbon-Parma. Archduchess Marie Anne wore this tiara to Zita's wedding in Schwarzau in 1911. According to a plaque inside its original case, the piece was originally set with a large blue diamond that belonged to the family, which has since been returned to the imperial treasury. The duke and duchess, who owned an impressive collection of jewellery, had eight children. This tiara remained in the family until very recently. **CV**

BIBLIOGRAPHY : Tokyo 2007, p. 120.

< Tiara of Queen Elisabeth of Belgium

Cartier, Paris, 1910

Platinum and diamonds, 55 x 150 mm

Geneva, Cartier S.A. (inv. HO 02 A10)

This tiara composed of diamonds mounted on platinum is an excellent example of the wreath style that jewellers brought back into fashion at the beginning of the twentieth century, borrowing a number of elements from the Louis XVI decorative style. It features an elegant combination of scrolls enclosed between a border of laurel leaves and a band of closely set stones serving as a base. A 5.84-carat diamond occupies the upper central part of this piece. The tiara was purchased in 1912 by Elisabeth (1876–1965), wife of Albert I, King of the Belgians (1875–1934). Born a duchess in Bavaria, this niece and goddaughter of Elisabeth of Bavaria (Sissi) acceded to the throne in 1909 and found herself in need of a larger jewellery collection. For this she looked to Cartier, 'jeweller to kings and king of jewellers', who was granted the title of Court Supplier in 1919. That same year, the sovereign acquired a lightweight bandeau of diamonds and turquoise set on a diamond-shaped base. Inherited by King Leopold III, the piece was sold in 1987 and added to Cartier's archive. In keeping with the fashion of the times, Queen Elisabeth wore the tiara across her forehead as a bandeau. She chose to wear it to the wedding of the future Leopold III as well as that of King Baudouin in 1960. The queen was highly intelligent and maintained friendships with many artists, researchers and scientists. Today her radiant personality is associated with a famous music competition and a renowned Egyptology foundation. CV

BIBLIOGRAPHY : Paris 1989, pp. 46, 124 ; Mexico City 1999, p. 105 ; Stockholm 2000, p. 178 ; Boston 2000, pp. 126–7 ; Vachaudez 2004, pp. 90–5 ; Lisbon 2007.

Queen Elisabeth of Belgium wearing her tiara.

Tiara of Archduchess Marie Valerie of Austria

Köchert, Vienna, 1913

Gold, silver, diamonds, pearls and sapphire cameo,

65 x 150 x 120 mm

Tokyo, Albion Art Collection

In 1913, Emperor Francis Joseph (1830–1916) presented a magnificent pearl and diamond tiara to his youngest daughter, Archduchess Marie Valerie (1868–1924). This piece, designed by imperial jeweller Köchert of Vienna, was originally composed of a diamond bandeau topped by five medallions linked together with small arches also set with diamonds. Each of these designs featured a central pear-shaped pearl in a fleuron setting. Today only three of these remain; they can be detached and worn separately as brooches or pendants. The favourite daughter of her mother Elisabeth of Bavaria (Sissi), Archduchess Marie Valerie married Archduke Francis Salvator (1866–1939) of Habsburg-Tuscany in 1890. Together they had nine children. **cv**

BIBLIOGRAPHY : Hauser-Köchert 1990 ; Tokyo 2007, pp. 172–3.

Tiara of Archduchess Marie Valerie in its original form.

Daughter of Archduchess Marie Valerie wearing her mother's tiara before the alterations, c. 1913.

Tiara of Grand Duchess Adelaide Marie of Luxembourg

c. 1865–1870

Gold, silver, sapphire and diamonds, 45 x 155 x 100 mm

Luxembourg, Collection Grand-Ducale

This sapphire and diamond tiara in the form of a bouquet – part of the 'Hausschmuck' of the house of Nassau-Weilburg – consists of a tapering band decorated with laurel leaves and berries set with brilliant- and rose-cut diamonds, arranged around a central large, pale blue, cushion-cut sapphire, which is in turn encircled by cushion-cut diamonds. The mount is in white gold on yellow gold (on the back) and the detachable sapphire is held in place by screws. Two loops on the base of the tiara allow an additional element to be attached. Grand Duchess Charlotte (1896–1985) would often wear this tiara embellished with a diamond rivière.

The tiara belonged to Grand Duchess Adelaide Marie (1833–1916), who bequeathed it to Grand Duchess Marie Anne (1861–1942), born Maria Ana of Braganza. Like many other pieces that had initially been personal property, it became part of the collection held in trust. Grand Duchess Marie Anne wore this tiara at the wedding of her daughter Elisabeth of Nassau (1901–1950) to Prince Ludwig Philipp of Thurn and Taxis (1901–1933) in November 1922. In the same year Grand Duchess Charlotte chose to wear it for an official photograph taken by Edouard Kutter. She continued to wear it regularly, although less frequently, notably after 1926, when she received the famous art deco tiara made by the Paris jewellers Chaumet. It was this latter piece that she wore at the wedding of Leopold, crown prince of Belgium, to Princess Astrid of Sweden on 10 November 1926. **MP**

Grand Duchess Charlotte of Luxembourg wearing the tiara of Grand Duchess Adelaide of Luxembourg.

Tiara associated with Queen Victoria-Eugenia of Spain

c. 1950

Platinum, diamonds and aquamarines

Private collection

King Alfonso XIII of Spain (1886–1941) loved to present jewels as gifts and his consort, Queen Victoria-Eugenia (1887–1969), a granddaughter of Queen Victoria through her mother Princess Beatrice, loved to wear them. From this point of view, it was a perfect match. The queen's collection was superb. Soon after the wedding, which took place in Madrid in 1904, she received from her husband a wonderful diamond and pearl tiara with open foliage garlands made by Ansorena, the Spanish court jeweller. Later, a set of impressive aquamarines was arranged to replace the pearls, as the queen favoured the stone for its sweet blue colour. The set was completed with a brooch and a matching necklace made later by Cartier and presented in 1935 by the queen to her elder daughter, Infanta Beatriz (1909–2002), as a wedding present. The princess married Don Alessandro Torlonia in Rome. He was fifth prince of Civitella-Cesi (1911–1986) and settled in the ancestral palace of his family. During the 1950s, the tiara was remodelled as a succession of intertwined diamond circles with the aquamarines hanging in the middle. The infanta wore the tiara without the aquamarines during the ceremonies organized in Athens for the wedding of her nephew Juan-Carlos in 1962, but she wore the full set in Portugal the day before the marriage of her niece, the Infanta Pilar in 1967. **cv**

Queen Victoria-Eugenia of Spain wearing her tiara before alterations made by the Infanta Beatrice.

Wedding of the future King Leopold of Belgium and Princess Astrid of Sweden, Duke and Duchess of Brabant, 10 November 1926.

Seated left to right : Princess Ingeborg, née Princess of Denmark, mother of the bride and Duchess of Vastergotland; Princess Margaretha of Sweden, wife of Prince Axel of Denmark and sister of the bride; Princess Astrid and Prince Leopold, Duchess and Duke of Brabant; Queen Elisabeth of Belgium, wearing the tiara made for her by Cartier in 1912; Queen Alexandrine of Denmark, wearing a diamond fringe tiara by Fabergé; Grand Duchess Charlotte of Luxembourg, wearing an emerald and diamond art deco tiara by Chaumet.

Standing left to right : Prince Charles of Sweden, father of the bride and Duke of Vastergotland; Prince Eugen of Sweden, Duke of Narke; Countess Bernadotte; Prince Charles of Belgium, brother of the groom (partially obscured); Princess Ingrid of Sweden, future queen of Denmark; Princess René of Bourbon-Parma, née Princess Margaret of Denmark; Prince Sigvard of Sweden, Duke of Uppland; Prince Carl of Sweden, brother of the bride; Princess Marie-José of Belgium, future queen of Italy and sister of the groom; Count Bernadotte; King Christian x of Denmark; King Albert I of Belgium; Prince Gustav Adolf of Sweden, Duke of Västerbotten; Prince Axel of Denmark; Princes François-Xavier and Sisto of Bourbon-Parma.

Bibliography

AALST 1980

Jaar Sint-Martinuskerk 500, exhib. cat., Aalst, 1980.

ACKERMANN 1855

G.A. Ackermann, *Ordensbuch sämtlicher in Europa blühender und erloschener Orden und Ehrenzeichen*, Annaberg, 1855.

AJUDA 1986

Ouros do Brasil no Palácio da Ajuda, Lisbon, 1986.

AKEN 1965

Karl der Grosse: Werk und Wirkung, exhib. cat., Aken, 1965.

ALCOUFFE 2001

D. Alcouffe, *Les Gemmes de la Couronne*, Paris, 2001.

ANDERSSON 1984

A. Andersson, *Treasures of Early Sweden*, Stockholm, 1984.

ANTWERP 1968

J. Walgrave, *Diamant, Geschiedenis en Techniek*, exhib. cat., Museum Sterckshof, Deurne-Antwerp, 1968.

ANTWERP 1977

J. Walgrave, *Diamantjuwelen uit Rubens' Tijd*, exhib. cat., Antwerp, 1977.

ANTWERP 1993

J. Walgrave, *Een Eeuw van Schittering – Diamantjuwelen uit de 17de eeuw*, exhib. cat., Antwerp, 1993.

ANTWERP 1995

J. Walgrave (ed.), *Sieraad-Symbool-Signaal*, exhib. cat., Antwerp, 1995.

ANTWERP 1997

From the Treasury, exhib. cat., Antwerp, 1997.

ANTWERP 1998

J. Walgrave, *Het Labo van de Verleiding*, exhib. cat., Antwerp, 1998, pp. 106–9.

ANTWERP 1999

J. Walgrave, *Een Vorstelijk Imago: het Beeld van de Heerser sedert Antoon van Dyck*, exhib. cat., Antwerp, 1999.

ANTWERP 2002

J. Walgrave, *Living Diamonds: fauna en flora in het diamantjuweel*, exhib. cat., Antwerp, Diamantmuseum, 2002.

ANTWERP 2004

S. Denissen and W. Luyckx, *Rubens & diamant: thematentoonstelling over broches vanaf de 17de eeuw tot nu*, exhib. cat., Antwerp, 2004.

ANTWERP 2004B

W. Luyckx and J. Walgrave, *De Man Versier(d)/(t). Diamantjuwelen voor de man*, exhib. cat., Antwerp, 2004.

ANTWERP 2006

B. van Beneden and N. de Poorter, *Réfugiés royalistes*, exhib. cat., Antwerp, 2006.

ANTWERP 2006B

W. Luyckx and B. Van Gelder, *Baburs Erfenis: de invloed van het Mogoljuweel*, exhib. cat., Antwerp, 2006.

ARBETETA MIRA 2004

L. Arbeteta Mira, 'La Corona Rica y otras joyas de estado de la reina Isabel', in *Isabel La Catolica, la magnificencia de un reinado*, Valladolid, 2004.

ARENENBERG 2003

D. Gügel and C. Egli (eds), *Was für ein Theater! Krönungen und Spektakel in napoleonischer Zeit*, exhib. cat., Napoleonmuseum, Schloss Arenenberg, 2003.

ARNOLD 1994

U. Arnold in D. Syndram (ed.), *Das Grüne Gewölbe zu Dresden. Führer durch seine Geschichte und seine Sammlung*, Munich/Berlin, 1994.

ARNOLD 2001

U. Arnold, *Die Juwelen Augusts des Starken*, Munich/Berlin, 2001.

ASPINALL 1963–1971

A. Aspinall, *Correspondence of George Prince of Wales 1770–1812*, London, 1963–1971.

AUCHINCLOSS 1972

L. Auchincloss, *Richelieu*, London, 1972.

BÄUMEL 1997

J. Bäumel, *Auf dem Weg zur Thron. Die Krönungsreise Augusts des Starken*, Dresden, 1997.

BABELON 1897

E. Babelon, *Catalogue des camées antiques et modernes de la Bibliothèque Nationale*, Paris, 1897.

BALLESTEROS-GAIBROIS 1964

M. Ballestros-Gaibrois, *Isabel la Catolica de España*, Madrid, 1964.

BÄUMEL 2004

J. Bäumel, *Rüstkammer. Führer durch die ständige Ausstellung im Semperbau*, 2nd edition, Munich/Berlin, 2004.

BEAULIEU/BAYLÉ 1956

M. Beaulieu and J. Baylé, *Le costume en Bourgogne de Philippe le Hardi à Charles le Téméraire*, Paris, 1956.

BEAUNE 2000

De Bruges à Beaune. *Marie, l'héritage de Bourgogne*, exhib. cat., Beaune, 2000.

BENNETT/MASCETTI 1989

D. Bennett and D. Mascetti, *Understanding Jewellery*, Woodbridge, 1989.

BIEDERMANN
G. Biedermann, 'L'art d'attraper les puces', in *L'Objet d'Art*.

BOIS-LE-DUC 1993
Maria van Hongarije, 1505–1558 : Koningin tussen keizers en kunstenaars, A.M. Koldeweij (ed.), Rijksmuseum, Het Catharijneconvent, Utrecht-Noordbrabants Museum, 's Hertogenbosch, 1993.

BONN/VIENNA 2000
Kaiser Karel v (1500–1558) : Macht und Ohnmacht Europas, Bonn/Vienna, 2000.

BÖNSCH 2001
A. Bönsch, *Formengeschichte europäischer Kleidung*, Vienna, 2001.

BORNER 1981
L. Borner, *Deutsche Medaillenkleinode des 16 und 17 Jahrhunderts*, Würzburg, 1981.

BÖRSCH-SUPAN 1986
H. Börsch-Supan, *Der Maler Antoine Pesne. Franzose und Preuße*, Friedberg, 1986.

BOSTON 2000
Crowning Glories : Two Centuries of Tiaras, exhib. cat., Boston, Museum of Fine Arts, 2000.

BOTT 1972
G. Bott, *Ullstein Juwelenbuch*, Berlin/Frankfurt/Vienna, 1972.

BOUCHER 1996
F. Boucher, *A History of Costume in the West*, London, 1996.

BOURGET 1905
A. Bourget, *Revue d'Histoire diplomatique*, XIX, 1905, pp. 441–7.

BOYADJIAN 1980
N. Boyadjian, *Le cœur : son histoire, son symbolisme, son iconographie et ses maladies*, Antwerp, 1980.

BREPOHL 2005
E. Brepohl (ed.), *Benvenuto Cellini. Traités sur l'architecture et la sculpture*, Cologne/Weimar/Vienna, 2005.

BRUGES 1962
La Toison d'Or : cinq siècles d'art et d'histoire, contenant la liste de tous les chevaliers depuis la première institution jusqu'en 1962, exhib. cat., Bruges, 1962.

BRUGES 2007
Schoonheid en Waanzin in Margareta's familie, exhib. cat., Bruges, 2007.

BRUSSELS 1972
Rhin et Meuse : art et culture 800–1400, exhib. cat., Cologne/Brussels, 1972.

BRUSSELS 1991
Magie des pierres précieuses, exhib. cat., Europalia 1991, Brussels, Galerie de la Kredietbank, 1991.

BRUSSELS 1991B
Triomphe du Baroque, exhib. cat., Europalia 1991, Brussels, Palais des Beaux-Arts, 1991.

BRUSSELS 1992
Specerijkelijk, exhib. cat., Brussels, 1992.

BRUSSELS 1998
L. Duerloo and W. Thomas, *Albert et Isabelle 1598–1621*, exhib. cat., Brussels, 1998.

BRUSSELS 2004
Magie de l'orfèvrerie. Cinq siècles d'orfèvrerie européenne dans les collections privées, Brussels, 2004.

BUDAPEST 1965
Anciens joyaux hongrois, Budapest, 1965.

BUDAPEST 1988
Periods in European Decorative Arts, Budapest, 1988.

BUDAPEST 2002
Jankovich Mikklós (1772–1846) gyjteményei, exhib. cat., Budapest, 2002.

BUDAPEST 2004
P. Farbaky and S. Serfözö (eds), *Mariazell und Ungarn*, Sz., Budapest, BTM Kiscelli Múzeuma, 2004.

BUDAPEST 2005
Mary of Hapsburg, Widow of Mohács : the Queen and her Court 1521–1531, O. Réthelyi (ed.), Budapest, Budapesti Történeti Múzeum, 2005.

BURCKHARDT 1931
R.F. Burckhardt, 'Ueber vier Kleinodien Karls des Kühnen', in *Anzeiger für Schweizerische Altertumskunde*, NF XXXIII, 1931, pp. 247–59.

BURKE 1992
P. Burke, *The Fabrication of Louis XIV*, New Haven/London, 1992.

BURY 2000
S. Bury, *Jewellery 1789–1910. The International Era, Vol. 1, 1789–1861*, Woodbridge, 2000.

CATALOGUE BERN 1969
Katalog der Ausstellung. *Die Burgunderbeute und Werke Burgundischer Hofkunst*, Bern Historisches Museum, 1969.

CHABOUILLET 1858
A. Chabouillet, *Catalogue général et raisonné des camées et pierres gravées de la Bibliothèque impériale*, Paris, 1858.

CHAVES 1989
F. Chaves Castelo-Branco (introduction and notes), *O Portugal de Dom João V visto por três forasteiros*, Lisbon, 1989.

CHERRY 1992
J. Cherry, *Goldsmiths*, 1992.

CHEVALIER/GHEERBRANT 1993
J. Chevalier and A. Gheerbrant, *Dictionnaire des symboles*, Paris, 1993.

CHRISTIE'S 1988
Catalogue d'enchères, Christie's, Geneva, 15 November 1988.

COLLIGNON 2004
J.-P. Collignon, *Ordres de chevalerie : décorations et médailles de France des origines à la fin du Second Empire*, Charleville-Mézières, 2004.

CONSTANT 1995
C. Constant, *Musée national du château de Versailles, Les Peintures*, vol. 1, Paris, 1995.

COPENHAGEN 1992
Aedle Stene og Magiske Farver, exhib. cat., Copenhagen, Christianborg Slot, 1992.

DALTON 2000
K.C. Dalton, 'The Black Emperor in the Drake Jewel and Elizabethan Imperial Imagery', in P. Erickson and C. Hulse (eds), *Early Modern Visual Culture : Representation, Race and Empire in Renaissance England*, Pennsylvania, 2000.

DAOULAS 1991
La Bretagne au temps des Ducs, exhib. cat., Daoulas, 1991.

DE AZCONA 1964
T. de Azcona, *Isabel la Catolica*, Madrid, 1964.

DE BREM 1993
A.-M. de Brem, *Louis Hersent*, exhib. cat., Paris, Musée de la Vie romantique, 1993–1994, p. 85.

DE CERVAL 1998
M. de Cerval, *Dictionnaire international du bijou*, Paris, 1998.

DENIS/KLEIN 1992
M.A. Denis and M. Klein, *Madame du Barry de Versailles à Louveciennes*, Paris, 1992.

DENISSEN 2002
S. Denissen, *De geschiedenis van het diamantjuweel*, Antwerp, 2002.

DENISSEN/DE REN 2001
S. Denissen and L. De Ren, *The Splendour of Diamonds : 400 years of Diamond Jewellery in Europe*, Antwerp, 2001.

DEUCHLER 1963

F. Deuchler, *Die Burgunderbeute*, Bern, 1963.

DEURNE 1968

J. Walgrave (ed.), *Diamant, Geschiedenis en Techniek*, exhib. cat., Deurne-Antwerp, 1968.

DEURNE 1977

J. Walgrave (ed.), *De Mode in Rubens' Tijd*, exhib. cat., Deurne-Antwerp, 1977.

DE WILDE 1996

P. De Wilde, *Een beknopte geschiedenis van de familie Vilain XIV*, Kruibeke, 1996.

DIDIER 2003

R. Didier, 'Couronne-reliquaire des Saintes Épines', in R. Didier and J. Toussaint, *Autour de Hugo d'Oignies*, Collection Monographies du Musée des Arts anciens du Namurois, no. 25, Namur, 2003, pp. 350–3.

DIJON 2004

L'Art à la cour de Bourgogne, exhib. cat., Dijon, 2004.

DISTELBERGER 2002

R. Distelberger, *Die Kunst den Steinschnitts : Prunkgefässe, Kameen und Commessi aus der Kunstkammer*, Milan/Vienna, 2002.

DOMANOVSZKY 1939

S. Domanovszky (ed.), *Magyar Müvelödéstörténet II. Magyar Renaissance*, Budapest, p. 302.

DRESDEN 2002

Gegen den Strom, exhib. cat., Dresden, 2002.

DUFRESNE 1986

C. Dufresne, *L'Impératrice Eugénie*, Paris, 1986.

EDINBURGH 1992

Leonardo da Vinci : The Mystery of the 'Madonna of the Yarnwinder', exhib. cat., Edinburgh, National Gallery of Scotland, 1992.

EGGER 1984

G. Egger, *Bürgerlicher Schmuck – 15. bis 20. Jahrhundert*, Munich, 1984.

ENGERAND 1900

F. Engerand, *Inventaire des tableaux commandés et achetés par la direction des Bâtiments du Roi (1709–1792)*, Paris, 1900.

ESTEVENIN-DAVENNE 1987

M. Estevenin-Davenne, 'Les Francs, les Abeilles et les Fleurs de Lis', in *L'Âge d'Or – Spiritualité et Tradition*, no. 8, Puiseaux, 1987.

ESTEVENS 1944

M.S. Estevens, *Subsídios para a história da Ourivesaria Portugesa*, I, Lisbon, 1944.

EVANS 1951

J. Evans, *A History of Jewellery* 1100–1870, London, 1951.

EVANS 1970

J. Evans, *A History of Jewellery* 1100–1870, New York, 1970.

EVANS 1989

J. Evans, *A History of Jewellery* 1100–1870, New York, 1989.

FALKINER 1968

R. Falkiner, *Investing in Antique Jewellery*, London, 1968.

FERGUSON 1966

G. Ferguson, *Signs and Symbols in Christian Art*, New York/Oxford, 1966.

FEUCHTMÜLLER 1974

R. Feuchtmüller (ed.), *Renaissance in Österreich : Geschichte-Wissenschaft-Kunst*, Horn, 1974.

FIELD 1987

L. Field, *The Queen's Jewels*, London, 1987.

FIERRO/PALLUEL-GUILLARD/TULARD 1995

A. Fierro, A. Palluel-Guillard and J. Tulard, *Histoire et dictionnaire du Consulat et de l'Empire*, Paris, 1995.

FLEISCHHAUER 1970

W. Fleischhauer, 'Der Edelsteinschnieder Hans Kobenhaupt in Stuttgart und seine Werkstatt', *Pantheon*, vol. 28, 1970.

FLORENCE 2006

Annamaria Giusti (ed.), *Arte e Manifattura di corte a Firenze dal tramonto die Medici all'Impero (1732–1815)*, Florence, 2006.

FRANKLIN 1885–1886

A. Franklin, *La vie privée d'autrefois. Arts et métiers, modes, mœurs, usages des Parisiens du XIIᵉ au XVIIIᵉ siècle*, 3 vols, Paris, 1885–1886.

FUCHS 1996

C.L. Fuchs, *Die Perlen der Medici. Weltkunst 17*, 1996, pp. 1853–7.

GAJEWSKA-PROROK 2001

E. Gajewska-Prorok, 'Skarb zlotych ozdob ze Srody Slaskiej', in *Bizuteria w Polsce*, Torun, 2001, pp. 25–56.

GAND 1999

Carolus Keizer Karel V 1500–1558, exhib. cat., Gand, 1999.

GANS 1961

H.M. Gans, *Juwelen en Mensen*, Amsterdam, 1961.

GENEVA 1983

Montres françaises 1580–1680, exhib. cat., Geneva, 1983.

GOLINSKI 2006

M. Golinski, 'Sroda Slaska w sredniowieczu', in *Sroda Slaska. Dzieje miasta wina i skarbow*, Wroclaw, 2006, pp. 67–70.

GREGORIETTI 1970

G. Gregorietti, *Jewellery through the Ages*, London/Sydney, 1970.

GRZIMEK 1973

B. Grzimek, *Het leven der dieren*, vol. VII, Utrecht/Antwerp, 1973.

GUIDE BUDAPEST 2005

Historical Exhibition of the Hungarian National Museum. Guide 2 : 11th to 17th centuries, Budapest, 2005.

GUIDE LISBON 2004

Museum-School of Portuguese Decorative Arts, Fundaçáo Ricardo do Espírito Santo Silva, Lisbon, 2004.

HACKENBROCH 1967

Y. Hackenbroch, 'Jewellery of the Court of Albrecht V at Munich', *The Connoisseur*, June 1967, vol. 165.

HACKENBROCH 1979

Y. Hackenbroch, *Renaissance Jewellery*, London/Munich, 1979.

HACKENBROCH 1996

Y. Hackenbroch, *Enseignes : Renaissance Hat Jewels*, Florence, 1996.

HAMANN 1988

B. Hamann, *Die Habsburger : ein biographisches Lexicon*, Vienna, 1988.

HAMM 2001

U. Härting (ed.), *Gärten und Höfe der Rubenszeit im Spiegel der Malerfamilie Brueghel und der Künstler um Peter Paul Rubens*, exhib. cat., Hamm and Mayence, 2001.

HANAU 1991

Schätze des Ungarischen Barock, exhib. cat., Hanau, 1991.

HAND 2004

J.O. Hand, *Joos van Cleve : The Complete Paintings*, New Haven/London, 2004.

HANSMANN/KRISS-RETTENBECK 1977

L. Hansmann and L. Kriss-Rettenbeck, *Amulett und Talisman – Erscheinungsform und Geschichte*, Munich, 1977.

HAUSER-KÖCHERT 1990

I. Hauser-Köchert, *Imperial Jewellers in Vienna : Jewellery Designs 1810–1940*, Florence, 1990.

HILTON PRICE 1902

F. Hilton Price, *The Marygold by Temple Bar*, London, 1902.

HLATKY 1939

M. Hlatky, *A Magyar Gyürü*, Budapest, 1939.

HUETE 1993

A.A. Huete, 'Dibujos de Joyas de MA de Sajonia', in *Reales Sitios*, vol. 115, 1993, pp. 33–9.

HUNT 1963

J. Hunt, 'Jewelled Furs and "Flohpelze"', *Pantheon*, XXI, 1963.

INNSBRUCK 1992

Hispania-Austria. Die Katholischen Könige, Maximilian I und die Anfänge der Casa de Austria in Spanien, Kunst um 1492, Innsbruck, 1992.

ISACSSON 1999

J. Isacsson, *Diadem, utvckling och bruk fram till 1830*, Stockholm, 1999.

KARLSRUHE 1986

Die Renaissance im Deutschen Südwesten, exhib. cat., Karlsruhe, 1986.

KISS 1994

E. Kiss, 'Arany kereszt és egy reneszánsz lánc töredéke', *Folia Historica*, XIX, 1994–1995.

KRAUTWURST 2003

M. Krautwurst, *Reinhold Vasters : ein niederrheinischer des 19 Jahrunderts in der Tradition alter Meister Sein Zeichnungskonvolut im Victoria & Albert Museum*, Trèves, 2003.

JACKSON, MISSISSIPPI 2004

D. Syndram, *The Glory of Baroque Dresden*, exhib. cat., Munich, 2004.

JOURDAN 1998

A. Jourdan, *Napoléon. Héros, Imperator, Mécène*, Paris, 1998.

KENYON 1992

J.P. Kenyon, *A Dictionary of British History*, Ware, 1992.

KOCKELBERGH/VLEESCHDRAGER/WALGRAVE 1992

I. Kockelbergh, E. Vleeschdrager and J. Walgrave, *The Brilliant Story of Antwerp*, Antwerp, 1992.

LANOTTE 1969

A. Lanotte, *Orfèvreries du Trésor de la Cathédrale de Namur*, Namur, 1969.

LEIPZIG 1997

Dresden, Unter einer Krone, exhib. cat., Leipzig, 1997.

LETKIEWICZ (FORTHCOMING)

E. Letkiewicz, 'Jewels of Izabella, Queen of Hungary', *Folia Historica*, XXIII, 2005–2006, (forthcoming).

LETTERS 1908

The Letters of Queen Victoria : a Selection from Her Majesty's Correspondence between the Years 1837 and 1861, vol. III, London, 1908.

LIGHTBOWN 1992

R. Lightbown, *Medieval European Jewellery*, 1992.

LISBON 1990

D. Luís, Duque do Porto, Lisbon, 1990.

LISBON 1992

I. Silveira Godinho, *Royal Treasures*, exhib. cat., Lisbon, Palácio Nacional da Ajuda, 1992.

LISBON 1993

Triunfo do Barroco, exhib. cat., Lisbon, Fundação das Descobertas, Centro Cultural de Belém, 1993.

LISBON 2007

Cartier, exhib. cat., Lisbon, Musée Gulbenkian, 2007.

LONDON 1987

Franz Xaver Winterhalter and the Courts of Europe, 1830–1870, exhib. cat., London, National Portrait Gallery/Paris, Musée du Petit Palais, 1987–1988.

LONDON 1988

The Power of Love : Six Centuries of Diamond Betrothal Rings, The Diamond Information Centre, London, 1988.

LONDON 2003

R. Marks and P. Williamson, *Gothic : Art for England 1400–1547*, London, 2003.

LONDON 2005

C. Hartop, Royal Goldsmiths, *The Art of Rundell and Bridge 1797–1843*, exhib. cat., Koopman Rare Art, London/Cambridge 2005.

LONDON 2006

Diamonds : the World's most Dazzling Exhibition, exhib. cat., London, 2006.

LOUVAIN 2005

D. Eichberger (ed.), *Women of Distinction : Margaret of York, Margaret of Austria*, Louvain, 2005.

MADRID 1998

La Joyería Española. De Felipe II a Alfonso XIII, exhib. cat., Madrid, 1998.

MADRID 1998B

F.A. Martin, Felipe II, *un monarca y su tiempo*, exhib. cat., Madrid, Monasterio de El Escorial, 1998.

MAGNIN 1883

Musée Magnin, *Catalogue du Musée*, Dijon, 1883.

MALINES 2005

D. Eichberger (ed.), *Dames met Klass : Margareta van York, Margareta van Oostenrijk*, exhib. cat., Malines, 2005.

MALMAISON 1993

La reine Hortense, une femme artiste, exhib. cat., Musée de Malmaison, 1993.

MALMAISON 2004

Bijoux des deux empires, 1804–1870, exhib. cat., Musée de Malmaison, 2004.

MANNHEIM 1999

Lebenslust und Frommigkeit. Kurfürst Karl-Theodor (1724–1799) zwischen Barock und Aufklärung, exhib. cat., Mannheim, 1999.

MARQUARDT 1983

B. Marquardt, *Klassizismus und Biedermeier 1780–1850 : Deutschland, Österreich, Schweiz*, Munich, 1983.

MAURICE 1665

J.-B. Maurice, *Le blason des armoiries de tous les chevaliers de l'Ordre de la Toison d'Or depuis la première institution jusqu'à…*, La Haye, 1665.

MEININGHAUS 2001

H. Meininghaus, 'Muskatreiben und Pomander für edle Gewürze', *Weltkunst*, no. 14, November 2001, pp. 2220–1.

MEXICO 1999

El Arte de Cartier. Resplandor del Tiempo, Mexico, Museo del Palacio de Bellas Artes, 1999.

MEYLAN 2002

V. Meylan, *Bijoux de reines*, Paris, 2002.

MICHAELIS 2003

R. Michaelis, *Antoine Pesne (1683–1757). Die Werke des preußischen Hofmalers in der Berliner Gemäldegalerie*, Berlin, 2003.

MOLINIER 1902

É. Molinier, *Catalogue de la Donation A. de Rothschild*, Paris, 1902.

MONGET 1898

C. Monget, *Publication de l'inventaire de la Chartreuse en 1791*, Dijon, 1898–1905.

MONTELIUS 1912

O. Montelius, *Mästerstycken i Statens historiska museum*, Stockholm, 1912.

MOREL 1988

B. Morel, *Les joyaux de la Couronne de France*, Paris/Antwerp, 1988.

MOSCO/CASAZZA 2004

M. Mosco and O. Casazza, *The Museo degli Argenti*, Florence, 2004.

MULLER 1972

P.E. Muller, *Jewels in Spain 1500–1800*, New York, 1972.

MUNICH 1970

Schatzkammer der Residenz München, exhib. cat., Munich, 1970.

MUNICH 1992

Friedrich der Große. Sammler und Mäzen, exhib. cat., Munich, 1992.

293

MUNICH 1995
R. Baumstark (ed.), *Das Goldene Rössel. Ein Meisterwerk der Pariser Hofkunst um 1400*, exhib. cat., Munich, 1995.

MUNICH 1999
Das Neues Hellas. Griechen und Bayern zur Zeit Ludwigs I, exhib. cat., Bayerisches Nationalmuseum, Munich, 1999.

MUNICH 2002
R. Eikelmann (ed.), *Der Mohrenkopfpokal von Christoph Jamnitzer*, exhib. cat., Munich, Bayerisches Nationalmuseum, 2002.

MUNN 2001
G.C. Munn, *Tiaras: a History of Splendour*, London, 2001, pp. 134–5.

NORDISKA 1952
Smycken i svensk ägo, Nordiska Museet, Stockholm, 1952.

OREY 1995
L. d'Orey, *Cinco Séculos de Joalharia no Museu Nacional de Arte Antiga*, Lisbon/London, 1995.

OTTAWA 1972
P. Verdier (ed.), *Art and the Courts: France and England from 1259 to 1328*, Ottawa, 1972.

PALMA 1995
F.A. Martin, *L'art de l'argenteria a les col·leccions reials*, exhib. cat., Palma de Majorca, 1995, no. 18, p. 45.

PARIS 1981
F. Baron (ed.), *Les fastes du Gothique: le siècle de Charles V*, Paris, 1981.

PARIS 1987
D. Gaborit-Chopin (ed.), *Regalia – Les instruments du sacre des Rois de France*, exhib. cat., Paris, 1987.

PARIS 1989
L'Art de Cartier, exhib. cat., Paris, Musée du Petit-Palais, 1989–1990/St Petersburg, Hermitage, 1992/Tokyo, Teien Art Museum, 1995.

PARIS 1998
Chaumet-Paris, deux siècles de création, exhib. cat., Paris, Musée Carnavalet, 1998.

PARIS 2000
P. Ayala (ed.), *Les bijoux romantiques 1820–1850*, Paris, Musée de la Vie romantique, 2000.

PARIS 2001
H. Bari and V. Sautter (eds), *Diamants. Au cœur de la terre, au cœur des étoiles, au cœur du pouvoir*, exhib. cat., Paris/Québec, 2001.

PARIS 2001B
J. Durand, *Le Trésor de la Sainte-Chapelle*, Paris, 2001.

PARIS 2002
X. Salmon (ed.), *Madame de Pompadour et les arts*, exhib. cat., Paris, Château de Versailles, 2002.

PARIS 2004
É. Taburet-Delahaye (ed.), *Paris 1400. Les Arts sous Charles VI*, exhib. cat., Paris, Musée du Louvre, 2004.

PARIS 2007
C. Descatoire (ed.), *Trésors de la Peste noire: Erfurt et Colmar*, Paris, 2007.

PFORZHEIM 1990
Veilingcataloog Henninger-Tarcar, Pforzheim, 1990.

PFORZHEIM 2003
Geschichten in Gold, Kostbarkeiten aus dem Ungarischen Nationalmuseum, Budapest, exhib. cat., Pforzheim, Schmuckmuseum, 2003.

PHILLIPS 2000
C. Phillips, *Jewels and Jewellery*, London, 2000.

PHILLIPS 2004
C. Phillips, *From Antiquity to the Present*, London, 2004.

PIETRUSINSKI 1996
J. Pietrusinski, 'Sredniowieczne klejnoty monarsze w zlotym skarbie ze Srody Slaskiej', *Klejnoty Monarsze, Skarb ze Srody Slaskiej*, Wroclaw, 1996, pp. 9–63.

PLOOS VAN AMSTEL 1990
G. Ploos van Amstel, 'Unde venis Ploos van Amstel? Verdichtsel en waarheid over een afstamming', *De Nederlandsche Leeuw*, no. 107, July–August 1990, pp. 178–283.

RENSON/CASTEELS 1979
G. Renson and M. Casteels, *Het kasteelmuseum van Gaasbeek*, Gaasbeek, 1979.

RENWICK 1972
J. Renwick (ed.), *Marmontel, Mémoires*, Clermont-Ferrand, 1972.

RIPA 1603
C. Ripa, *Iconologia*, Rome, 1603.

ROBIJNS 1980
L. Robijns, *500 Jaar Sint-Martinuskerk*, Aalst, 1980.

ROBIJNS 1980B
L. Robijns, 'De Sint-Martinuskerk te Aalst', in *Inventaris van het Kunstpatrimonium van Oost-Vlaanderen*, XV, Gand, 1980.

ROSAS JUNIOR 1954
J. Rosas Junior, *Catálogo dos Jóias e Pratas da Coroa*, Lisbon, Palácio Nacional da Ajuda, 1954.

ROSENBERG 1918
M. Rosenberg, *Geschichte der Goldschmiedekunst auf technischer Grundlage*, Darmstadt, 1918.

SACHS 1991
R. Sachs, 'Der Schatzfund von Neumarkt/Schlesien. Ein Zwischenbericht', *Schlesien Kunst Wissenschaft Volkskunde*, vol. 36, 1991, pp. 71–5.

SAMET 2000
J. Samet, *Chaumet*, Paris, 2000.

SÃO PAULO 2007
X. Salmon, *Images du souverain*, exhib. cat., São Paulo, Pinacoteca do Estado, 2007.

SAVOIE 2003
M.-G. de Savoie and S. Papi, *Gioielli di Casa Savoia*, Milan, 2003.

SCARISBRICK 1993
D. Scarisbrick, *Rings: Symbols of Wealth, Power and Affection*, London, 1993.

SCARISBRICK 1994
D. Scarisbrick, *Jewellery in Britain 1066–1837: A Documentary, Social, Literary and Artistic Survey*, Norwich, 1994.

SCARISBRICK 1998
D. Scarisbrick, *Tudor Jewellery*, London, National Portrait Gallery, 1998.

SCARISBRICK 2000
D. Scarisbrick, *Tiara*, exhib. cat., Boston, Museum of Fine Arts, 2000.

SCHALLABURG 2000
R. Zedinger (ed.), *Lothringens Erbe. Franz Stephan von Lothringen (1708–1765) und sein Wirken in Wirtschaft, Wissenschaft und Kunst der Habsburgermonarchie*, exhib. cat., Schallaburg, St. Pölten, 2000.

SCHIEDLAUSKY 1987
D. Schiedlausky, *Wie man Floehe faengt*, Kunst & Antiquitäten, II, 1987.

SCHIFFER 1988
N. Schiffer, *The Power of Jewelry*, West Chester, 1988.

SCHMUCKMUSEUM 1981
Schmuckmuseum Pforzheim. Von der Antike bis zur Gegenwart, Stuttgart, 1981.

SCHMUCKMUSEUM 2001
Schmuckmuseum Pforzheim. Museumsführer, Stuttgart, 2001.

SCHMUCKMUSEUM 2006
Schmuckmuseum Pforzheim. Museumsführer, Stuttgart, 2006.

SCHULZE 1995
S. Schulze (ed.), *Sehnsucht nach Glück: Wiens Aufbruch in die Moderne: Klimt, Kokoschka, Schiele…*, Ostfildern-Ruit, 1995.

SEELIG 1987

L. Seelig, *Pretiosen in der Münchner Schatz-kammer. Teil 2. Wittelsbacher Schmuck vom Spätbarock bis zum Historismus sowie Orden und Insignien, Kunst & Antiquitäten* 6, 1987, pp. 46–57.

SEIDEL 1901

P. Seidel, 'Die Prunkdosen Friedrichs des Großen', *Hohenzollern-Jahrbuch* 5, Berlin, 1901, pp. 74–86.

SFRAMELI 2003

M. Sframeli, *I Gioielli dei Medici*, Florence, 2003.

SILLO CORTES 1960

C. Sillo Cortes, *Isabel la Catolica*, Madrid, 1960.

SOMERS COCKS 1980

A. Somers Cocks (ed.), *Princely Magnificence – Court Jewels of the Renaissance 1500–1630*, Victoria & Albert Museum, London, 1980.

SOMERS COCKS/TRUMAN 1984

A. Somers Cocks and C. Truman, *Renaissance Jewels, Gold Boxes and Objets de vertu – the Thyssen-Bornemisza Collection*, London, 1984.

SRODA SLASKA

Guidebook of the National Museum of Sroda Slaska, Poland.

STEINGRÄBER 1956

E. Steingräber, *Alter Schmuck*, Munich, 1956.

STEINGRÄBER 1957

E. Steingräber, *Antique Jewelry*, New York, 1957.

STETTINER 1916

R. Stettiner, *Das Kleinodienbuch des Jakob Mores inder Hamburgischen Stadsbibliothek*, Hamburg, 1916.

STOCKHOLM 1949

Smycken, exhib. cat., Stockholm, Nordiska Museet, 1949.

STOCKHOLM 1999

M. Olausson, 'Gustave III, A Bejewelled Monarch', in *Catherine the Great and Gustave III*, exhib. cat., Nationalmuseum, Stockholm, 1999.

STOCKHOLM 2000

E Welander-Berggren, *Precious Gems: Jewellery from Eight Centuries*, exhib. cat., Stockholm, 2000.

SYNDRAM 2006

D. Syndram, *Die Juwelen der Könige: Schmuckensembles des 18. Jahrhunderts aus dem Grünen Gewölbe*, Berlin/Munich, 2006.

SZILÁGYI 1991

A. Szilágyi, *Periods in European Decorative Arts*, Budapest, 1991.

SZILÁGYI 2006

András Szilágyi, *Die Esterházy Schatzkammer*, Budapest, 2006.

TAIT 1986

H. Tait, *Catalogue of the Waddesdon Bequest in the British Museum, 1, The Jewels*, London, 1986.

TENZEL 1740

W.E. Tenzel, *Saxonia Numismatica, 1*, Frankfurt, 1740.

THOMAS/LEITER 1999

U. Thomas and A. Leiter, *Taschenuhren: Sammlung Philipp Weber*, Pforzheim, Sparkasse Pforzheim, 1999.

THOMAS/STOLZ 1995

W. Thomas and E. Stolz, 'Vlaanderen en Castilië, twee eeuwen gekruiste levenswegen', in *Vlaanderen en Castilla y Leon*, Antwerp, 1995.

TILLANDER 1995

H. Tillander, *Diamond Cuts in Historic Jewellery 1381–1910*, London, 1995.

TIMMERS 1993

J.J.M. Timmers, *Christelijke Symboliek en Iconografie*, Houten, 1993.

TOKYO 2003

Jewellery from Renaissance to Art Deco 1540–1940, Tokyo, Metropolitan Teien Museum; Fukuoka, City Museum; Nagoya, Mitsuzakaya Art Museum; Kyoto, Art Museum Eki, 2003.

TOKYO 2003B

J. Walgrave, *The Splendour of Diamond: 400 years of Diamond Jewellery in Europe*, exhib. cat., Tokyo, National Museum, 2003.

TOKYO 2007

Tiara: Dignity and Beauty, Tokyo, Bunka-mura Museum; Museums of Kyoto, Niigata Bandaijima Art Museum, 2007.

TRUMAN 1991

C. Truman, *The Gilbert Collection of Gold Boxes*, New York, 1991.

TWINING 1960

Lord F. Twining, *A History of the Crown Jewels of Europe*, London, 1960.

TWINING 1967

Lord F. Twining, *European Regalia*, London, 1967

UTRECHT 1993

B. Van den Boogert and J. Kerkhoff (eds), *Maria van Hongarije 1505–1558: koningin tussen keizers en Kunstenaars*, exhib. cat., Utrecht and Bois-le-Duc, 1993.

VACHAUDEZ 2004

C. Vachaudez, *Bijoux des reines et princesses de Belgique*, Brussels, 2004.

VALENCIA 2007

À la recherche de la Toison d'Or: l'Europe des Princes, l'Europe des villes, Valencia, Almudin, Museo de la Ciudad, 2007.

VALLADOLID 2004

Isabel la Catolica: a magnificencia de un reinado, exhib. cat., Valladolid, 2004.

VAN DER VELDEN 2000

Hugo van der Velden, *The Donor's Image: Gerard Loyet and the votive portraits of Charles the Bold*, Turnhout, 2000.

VARSOVIE 2001

Skarb ze Srody Slaskiej, exhib. cat., Varsovie, 2001.

VAN ZELM 1988

J.P.A.E. van Zelm van Eldik-Kuneman and J.A. van Zelm van Eldik, *Paleis Het Loo Nationaal Museum. Collectie Museum van de Kanselarij der Nederlandse Orden*, Appeldoorn, 1988.

VENTE FUGGER 1504

Documents from the sale of Jacob Fugger's jewellery, 16 September 1504, Archives de la Ville de Basle, Städtische Urkunde 2604.

VENTE 'TROIS FRÈRES' 1398

Facture et quittance des 'Trois Frères', Paris, 11 October and 24 November 1398, Dijon, Archives départementales de la Côte d'Or, in É. Kovács (ed.), *L'âge d'or de l'orfèvrerie parisienne au temps des princes de Valois*, Dijon, 2004, pp. 388–9.

VEVER 1975

H. Vever, *La bijouterie française au XIXe siècle, vol. 1, Consulat, Empire, Restauration, Louis-Philippe 1800–1850*, Paris, 1906, revised edition Florence, 1975.

VIENNA 1980

Maria Theresia und Ihre Zeit, exhib. cat., Schloss Schönbrunn, Vienna, 1980.

VIENNA 1988

Kunst und Kultur am Hofe Kaiser Rudolfs II, exhib. cat., Vienna, 1988.

VIENNA 2000

W. Seipel, *Kaiser Karl V (1500–1558). Macht und Ohnmacht Europas*, exhib. cat., Vienna, 2000.

VIENNA 2003

L. Fornari Schianchi and S. Ferino-Pagden (eds), *Parmigianino und der europäische Manierismus*, Vienna, Kunsthistorisches Museum Mailand, 2003.

VON RODA 1983

B. von Roda, *Aus dem Nechlass der griechischen Majestäten, 1. Teil: Das Bamberger Exil und die Bildnisse von König Otto und Königin Amalie*, Kunst & Antiquitäten 5, 1983, pp. 68–74.

WACKERNAGEL 1894

R. Wackernagel, 'Basels Anteil an der Burgunderbeute', *Basler Jahrbuch* 1894, pp. 57–68.

WACHOWSKI/WITKOWSKI 1996

K. Wachowski and J. Witkowski, '*Klejnoty*', *Klejnoty Monarsze, Skarb ze Srody Slaskiej*, Wroclaw, 1996.

WALGRAVE 1973

J. Walgrave, *Antwerp World Diamond Centre: Diamantfestival*, Antwerp, 1973.

WALGRAVE 1995

Jan Walgrave (ed.), *A Sparkling Age*, Antwerp, 1995.

WASHINGTON 1993

The Age of the Baroque in Portugal, exhib. cat., Washington, National Gallery of Art, 1993–1994.

WEBER 1999

G.J.M. Weber, *Pietro Graf Rotari in Dresden: ein italienischer Maler am Hof König Augustus III*, Emsdetten/Dresden, 1999.

WESTKUNST 1989

Westkunst, October 1989.

WILHELMY 2004

W. Wilhelmy, 'Krone eines Kaisers des lateinischen Kaiserreichs (Heinrich von Flandern?)', in *Die Kreuz-Züge*, H.G. Kotzur (ed.), Mayence, 2004, pp. 381–4.

WILHELMY 2004B

W. Wilhelmy, 'Die Kaiserkrone des Musée diocésain in Namur: Entstehung, Funktion und Stiftungsumstände', in *Actes du colloque Autour de Hugo d'Oignies*, Collection Monographies du Musée des Arts anciens du Namurois, no. 26, 2004, pp. 203–8.

WROCLAW 1996

Skarb ze Srody Slaskiej, exhib. cat., Wroclaw, 1996.